The European Union b

The European Union is undergoing a period of fundamental change. With the next stages of enlargement and debates to determine the financial contributions of each member state underway, the European Union faces painful and protracted negotiations over its evolution and its future.

The European Union beyond Amsterdam explores the fundamental structural challenges that the EU will continue to face in the twenty-first century. The contributors – all acknowledged experts in their field – look beyond the 1997 Amsterdam Intergovernmental Conference and such current problem areas as Economic and Monetary Union. They explore those crucial issues which they feel will be the subject of debate long after the pressing issues of today have been resolved. In the search for the factors that will determine the shape of the EU the contributors examine key problems and issues such as: democratising the Union; establishing a common foreign policy; the rule of law; and constitutional change.

The theoretical approaches developed in this volume offer fresh and far-reaching contributions to the continuing debates surrounding the European integration process. Including a preface by Jacques Delors, it will be valuable reading to students, teachers, politicians, and journalists seeking insights into the evolution of the EU in the twenty-first century.

Martin Westlake is Head of Unit for Institutional Relations in the European Commission, an Associate Member of the Centre for Legislative Studies at the University of Hull, and author of several authoritative works on the European Union and its institutions.

The European Union beyond Amsterdam

New concepts of European integration

Edited by Martin Westlake

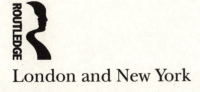

London and New York

First published 1998
by Routledge
11 New Fetter Lane, London EC4P 4EE

Simultaneously published in the USA and Canada
by Routledge
29 West 35th Street, New York, NY 10001

© 1998 Martin Westlake for the collection; individual chapters the contributors

Typeset in Baskerville by
Ponting–Green Publishing Services,
Chesham, Buckinghamshire
Printed and bound in Great Britain by
T.J. International, Ltd, Padstow, Cornwall

All rights reserved. No part of this book may be reprinted or reproduced or utilised in any form or by any electronic, mechanical, or other means, now known or hereafter invented, including photocopying and recording, or in any information storage or retrieval system, without permission in writing from the publishers.

British Library Cataloguing in Publication Data
A catalogue record for this book is available from the British Library

Library of Congress Cataloguing in Publication Data
The European Union beyond Amsterdam: new concepts of
  European integration / edited by Martin Westlake.
      p.   cm.
    Includes index.
      ISBN 0–415–16879–1   ISBN 0–415–16880–5 (pbk.)
      1. European Union.   I. Westlake, Martin.
   JN30.E9415   1998
341.242'2–dc21 98–5089
CIP

ISBN 0–415–16879–1 (hbk)

ISBN 0–415–16880–5 (pbk)

'Point n'est besoin d'espérer pour entreprendre ni de réussir pour persévérer.'

(William of Orange)

A CELEBRATION OF THE LIFE AND WORK OF JACQUES VANDAMME

Photograph: Jacques Vandamme (centre) presiding over a recent TEPSA Conference. To his right are: Jacques Santer, President of the European Commission, and Wolfgang Wessels, Professor at the University of Cologne and TEPSA President. To his left are: Gil Carlos Rodriguez Iglesias, President of the Court of Justice, and Jean-Victor Louis, Professor at the Free University of Brussels and long-standing TEPSA member.

Contents

Contributors		xiii
Foreword Jacques Delors		xv
Editor's note		xvii
1	**The book and the man** Martin Westlake	1
2	**The European Union's 'blind watchmakers': the process of constitutional change** Martin Westlake	16
3	**Britain and Europe: the different relationship** Andrew Duff	34
4	**From closed doors to European democracy: beyond the intergovernmental conferences** John Pinder	47
5	**Making European foreign policy work** Gianni Bonvicini	61
6	**Flexibility, differentiation and closer cooperation: the Amsterdam provisions in the light of the Tindemans Report** Wolfgang Wessels	76
7	**The rule of law** Jean-Victor Louis	99
8	**For a democratic Europe** Robert Toulemon	116
9	**Dreams come true, gradually: the Tindemans Report a quarter of a century on** Leo Tindemans	130
10	**European federalism: opportunity or Utopia?** Jacques Vandamme	142
Index		154

Contributors

Gianni Bonvicini is Director of the Institute for International Affairs, Rome

Jacques Delors, former President of the European Commission, is President of the College of Europe, Bruges, and Head of 'Notre Europe'

Andrew Duff is the Director of the Federal Trust, London

Jean-Victor Louis is Professor of Law at the Free University of Brussels

John Pinder, OBE, is Professor at the College of Europe, Bruges

Leo Tindemans, a former Belgian Prime Minister, is a Member of the European Parliament

Robert Toulemon, a former Commission Director-General, is President of the French Association for European Union Studies, Paris

Jacques Vandamme, Honorary President of the Trans-European Policy Studies Association, is Professor Emeritus of European Law at Leuven University

Wolfgang Wessels is Professor at the University of Cologne and President of the Trans-European Policy Studies Association

Martin Westlake is Head of Unit for Institutional Relations in the European Commission and Associate Member of the Centre for Legislative Studies at the University of Hull

Foreword

We are all Europeans but – if I may paraphrase George Orwell – some are more European than others. This book is a tribute to a man whose life and work sum up the richness and diversity that makes we Europeans what we are. In another time, Jacques Vandamme's career could, like his ancestors', so easily have gone another way; scion of two good military families, resistance member, British soldier . . . The tradition seemed set yet, as with so many of his contemporaries, Jacques emerged from the war period imbued not with militaristic fervour but with European militancy.

Over many years, and in various guises, Jacques has fought for a good Europe. In his vision, Europe is strong and united, prosperous and competitive, firm and fair. But his Europe is also compassionate and understanding, consensual and inclusive, and – perhaps above all – culturally diverse. Jacques' life has mirrored this vision, as all who know him and his family will attest.

In intellectual terms, Jacques has devoted his energies to furthering his general vision, not by force-feeding his views on a potentially sceptical audience, but simply by encouraging exchanges of views and ideas in a European context. To give an example, TEPSA, the think-tank he helped found, now has a long-established tradition of pre-Presidency conferences in the member state concerned. Given the frequently fervently-held views of the participants, these conferences could so easily degenerate into pontification, with pro-integrationists earnestly telling forthcoming Presidencies what they should do. The reality is far from this. The exchanges are never less than two-way. TEPSA learns as much as the Presidency. It was ever thus: Jacques has always been a good teacher, but he has also always been a good listener.

In this volume Martin Westlake has brought together contributions from a selection of some of Jacques' closest friends and associates. Each contributor was given the same brief; to look beyond Amsterdam, beyond the obvious challenges of EMU and enlargement, to the underlying structural challenges which the EU will continue to confront as it advances into the twenty-first century. The result is a rich and rewarding collection of analyses, stretching from consideration of the process of constitutional change itself, through to the vital importance of democratisation and the rule of law, to the concept of differentiated integration. The contributors push boundaries and explore limits. They write very much in the tradition of Jacques' quest for honest exchange. I cannot pretend to agree with everything they write, but I do agree with their general approach and, indeed, with the underlying theme of this work.

Many of us might wish for some sort of constituent assembly and a fixed constitutional settlement. The frustrations of Maastricht and Amsterdam and of the 'diplomatic method' in general have led to repeated calls for such a settlement, and these calls will continue. It is no secret that I myself found the Amsterdam Treaty deeply disappointing. However, realism dictates a two-pronged approach. We could and should address ourselves to the question of what an ideal fixed European constitutional settlement might be. But, as Leo Tindemans' chapter reminds us, we are unlikely to see such a constituent assembly process in the near future. In the absence of a fixed settlement, we can expect to continue to live in a state of flux. To take but the most recent example, as the ink dries on the Treaty of Amsterdam, we know that there will almost certainly be another intergovernmental conference in the near future.

In other words, Europe is constantly evolving, and the fundamental question which the contributors confront is how the integration process can be kept on course in a situation of perpetual flux. The collective answer they give is that, like the navigation of a ship, we can only keep to a course by reference to a set of fixed values. The set includes a mix of normative and positive values, most found in the treaties themselves: peace, prosperity, non-discrimination, pluralism, democracy, economic freedom, solidarity and social cohesion. The existence of this – particularly European – mix gives the lie to the accusations of those who declare the goal of European Union to be vague and insubstantial.

Herein lies the deepest truth of this book. Europe will, sooner or later, in one way or another, witness a fixed constitutional settlement. The 'good old bad old days' of diplomacy and the balance of power, of war as an extension of diplomacy by other means, are long since over. Some forty years ago, Europe embarked upon an evolutionary constitutional process. We may not – cannot – know exactly what form Europe's definitive constitutional settlement will take. But we can already say what values it should embody, what traditions it should uphold.

To my mind, Jacques Vandamme personally embodies all that is most attractive about Europe. I recommend this book to its readers as a reflection of the man it honours.

Jacques Delors

Editor's note

The final version of the Amsterdam Treaty, signed on 2 October 1997, renumbered all of the existing articles of the Treaty of European Union and its component Treaties. However, the old numbering will remain familiar to many commentators. In the interests of the greatest possible accuracy and access, I have therefore decided that, where reference is made to Treaty articles, the text will give both the old numbers/letters (in ordinary font) and the new numbers (in bold).

MW

1 The book and the man

Martin Westlake

THE BOOK

This book is intended to honour the work of Jacques Vandamme, a Belgian federalist, whose varied career I shall describe below. Such Festschrifts frequently consist of collections of re-cycled articles and essays whose only common theme, it sometimes seems, is the relationship between their authors and the person in whose honour the work is published. I should therefore stress at the outset that this book consists of original contributions, published nowhere else, written specifically to the editor's instructions and addressing a common theme. In editing this work, my first guiding principle has been that the best way to honour an individual is to produce something of high and lasting quality. I am convinced that the analyses in this book will be of enduring relevance.

The book brings together a number of highly experienced individuals, all acknowledged experts in their fields. Most of them are members of the Trans-European Policy Studies Association, a Brussels-based think-tank which Jacques Vandamme helped found. Jacques Vandamme has worked with all of the contributors in the furtherance of the European ideal. My second guiding principle as editor was therefore that the work should somehow address the central theme of furthering the European ideal.

The bulk of the book was written during the closing stages of the Amsterdam Intergovernmental Conference, but I wanted the contributors to look beyond the IGC and to address themselves to lasting themes. My third and last guiding editorial principle was therefore that the contributors should not concentrate on the impending issues – enlargement, Economic and Monetary Union, the financial perspectives – which we all know are just around the corner. Rather, I wanted them to concentrate on problems or issues – democratising the Union, establishing a common foreign policy, the rule of law, to take but a few examples – which will still be the focus of debate ten or fifteen years hence.

In his foreword, Jacques Delors identifies the central theme of this book. He points out that soon it will be time to look *beyond* the pressing issues of the next few years to the relative calm which awaits us on the other side. In the foreseeable future, the Union will have reached its maximum size and some sort of stable equilibrium will have been reached with those European states which cannot or will not participate. What would that Union look like? And how will we get there? Whatever the answer to these questions, Delors feels that we should already be able to say what values the Union will embody, and what traditions it will uphold.

In my chapter I use the parallel of neo-Darwinian evolutionary theory to show, first, how the Union is an organic constitutional arrangement and, second, how its evolution is influenced by what I term the Union's 'blueprint draftsmen'. Much dissatisfaction has been expressed at the 'diplomatic method' which resulted in the Amsterdam Treaty, but there was never any initiative during the IGC to alter the rules of the game and we could in any case expect them to remain the same for the foreseeable future. In practical terms, this means that constitutional change will continue to require the unanimity of all of the member states, with all that this implies for the negotiating process. All the more need, then, for Europe's blueprint drafters to keep a weather eye on proceedings and to make sure that the European Union's constitutional development is kept to a reasonably coherent course.

That course is decided primarily by the member states, acting together. In recent years, the United Kingdom has seemed to act more like a sheet anchor than a helmsman. In the first part of his chapter, Andrew Duff casts a critical eye over the problem of Britain and its traditionally troubled relations with Europe. He identifies the idiosyncratic British electoral system as one of the principal villains of the piece; it distorts results and, by exaggerating swings, creates inconsistency in government policy. By exaggerating the importance of short-term electoral advantage, it puts the accent on tactics at the expense of longer-term strategy. By excessively penalising parties which do not retain a critical mass, it has obliged the two major political parties to absorb contradictory elements (particularly on European issues) which, under another system, would exist separately: Eurosceptical 'tails' cannot wag broadly Euro-sympathetic 'dogs' if they have been severed from them. Duff goes on to examine the development of the concept of flexibility which, as he points out, has accompanied European integration since the inception of the EEC, but which has taken on increasing importance as the integration process has deepened. Perhaps crucially, the 'British problem' resurfaced during the Amsterdam negotiations on the flexibility theme, and the resulting treaty amendments can be seen very much as a response to it. The European Union seems condemned to live with a 'double indemnity'; the 'British problem' and the cumulative effect of the responses to it.

John Pinder (like Andrew Duff, one of the United Kingdom's front-ranking federalists) chooses to focus not on the states, but on their peoples. He lucidly describes today's European Union as a combination of federal powers and pre-federal institutions. He confronts the federalists' dilemma –

should the aim be a federal union or a federal state? – and pragmatically concludes that the best solution would be a fully democratic federal union, accompanied by partial integration in the field of security. But the Union's institutions can only be democratically reformed with the support and the involvement of the European people. Pinder suggests that the European Parliament could use its assent powers in relation to the next waves of enlargement to force a constitutional conference which would involve representatives not only of the member state governments but also of national parliaments and the European Parliament. He points out that opinion polling has consistently demonstrated generalised majority support among the public at large for continued integration (levels of support which, incidentally, go up with levels of knowledge) and urges the Parliament to use its powers and the strength of its convictions to force the issue before the next wave of accessions can occur.

One of the policy areas in which the European Union has clearly fallen short of public expectations is foreign policy. Gianni Bonvicini examines why it is proving so difficult to get a genuine European foreign policy up and running. He rejects traditional arguments about foreign policy being a vital component of national sovereignty – surely no more so than economic and monetary policy – and describes how, for a variety of historical reasons, European foreign policy has fallen into a particular ideological context. Thus it has become, he writes, 'the involuntary object of the battle over the type of Europe to be built that has divided entire generations of politicians and intellectuals'. Bonvicini argues that it is this political and ideological context which accounts for the structural differences between the highly successful Community method and the hybrid 'second pillar' created at Maastricht. Amsterdam showed that the intergovernmental approach and sensitivities about national sovereignty are still so deeply ingrained that a decisive 'Communitarisation' of the European Union's foreign policy remains unlikely in the foreseeable future. As Bonvicini points out, the great paradox is that, at the outset of the IGC, virtually all of the member states were agreed on the need for fundamental improvements to be made. Worse, the imbalance is destined to grow, as the introduction of the euro will have unavoidable repercussions on the Union's foreign policy. In turn, the existence of an economic 'government' and the absence of a 'government' for foreign policy means that, in Bonvicini's expressive metaphor, the two main pillars of the Union will support a 'dangerously inclined roof'. What should be done? He argues that another Amsterdam is needed to focus on the creation of clear mechanisms between the two pillars.

One of the problems which renders the realisation of a common foreign policy so difficult is the difference in the stances of the member states with regard to the pace of integration. Some wish to move forward faster than others. Should they do so? Wolfgang Wessels focuses his analysis on the concepts of flexibility and differentiated integration, together with their logical corollary, closer cooperation. He examines critically the outcome at Amsterdam in the light of the recommendations of the 1974 Tindemans Report on European Union (an exercise in which Jacques Vandamme was deeply involved). It was in the Tindemans Report that a 'new approach' was first explicitly outlined, according to which 'those states which are able to progress have the duty to forge ahead'. In the Tindemans approach, as revisited by Amsterdam, Wessels identifies three fundamental dilemmas: first, the uneasy dialectic between progress and solidarity; second, the contradiction between the politically necessary complexity of the Amsterdam outcome and the constitutional necessity for transparency and effectiveness; third, the fact that the very existence of the provisions for closer cooperation will almost certainly lead to them not being applied. Wessels predicts that member states' cost-benefit analyses will continue to lead them to seek the broadest possible consensus even at the cost of policy satisfaction – a sort of rolling application of the prisoners' dilemma. Ultimately, Wessels argues, the 'second best options' negotiated by the Amsterdam draftsmen will only be rendered superfluous by further, and far more fundamental, constitutional reform.

The primacy of the rule of Community law has been considered one of the mainstays of the European integration process so far, but can such a universal principle continue to survive in a differentiated system? With a lawyer's eye, Jean-Victor Louis first assesses the implications for the rule of law of the flexibility provisions created at Maastricht and Amsterdam. Critical of their existence, sceptical of their practicability, he argues that they will be difficult to implement and will prove short-lived. But he underlines the need for the Court of Justice to be vigilant, particularly in regard to the attribution of competences and the obligations deriving from the so-called loyalty clause (Article 5(**10**) in the Treaty). Louis argues forcefully that failure to ensure the rule of law as it has existed until now would lead, slowly but inexorably, to a decline into purely intergovernmental cooperation. With or without flexibility clauses, the law will have to be applied in an increasingly large and complex Union. Arguing strongly that the basic features of Community law should be maintained, Louis calls for in-depth reflection on how the work capacity of the Courts can be enhanced in a Union of twenty or more member states. He calls for a reflection procedure which would involve the participation of the Courts, as well as of the member state governments. Expedient solutions for cutting the Courts' workloads, such as limiting the rights for national courts to seek preliminary rulings or the access of private parties, are to be avoided, but organisational reforms will be required if the system is not to collapse.

The consequences of the 1992 Danish 'no' are still reverberating around the European Union and its institutions. The citizen, benignly forgotten for so long, is climbing back into the saddle. Robert Toulemon argues that a major reduction in the democratic deficit is vital if the European Union is to progress further. He articulates his argument around three observations:

the European Union can only be of substance if it involves some sort of transfer of sovereignty; democratisation of the European Union's institutions will inevitably lead to the creation of a European political class; last but not least, the European Union can no longer advance or even consolidate its role if it does not respond to the needs and expectations of its citizens. Toulemon goes on to list a series of reforms which would democratise the institutions and hence the Union. He argues that a true citizens' Europe must be created, with the entrenchment of moral and economic rights. Europe, he concludes, cannot be a panacea for all our ailments, but it does provide a framework for problem solving which has worked remarkably well in the past, and which is increasingly seen as a model by nascent groupings of states elsewhere in the world. Europe's traditional democratic values must be reflected in that model.

What is European integration about? Where, ultimately, are we heading? Jacques Vandamme passes in review some of the more enduring integration theories and examines what they might tell us about the future direction of the European Union's development. To the same end, he examines attempts to define the concept of European Union, but concludes that the term is destined to remain vague and amorphous precisely because it reflects the fluid nature of the integration process itself. Giving his own considered view of the future, he concludes that 'we are no longer very far from a federal model adapted to European reality'. However, like Pinder, he distinguishes between the concept of a federal union and one of a federal state. Europe's constitutional development will remain *sui generis* (pace Wessels' comments below) and, whilst some are disappointed at how slow the process is, others are happy that the Union has managed to come so far so fast. Vandamme concludes with his own by-word; persevere.

THE MAN

Having written at some length about the book and its contents, it is time to turn to the man in whose honour the book has been written. I should immediately declare an interest; I am Jacques Vandamme's son-in-law. For somebody working in and writing about the European Union institutions, this has been a privileged relationship, for Jacques is passionately interested in European affairs and has witnessed or participated in many of the developments which I can only write about. He is also extraordinarily openminded and he adores discussion and debate, perhaps particularly, over the past decade, with his British son-in-law! I have good reason to feel affection for the man. I also admire his indefatigable enthusiasm and his optimistic resilience. As the closing sentence of Chapter 10 shows, these are characteristic qualities of the man. In the remainder of this introduction, I would like briefly to share with the reader the main themes of the life of somebody whom I consider to be a quintessentially *European* European. Jacques Vandamme's life is also a case study of the *good* European. With Europe's last major conflagration now so far away, we have perhaps forgotten how badly we sometimes need good Europeans.

Military antecedents

As perhaps befits a militant European, Jacques Vandamme is the scion of two military families. His paternal grandfather was a Flemish, but Francophone, captain in the Belgian Army. An independent and creative spirit, the captain would often pack his easel and paints and set off to the dunes of the Flemish coast or rural Limbourg. Captain Vandamme was married to the sister of a Belgian Army general. Jacques' maternal grandfather was a Belgian Army colonel and a fierce patriot. Left for dead on a First World War battlefield, he was nursed back to life by Dutch nuns whence, as soon as he was able, he raced to London and from there returned to the front.

Jacques' father, Charles Vandamme, grew up as a Francophone citizen of the city of Antwerp (in Flanders). Wanting to be a soldier like his father, he signed on at the military cadets school at Namur (in Wallonia). He was seventeen years old when Germany invaded in 1914. He walked for four days across country to reach the Belgian Free Army and saw active service on the Western Front. But by 1917, the Front was stagnating. Charles Vandamme volunteered for service in the Belgian Congo, where he served until 1919. He returned to Belgium and met and fell in love with Elsa Bouvier. The two were married in 1922.[1]

Childhood

The newly-wed Vandammes were determined to do something different with their children. Jacques, their first, was born in 1923. Another son, Daniel (1929), and two daughters, Lilianne (1926) and Yolande (1941), were to follow. In those early postwar years, there was a sense abroad on the Continent of having survived Armageddon. The proportion of men in the population had been savagely reduced by four years of attritional trench warfare and the young were the object of relieved affection. Life for the young Vandamme children seemed idyllic. Jacques' father had left the army and begun a career as a stockbroker at the Belgian *bourse*. He enjoyed considerable success. A town house in Brussels was complemented by a summer house at Hastière, on the banks of the Meuse. In 1929, disaster struck, with the collapse of stockmarkets throughout the world. Extraordinary as it seems, the young Jacques was kept in the dark, and his parents never admitted to the financial hurt they must have endured. Thus, the young Jacques, first-born, an object of unlimited parental affection, shielded from the bad times, was to gain a bedrock of confidence and optimism which has never left him since, not even in his darkest hours.

Charles Vandamme eagerly shared with his eldest son his passion for history and contemporary politics. From the earliest age, Jacques was encouraged to keep an open mind and to engage in debate. At the precocious age of twelve, Jacques began to organise political meetings at home, to which he would invite his aunts and uncles to discuss given themes. Nobody mocked him. It was also from his father that Jacques first gained a sense of injustice about the situation of the Flemish population.

Jacques had his mind set on following his forebears into the army. His parents had already decided on the form that Jacques' education should take, and he began his secondary education at the elite Jesuit-run college of St Michel in Brussels. Extraordinarily, Jacques insisted on quitting St Michel for a Flemish education, and so in 1938, at the age of fifteen, Jacques left for the prestigious Catholic boarding school of St André at Loppem, near Bruges. This was a super-elite college – the Belgian equivalent of, say, Ampleforth. There were only one hundred students, fifteen per class. Despite the generally privileged atmosphere, St André's was an austere community of prayer which put the primary emphasis on religious education. Pupils were allowed home once a month and the young Jacques might have been expected to suffer a little. But his letters to his parents (hoarded by his adoring mother) display confident self-assurance and a paternalistic concern for his brother and sisters. In one important respect, St André's provided significant continuity; debate and discussion were encouraged. And in continental Europe, as in Britain, this was a period characterised by increasingly anxious debate, with most European states caught in episodes of social and economic unrest, and a German invasion once more looming as a growing possibility. Loppem opened Jacques' intellectual world, with much emphasis on the arts and the sciences. It was also at Loppem that Jacques first encountered the left-wing Catholic philosophy of personalism, later to play an important part in his life.

War

On 10 May 1940, the Germans once again invaded Belgium. Fearing the worst this time, Charles Vandamme took up his whole family (including the governess) and fled to France. At St Nazaire, the Vandammes only just missed the last boat to the United States. Resigned to remaining on the Continent, Vandamme père rented a house on the Belgian coast at Wendune, near Zeebrugge, and the family were promptly caught up in the German 'pocket', as the invaders raced to cut off the retreating British Expeditionary Force at Dunkirk. In July 1940, the family came back to Brussels, and Jacques went back to finish his last year at school. Throughout this period, as his children recall, Charles Vandamme never faltered in his belief that Britain would win through. Like his grandfather and his father (and unlike the traditionally suspicious French), Jacques has always felt confident about the basic commitment of the Anglo-Saxon world to the future of the Continent.

In October 1941, Jacques went up to the University of Leuven to study law. Those years were shared with a clan of young, committed students who, whilst outwardly content to carry on as normal under the occupiers' regime, were inwardly seething. The student population could be divided into three categories. A minority, to which Jacques belonged, were impatient for the Allied victory they were sure would come and addressed themselves to the problems which would follow. The vast majority settled down uneasily to study, whilst another minority more or less collaborated with the occupiers. Passive resistance took many forms, with unspoken sentiments shared through such apparently innocuous networks as the Scout movement and ramblers' associations. With characteristic fervour, Jacques sought a more active role, and for six months (1943–4) he worked in the Belgian resistance movement, *le Mouvement national belge*, or '*L'armée blanche*', near the old Vandamme family haunt of Hastière. For those six months, Jacques smuggled information to and fro and, in one fraught episode, through the German lines to the advancing allies about gun emplacements and tank positions. It might have seemed relatively unromantic work but, for a twenty year-old man, capture would have meant certain deportation to a concentration camp, if not immediate execution.

Like all people of his generation, Jacques saw enough of war to be convinced of its futility and of its repugnance. The need to avoid war became another constant strand in his philosophy.

As the war dragged on, Jacques and his like-minded university contemporaries turned their thoughts increasingly to *l'après guerre*. In the Belgian case, there were three distinct, complicated layers to be considered. The first was the Belgian state: rightly or wrongly, the monarchy had been discredited and social and economic divisions had become more pronounced. How could the Belgian state be reconstituted? The second was the community-within-the-state. Both in the First and the Second World Wars, the German occupiers had adeptly exploited the sense of grievance in the Flemish community and encouraged a degree of autonomy previously unknown. The question of how to accommodate more autonomous linguistic communities within a gradually federalising state was to become the *leitmotif* of Belgium in the postwar years. The third layer was the community of states. Itself created as a buffer state, Belgium would always suffer when its larger neighbours went to war. The avoidance of war was an absolute imperative for those reflecting on the postwar world order and how future relations between European states could be arranged.

Jacques Vandamme was deeply involved in all of these debates, but first there was the matter of the war to be won. In the winter of 1944, it seemed as though Von Rundstedt's daring counter-offensive in the Ardennes might pay off. Characteristically impatient to lend a hand, Jacques dropped his studies and enrolled as a volunteer in the 'Piron Brigade' (an ad hoc brigade which enabled Belgian volunteers to be recruited into the British Army after Belgium had been liberated), together with some 800 other young Belgians. To their frustration, the new recruits were obliged to embark on a lengthy period of training, and it wasn't until April 1945 that Jacques reached the war zone. No sooner had he arrived than the European armistice was declared, in May 1945, and Vandamme found himself carrying out various anodyne chores near Cologne in occupied Germany. His studies suddenly seemed more important again. He was able to take two months' sabbatical leave from his British Army duties to cram for his exams, and in 1946 he passed out with a degree in law.

Peace and early career

Now twenty-three years old, Jacques began his career as a lawyer with a Brussels-based law firm. But there was always a life in parallel. His formative periods with the monks of St André, with the frustrated intellectuals of occupied Leuven, with the patriots of the resistance, and with his fellow volunteers in the British Army had left him a component part of a vast and overlapping network of committed thinkers and practitioners who shared the common objective of learning from the past to address the future. He was to become particularly active in a broadly centre-left discussion group, aptly named '*La Relève*', which for most of its early life actively sought out iconoclastic free thinkers and which therefore well suited Jacques' intellectual temperament. Thus, outside office hours, Jacques found himself in the thick of intellectual and political debate on such thorny and vital topics as the reform of the Belgian social security system, a topic still at the centre of the political stage today (and one combining problems of redistribution, social justice, and communities-within-the-state – all topics of particular interest to Jacques). It was through these debates that Jacques found himself appointed to the *cabinet* of the Belgian Minister for Public Health and the Family and, later, as Secretary of the Belgian Minister for Work and Social Security.

In 1948, the year after he came to the Brussels Bar, Jacques struck up a conversation with a young and vivacious fellow guest at a wedding, Marguerite Bondue. The following year, they were married. It was difficult to imagine a couple of greater contrast. Despite his Brussels' origins and Hastière sojourns, Jacques considered himself to be of Flemish descent and his periods of study at Loppem and Leuven had transformed him into a committed supporter of the Flemish cause. The Bondue family, on the other hand, were quintessentially Francophone and, whereas the Vandammes were soldiers, the Bondues were proud to be part of the extended family of Thomas Braun, a renowned Belgian fin-de-siècle poet. Jacques and Marguerite shared the attraction of opposites and, over the next two decades set up a happy home for a large family[2] in Uccle, a Brussels suburb.

Personalism

It was in the 1950s that Jacques fell under the influence of personalism. As expounded by its founder and principal proponent, Emmanuel Mounier, personalism emphasised the voluntarist dimension of the human being. It stressed the existence of a 'third way' or 'middle way' between Communism, with its denial of the individual, and liberalism, with its denial of the community ('we must liberate liberty from liberalism'). Personalism stressed the individual's responsibility to the society about him; 'Man masters himself through his relationship with other people and things, in work and in camaraderie, in friendship, in love, in action, in meeting, and not in standoffishness' (Mounier, 1947).

But Mounier held that a new social order would be insufficient in itself. He argued that a spiritual transformation was also necessary. 'The classical notion of man has been broken up; people affirm the absolute of the individual, the race, the class, the nation ... Each broken fragment withers on its own: we search to rebuild him, to bring together his body and mind, meditation and works, thought and action' (ibid.) Mounier admired the socio-economic analyses of the younger Karl Marx, particularly his theory of human alienation and, like Marx, he fused theory and practice; 'Man', he wrote, 'is only man when committed.'

Last but not least, Mounier's stress of community went far beyond the purely local. For him, the pre-Reformation Christian tradition had been *communautaire*, and he was interested in reviving the Catholic values of fraternity and internationalism – values which chimed strongly with the political clarion calls of the socialist left in the 1930s.

Jacques Vandamme's life has been deeply affected by these early personalist influences. In political terms, Jacques has always resided to the left of centre, comfortably at home in the idiosyncratic Belgian tradition of Christian Socialism. He harbours a deep belief in social justice and sees the law as a protective mantle for the needy. He is convinced of the need, morally and politically, for re-distributive mechanisms (his favourite parable is of the loaves and the fish). He wears an easy-going, urbane spirituality which has nevertheless been tempered in the flames of great personal sorrow. He is characterised by his commitment and involvement, tinged with a sense of urgency. As one of his nephews described it: 'Jacques has combined a talent for seeing things that need to be done with a talent for identifying those that can be done.'

Europe: steel and competition

In 1952, Jacques' career took a characteristically abrupt change of direction when he was appointed as Deputy Secretary to the Professional Council of the Belgian Steel Industry. The date was significant, for it was in 1952 that Europe's first major integration experiment got under way with the creation of the European Coal and Steel Community (ECSC). Through his new position, Jacques enjoyed a ringside view of the birth and evolution of the ECSC, and of the negotiations which were to lead to the creation, in 1958, of the European Economic Community (EEC). Among the many radical innovations of the EEC Treaty was the provision for an independent competition policy. The prospect fascinated Jacques, and in 1960 he was appointed as Head of Division in the three years-old European Commission, in the Directorate-General for Competition policy, a position he was to hold happily for the next thirteen years.

Tragedy

We live in a mechanised world which, by its very nature, brings great advantages and considerable risks. On the afternoon of 10 September 1970, Jacques and his wife were driving near Renaix (Ronse) when a driver in an oncoming car suffered a heart attack. His car veered suddenly across the road and a head-on, frontal collision occurred. Marguerite died the next day. Jacques was grievously injured, his chest crushed by the steering wheel. He was still in intensive care when his beloved Marguerite was buried. At fifty years of age, he found himself alone with five children to bring up. He took advantage of British accession to take an early pension, and was resolved on devoting himself to looking after his children and focusing more on his parallel academic career.

It was at this time that Jacques bought an old and delapidated former presbytery in the little Famennes village of Froidlieu, on the border with the Ardennes, and not far from Hastière. With the help of his children and friends, Jacques restored the presbytery and over the years it has become something of an institution, with frequent visits from family, friends, academics, diplomats and the occasional minister.

The Report on European Union

Within a year, with a demonstration of the extraordinary physical and psychological resilience for which he is renowned, Jacques had bounced back into professional life. His mother, a long-standing widow, had temporarily moved into the Uccle family home to look after the children who were, in any case, all of school age by then. As he recounts in Chapter 9, the Belgian Prime Minister, Leo Tindemans, had been charged by the 1974 Paris summit with the task of drawing up a report on European Union. He asked Jacques Vandamme to help him in the task and for the next three years Jacques served as Tindemans' special adviser on European and international affairs.

As an ardent supporter of the integration process, Jacques saw the Tindemans Report as a potential watershed. Of particular importance was the very broad consultative exercise which the Heads of Government had requested. As Jacques himself points out in Chapter 10, the forces of intergovernmentalism had emerged victorious in the late 1940s and early 1950s. The ECSC and the EEC had represented hybrid, organic compromises, but had been built top-down rather than grass-roots up. Now the European Heads of State had asked Tindemans not only to go to the member states and the European institutions, but also to go back to the grass roots. As Leo Tindemans was to write in his 29 December 1975 letter to his European Council colleagues, 'almost all the people to whom I spoke stated that they could not imagine a better future for their country than that offered by the building of Europe. They could not conceive of doing this other than by strengthening the Community' (Tindemans, 1976). Could this be another possibility to tap into popular sentiment in favour of greater integration? Jacques Vandamme believed so and threw himself into his work with great fervour.

The consultations which led to the Tindemans Report involved prodigious amounts of work. Having first consulted academic specialists, Tindemans drew up a questionnaire which was sent to all of the participants in the exercise. Tindemans, Jacques, and a few other colleagues visited each member state in turn. They camped in the Belgian Embassy in each capital and organised intensive schedules of interviews and meetings with as broad a spectrum of representatives as possible. In between, Tindemans would visit the chief members of the government of the member state concerned. He also received vast quantities of written submissions. Simply to digest and analyse all of this information involved a major logistical exercise. Jacques was at the heart of it.

When all of the consultations had been made, and the various contributions digested, Tindemans, who was himself a convinced federalist, was confronted with an agonising choice between three possible roads of action. The first, as later described by Jacques,

> was to make a report relying on the majority tendency which had emerged from the 'popular consultation', and which was in favour of substantially strengthening the European construction, with regards both to the powers and the working of the institutions. Such a report would have identified the new challenges facing the Community, and the solutions with which to deal with them, in the short and medium term. It would have been a kind of 'message' to the European people, looking further afield than the immediate prospects.
>
> Vandamme, 1989, p. 158

A second possibility would have been to draft a report similar to the Spaak Report which followed the 1955 Messina Conference. Such an approach would have set out the basis for future negotiations to draw up a Treaty of European Union. As such, it would have been predicated on a generalised political will among the member states which, if it had existed at the December 1974 Paris Conference, had since rapidly waned.

The third possibility was to take a far more pragmatic approach, perhaps better adapted to the prevailing political winds, an approach which would seek agreement on broad guidelines which could then serve as the basis for the gradual elaboration of legally binding texts in such areas as European Political Cooperation, Economic and Monetary Union, and Social Policy. The ultimate aim of such an incremental approach would be European Union, but any immediate definition of the end state would be eschewed.

As an idealistic pragmatist, Jacques preferred the first option. As a pragmatic idealist, Leo Tindemans preferred the third. As Tindemans put it,

> I had to make a difficult choice. My proposals do not directly concern the final phase of European development. They state the objectives and the methods whereby Europe can be invested with a new vitality and current obstacles can be overcome . . . it represents a realistic yet feasible approach.
>
> Tindemans, 1976, p. 8

There was no dramatic parting of the ways. Jacques was an adviser, and he gave his advice. Tindemans was the author of the report, and on the basis of his political judgement he decided to take a balanced approach. Nevertheless, the idealist in Jacques was frustrated. He had always been a free spirit and – although I am speculating here – it might be that he thought that Tindemans' mandate had genuinely given federalists a chance to appeal directly to the European peoples over the heads of the member state governments.

In Chapter 9, Tindemans describes what happened to his report. By 1976, the general *relance* he had sought seemed more distant than ever, and attention was more narrowly focused on the advent of direct elections to the European Parliament. At the end of 1977, with the Belgian Presidency (in the second half of that year) out of the way, Jacques felt he had done all that he could and resigned his position as adviser.

Academia, GEPE and TEPSA

Jacques had been a professor at the University of Leuven since 1961, where he taught European economic and social law. He was also a visiting professor at Nancy University's European Studies Centre, and at the Economic and Social Sciences faculty of the University of Lille I. He had become increasingly involved in research and academic studies relating to the European Community, and was part of a network of interested academics throughout Belgium. Now freed from his *cabinet* duties, Jacques began to devote himself more fully to research and writing, but it also occurred to him that it would be useful to formalise this network by transforming it into an academic association. Jacques thus became a founding member of the Belgian *Groupe d'Etudes Politiques Européennes* (GEPE), and was appointed its Chairman in 1981. The creation of GEPE led rapidly to contacts with similar organisations in other member states.

Jacques' involvement in the wide-ranging consultative process which had led to the Tindemans Report had already given him direct insights into the value of international cooperation. Once again, Jacques saw the potential for a more formal and structured association which could maximise the advantages of cooperation. Thus, his enthusiasm began to infuse the Trans-European Policy Studies Association, TEPSA, a network which today comprises research institutions in all fifteen member states and which has become one of the major Brussels-based think-tanks. Jacques served as President of TEPSA until 1995. (With the exception of Jacques Delors and Leo Tindemans, the contributors to this book are all long-standing TEPSA members.) Over the years, TEPSA has proved a fertile breeding ground for conceptual innovation and the exchange of ideas. It has also produced a large number of wide-ranging publications. It has become particularly well-known for the conferences it organises before each Presidency in the member state concerned.

'Retirement'

Jacques is now a *pater familias par excellence*, with an extended family. In the early 1980s this long-standing widower found renewed happiness when he met and married Maïna Van Heike, a book-binder. Of his five children, three married non-Belgians, giving his family life the same sort of international atmosphere he so much enjoyed in his professional life. He has twelve grandchildren on whom he dotes. Five of these children are adopted, two from India, two from Vietnam and one from China, and nothing has given Jacques greater joy than to welcome to his family members of the greater world community. In 1988, at the age of 65, Jacques invited all of his family to a Burgundy hotel to celebrate his 'retirement'. His disbelieving audience were told of his intentions to cut down on his professional activities, and of how he intended to devote himself increasingly to two research projects; a study of his military ancestors and, above all, a study of the Dukes of Burgundy, whom Jacques considers to have been the first 'true' Europeans.

Whilst it was true that Jacques spent more time at Froidlieu, his GEPE and TEPSA activities showed no signs of slowing down. He seemed to travel just as frequently, and when he was not travelling on academic business, there were his holidays to the Alps (Jacques continued playing tennis until the age of 70 and he continued skiing until the age of 74), and he could always find good reason to visit one or other of his children in Ispra or Geneva.... Nevertheless, in 1997 Jacques finally handed over the Presidency of TEPSA to Wolfgang Wessels, a Professor at the University of Cologne and a long-standing TEPSA member. In the same year, Guy Vanhaeverbeke became TEPSA Secretary General. These developments at last enabled Jacques to slow down his professional life a little, though his passionate intellectual interest in all matters European continues unabated. This book has been published to coincide with Jacques' seventy-fifth birthday. Longevity runs in his family. We still hope to read one day about the military Vandammes and the Dukes of Burgundy. In the meantime, we hope this book will stand as a monument to a life devoted, in best European tradition, to family, friends, and the numerous communities to which Jacques belongs and to which he has given so much.

NOTES

1 Elsa, who lived on to the ripe old age of 93, had vivid memories of Zeppelins over London, the sound of the big guns on the Western Front carrying over the English Channel to Brighton (where her convalescing father was briefly billetted), and of the bombardments of Paris and Calais (where the Bouvier family had moved to be near the Front). She later wrote up a journal of her early life which includes a particularly poignant passage about military medals tinkling in the wind on the massed graves of the war dead.
2 François was born in 1950, Elizabeth in 1951, Godelieve in 1956, and the twins, Myriam and Damien, in 1958.

REFERENCES

Gelard, Joseph, 1986, *L'artillerie Belge en Grand-Bretagne et dans les Combats de la Libération, 1941–1945: First Belgian Field Battery*, Cabay, Louvain-la-Neuve

Mounier, Emmanuel, 1947, *Qu'est-ce que c'est le personalisme?*, Seuil, Paris

Pryce, Roy (ed.), 1989, *The Dynamics of European Union*, Routledge, London

Struye, Paul, 1945, *L'évolution du sentiment public en Belgique sous l'occupation allemande*, Editions Lumière, Brussels

Tindemans, Leo, 1976, 'European Union. Report by Mr Leo Tindemans, Prime Minister of Belgium, to the European Council', *Bulletin of the European Communities*, 1/76, Brussels

Vandamme, Jacques, 1989, 'The Tindemans Report (1975–6)', in Pryce, Roy (ed.), op. cit.

2 The European Union's 'blind watchmakers'[1]
The process of constitutional change

Martin Westlake

In his 1802 *Natural Theology – or Evidences of the Existence and Attributes of the Deity collected from the Appearances of Nature,* William Paley gave perhaps the best-known exposition of the 'argument from design' for the existence of God.

> In crossing a heath, suppose I pitched my foot against a *stone*, and were asked how the stone came to be there; I might possibly answer that, for anything I knew to the contrary, it had lain there forever: nor would it perhaps be very easy to show the absurdity of this answer. But suppose I had found a *watch* upon the ground, and it should be inquired how the watch happened to be in that place; I should hardly think of the answer which I had before given.
>
> Paley, 1828

Having described the precise nature of the watch's cogs and springs and the complexity of the mechanism of which they form a part, Paley went on to argue that, even if we had never come across a watch before, these qualities would force us to conclude:

> that the watch must have had a maker: that there must have existed, at some time, and at some place or other, an artificer or artificers, who formed it for the purpose which we find it actually to answer, who comprehended its construction, and designed its use.
>
> Paley, idem.

Until 1859, when Darwin's *Origin of Species* was published, Paley's argument both reflected and reinforced the conscious designer theory which virtually everybody in the Western world accepted as the only logical explanation of man's and the world's existence. Darwin's theory proposed the blind creativity of physics:

> A true watchmaker has foresight: he designs his cogs and springs, and plans their interconnections, with a future purpose in his mind's eye. Natural selection, the blind, unconscious, automatic process which Darwin discovered, and which we now know is the explanation for the

existence and apparently purposeful form of all life, has no purpose in mind. It has no mind and no mind's eye. It does not plan for the future. It has no vision, no foresight, no sight at all. If it can be said to play the role of watchmaker in nature, it is the *blind* watchmaker.

Dawkins, 1986, p. 5[2]

This chapter is inspired by the neo-Darwinian approach, as most lucidly extolled by Richard Dawkins. It should be stressed that the spirit of the chapter is *descriptive* and not, with the exception of the conclusions, *normative*. My chief argument is that the process of constitutional change in the European Union is organic and evolutionary in nature. Using the parallel of neo-Darwinian evolutionary theory, I hope to show how the dynamics of the integrative process can be both positive and negative, progressive and regressive.[3] I will argue that the key to understanding constitutional change in the European Union is not so much by reference to any underlying constitutional blueprint, but through an understanding of the restraints facing participants in the process of constitutional change (principally intergovernmental conferences) *at the time of that change*. But in conclusion I shall argue that constitutional blueprints, seen as evolutionary forces, have a vital role to play in the European Union's development.

Let me begin with an adaptation of William Paley's colourful metaphor. Supposing the wandering Paley were to stub his toe not on a stone or a watch but on the German Basic Law or the constitution of the French Fifth Republic. Paley would argue that the complexity of these constitutional mechanisms provides incontrovertible proof that they were the creations of an intelligent constitution-builder. Whilst Darwin (and Hume) might disagree with Paley's logical processes, the fact is that Paley's imagined conclusion, even if based on an erroneous assumption, would be right: the Basic Law and the modern French constitution *were* the conscious creations of intelligent constitution builders – the Allies and German constitutionalists finalising their work through a West German constituent assembly on the one hand, De Gaulle, Debré and French constitutionalists on the other. The same could be said of the US constitution and the Philadelphia Congress.

But what of the emerging constitutional arrangement of the European Union? Supposing the wandering Paley were to stub his metaphorical toe on the Treaty on European Union and all the accompanying amending Treaties. Would he be right to assume that this complex mass was the conscious result of a process of constitution building? Of course not! The European Union has never seen the equivalent of a Philadelphia Congress, a German constituent assembly or a Charles de Gaulle. As Jacques Vandamme points out in the last chapter in this volume, moves which *might* have led to the creation of federalist permanent constitutional settlements were seen off in the 1940s by the British preference for intergovernmentalism (leading to the creation of the Council of Europe) and in the

1950s by the French Assemblée Nationale's refusal to countenance a European Army. True, the Rome Treaty is commonly portrayed as the European Union's foundation stone, but Messina was never on a constitutional par with Philadelphia. Indeed, the 'founding fathers' consciously eschewed any concept of a finished constitutional settlement in favour of an organic framework treaty. This is not to argue that 'intelligent processes' have not been at work over the past forty years, but more in the relatively short-term, and short-sighted, work of intergovernmental conferences, Court rulings, inter-institutional agreements, and other pseudo-constitutional mechanisms. Despite the undoubted intelligence of the human actors involved, these various mechanisms are, I would argue, the European Union's equivalent of Dawkins' 'blind watchmakers'.[4]

HOW EVOLUTION WORKS

> Natural selection is the blind watchmaker, blind because it does not see ahead, does not plan consequences, has no purpose in view.
>
> Dawkins, 1986, p. 21

One of the central planks of neo-Darwinian theory is the power of cumulative selection. Dawkins describes this as:

> gradual, step-by-step transformations from simple beginnings ... Each successive change in the gradual evolutionary process was simple enough, relative to its predecessor, to have arisen by chance. But the whole sequence of cumulative steps constitutes anything but a chance process, when you consider the complexity of the final end-product relative to the original starting point.
>
> Dawkins, 1986, p. 43

To take one example, the human eye could not have arisen directly from no eye at all, but even such a highly complex organ could be the end state of a series of mutations, stretching back to the state of no eye at all. If all animal life is examined, we quickly realise that there is not one model of human eye at all, but many different ones; the lensless eye of the Nautilus, the compound eyes of some crustaceans and insects, the four eyes of the snail and the eight eyes of the spider, the eye of the chameleon, and mammalian eyes such as our own. All are end products of very different evolutionary processes, and yet all have the same function and all, with varying degrees of sophistication, work in similar ways.

Dawkins provides another good example from the natural world in the form of the two very different sorts of flatfish which live in the oceans. In the case of skates and rays (biological relatives of sharks), their bodies have gradually grown out sideways. Although their bodies are now flattened, they remain symmetric. But in the case of bottom-feeders such as plaice, sole, halibut and turbot, the fish has gradually, over thousands of years, turned over on to one side. Since this process left one eye on the 'blind', or bottom, side, evolution has gradually shifted the bottom eye around to the top side. This migration of the bottom eye can still be observed as it takes place in every young flatfish. As Dawkins puts it,

> The whole skull of a bony flatfish retains the twisted and distorted evidence of its origins. Its very imperfection is powerful testimony of its ancient history, a history of step-by-step change rather than of deliberate design. No sensible designer would have conceived such a monstrosity if given a free hand to create a flatfish on a clean drawing board.
>
> Dawkins, 1986, p. 92

I would argue that very similar observations could be made about the current constitutional arrangement of the European Union and its institutions. As I have written elsewhere, 'the initial blueprint of the European Union's "founding fathers" is still visible, a little like the way we can still see the Roman street plans in maps of our modern cities'. (Westlake, 1996–7, p. 150). I shall return to a consideration of the role of constitutional blueprints in the final section of this chapter, but I first want to show how the parallel of evolutionary theory can give us important insights into the integration process.

THE EUROPEAN UNION'S EVOLUTIONARY PROCESS AT WORK – TWO EXAMPLES

Anyone who has seen a detailed diagram of the so-called 'co-decision procedure'[5] which emerged from the Maastricht Treaty would agree, to paraphrase Dawkins, that 'no sensible engineer would have conceived such a monstrosity if given a free hand'. But the point here, as this section will show, is that the Maastricht Treaty's draftsmen decidedly did *not* have free hands.

The 1957 Rome Treaty provided for the consultation of the European Parliament in certain policy areas. Under pressure from the Parliament, and with Commission backing, the Council agreed gradually to extend such consultation to other policy areas. Whether facultative or obligatory, such consultation was rarely more than perfunctory, and the European Parliament's opinions were largely ignored.

The advent of direct elections to the European Parliament in 1979 did not alter these circumstances, though direct elections did give the Parliament the moral status and the political impetus to pursue its claims. An unexpected 1980 ruling of the European Court of Justice[6] suddenly created the possibility for the Parliament to play a more influential, if negative, role in the European Community's legislative processes. The Council had definitively adopted a decision before the Parliament had delivered its opinion. Since the consultation of Parliament was obligatory, the Court ruled that the Council's decision should be annulled and Parliament's opinion sought.

With ingenious use of its internal rule-making autonomy, the Parliament turned this right to consultation into a de facto power of indefinite delay.[7] Where it was unhappy with the legislative text emerging from the Council's drafting bodies (the working groups and COREPER), the Parliament gave itself the right to refer its draft opinion back to committee for further consideration.

Parliament was not naïve enough to suppose that such action could have direct influence on the member state governments. However, under the Treaties the Commission may amend or withdraw its draft proposals at any time and, under the provisions of Article 189a (**250**), the Council requires unanimity to amend a Commission proposal. Parliament's target was the initial draftsman of the legislative proposal, the Commission. Delay might force the Commission into amending its proposal. It is clear that, in amending its rules to create such a de facto power of delay, the Parliament was not intent on laying the definitive foundations of its future legislative role. On the contrary, the so-called 'consultation procedure' was improvised precisely because the European Parliament did not have *any* legislative role. It was never intended to be anything more than a stop-gap, ad hoc device.

The 1985 Intergovernmental Conference enshrined the policy goal of the completion of the internal market in the Treaty. The Commission had set out a vast raft of legislation (about 300 legislative proposals) in its White Paper, and proposed a deadline – 31 December 1992. It was commonly recognised that such a plan would remain hopelessly ambitious unless some form of majority voting were introduced to the Council of Ministers, which had stagnated since the 1966 crisis because of a generalised insistence on unanimity. The draftsmen therefore agreed on the explicit provision for qualified majority voting in certain policy areas, but they were obliged to find a democratic, parliamentary quid pro quo for what was, after all, a highly significant constitutional innovation. Understandably, they built on what already existed. A new procedure was introduced, with two readings for the Parliament and an important gate-keeping role for the Commission. The first reading of the resulting cooperation procedure was identical to the consultation procedure. Five years later, the draftsman of the Maastricht Treaty continued to build on the same basic block. Under the co-decision procedure, potential for a third reading was introduced, but the first reading remained virtually identical to the old consultation procedure.[8] Similarly, though the architects of the Amsterdam Treaty streamlined the co-decision procedure, the first reading stage – and hence the implications of the Isoglucose ruling – remained unchanged.

The evolution of the Parliament's legislative role (summarised in Table 2.1) provides a good example of the way in which the Union's constitutional development is a cumulative process, based on incremental change. The evolution of the Parliament's 'elective function', summarised in Table 2.2, provides another good example of the same phenomenon at work.

Table 2.1 The evolution of the European Parliament's Legislative Role[9]

Year	Event
1957	Rome Treaty provides for consultation of the European Parliament on legislative proposals in certain policy areas (the so-called 'consultation procedure')
1979	Direct elections create new, more autonomous, dynamic and ambitious full-time Parliament enjoying direct legitimacy
1980	Unexpected Isoglucose ruling by the Court of Justice obliges the Council to await formal parliamentary opinion before definitive adoption of legislative acts where consultation of the Parliament is provided for by the Treaty
1981	Using internal rule-making autonomy, the Parliament creates a mechanism providing for indefinite 'referral back to committee' – creating a de facto, open-ended power of delay
1986	Single European Act radically expands explicit qualified majority voting in the Council. The Parliament is granted a positive input into the legislative process as a democratic quid pro quo. The cooperation procedure consists of two readings. The first is identical to the consultation procedure
1993	The Treaty on European Union creates the so-called 'co-decision procedure', involving three readings. The first reading is identical to the consultation procedure. The second reading is borrowed from the cooperation procedure
1997	The Amsterdam Treaty refines and extends the scope of the co-decision procedure. The consultation procedure-type first reading remains intact

Table 2.2 The evolution of the European Parliament's 'Elective Function'[10]

Year	Event
1975	Luxembourg Treaty creates the Court of Auditors and grants the European Parliament a consultative role in regard to the appointment of the members of the Court. The Parliament institutes a committee hearing procedure
1979	Direct elections create new, more autonomous, dynamic and ambitious full-time Parliament enjoying direct legitimacy
1981	Gaston Thorn, President-elect of the European Commission, comes before the European Parliament, together with his new Commission colleagues in what is styled as a 'confirmation hearing'
1983	The Stuttgart Solemn Declaration on European Union codifies Thorn's precedent and grants the Parliament's then 'enlarged Bureau' a consultative role in relation to the nomination of the Commission's President
1985	Jacques Delors and his Commission colleagues, respecting the Stuttgart provisions, repeat Thorn's gesture at the beginning of the Delors I Commission
1989	At the beginning of the Delors II Commission, Jacques Delors and his Commission colleagues refine the procedure by participating in the Parliament's 'confirmatory hearing' before they take the oath before the Court of Justice
1993	The Treaty on European Union grants the Parliament a consultative role in relation to the appointment of the European Monetary Institute's President. The Parliament exploits its internal rule-making autonomy to create a refined committee hearing process based on the US model
1995	The Parliament, building on its past experience and the new provisions in the Treaty on European Union for a vote of confidence on the Commission college as a whole, again exploits its internal rule-making autonomy and the political situation to create individual parliamentary committee hearings for the Commissioners-elect. The President-elect's 'hearing' consists of a refined confirmatory debate and vote in a plenary session of the Parliament
1997	The Amsterdam Treaty transforms Parliament's consultation on the nomination for Commission President into approval

The consequences of this process, of building on precedent whilst satisfying short-term pragmatic requirements, are everywhere present in the European Union's structure. One need only think, for example, of the snake, the snake-in-the-tunnel, the Exchange Rate Mechanism and the first stage of Economic and Monetary Union. . . . But there is another aspect to this process; things are frequently used for ends for which they which were not originally intended.[11]

THE MECHANISM FOR CONSTITUTIONAL CHANGE

Tabling amendments

Box 2.1 compares the EU and US mechanisms for constitutional change (respectively, Article N- **48** of the Treaty on European Union and Article V of the US Constitution). As can immediately be seen, the framers of the US Constitution made it very difficult to get the amending process under way; a proposed amendment must be passed either by a two-thirds majority of both Houses of Congress or a convention called by Congress at the request of two-thirds of the States. In the European Union, on the other hand, any member state government, or the Commission, may 'get the ball rolling' by tabling amendments. The Council will then decide (after due consultation of the Parliament and, where necessary, the Commission), whether to convoke an intergovernmental conference. Only a simple majority is required to take such a decision; member states can be, and have been, outvoted. Notably, Greece, Denmark and the United Kingdom (three out of the then ten member states or, in terms of weighted votes, eighteen out of sixty-three votes – 28.5 per cent) were outvoted in relation to the convocation of the 1985 intergovernmental conference which led to the 1986 Single European Act.

The fact that member states may be outvoted brings its own dynamics to the intergovernmental conference process itself, but the point here is that it is very much easier to get the amending process under way in the European Union than in the United States. This explains why, and how, the European Union has managed to hold three major intergovernmental conferences in the space of little more than a decade (not counting the mini-intergovernmental conferences which accompanied the 1986 and 1995 enlargements).

Passing amendments

Contrarily, at first sight, it seems easier to *pass* constitutional amendments in the United States than in the European Union. In the United States, an amendment need 'only' be ratified by three-fourths of the State legislatures or by conventions in three-fourths of the States (the method used for all but one of the twenty-six amendments passed to date has involved a proposal by Congress and ratification by State legislatures).

Box 2.1 The EU and US mechanisms for constitutional change compared

---

Article N-(48) of the Treaty on European Union *(excerpt)*
'1 The government of any Member State or the Commission may submit to the Council proposals for the amendment of the Treaties on which the Union is founded.
If the Council, after consulting the European Parliament and, where appropriate, the Commission, delivers an opinion in favour of calling a conference of representatives of the member states, the conference shall be convened by the President of the Council for the purpose of determining by common accord the amendments to be made to those Treaties . . .'
Article V of the US Constitution
'The Congress, whenever two-thirds of both houses shall deem it necessary, shall propose amendments to this constitution, or, on the application of the legislatures of two-thirds of the several States, shall call a convention for proposing amendments, which, in either case, shall be valid to all intents and purposes, as part of this Constitution, when ratified by the legislatures of three-fourths of the several States, or by conventions in three-fourths thereof, as the one or the other mode of ratification may be proposed by the Congress.'

In the European Union, on the other hand, amendments must be adopted by 'common accord' (that is, unanimity) of the representatives of the governments of the member states *and* ratified by all of the member states according to their various constitutional requirements. Such requirements may involve parliamentary ratification (for example, the United Kingdom), special parliamentary congresses (for example, France), and/or direct consultation of the people (for example, Ireland).

At face value, these requirements seem far more daunting than a three-fourths majority of State legislatures, particularly since the European Union contains a number of states habitually sceptical about the need for further constitutional change; the Danish Folketing rejected the Single European Act by five votes (although this was later overthrown by a 56 per cent majority in a referendum); the Danish people rejected the Treaty on European Union by 50.7 per cent to 49.3 per cent (this was later overthrown by a 56.8 per cent to 43.2 per cent majority in a second referendum).

And yet, despite all of these apparent difficulties, every single European Union intergovernmental conference held to date has been entirely successful, in the sense that the results of each have been agreed by all of the representatives of the governments of the member states and, ultimately, ratified by all of the member states according to their respective constitutional requirements. In the United States, on the other hand, of the more than 6,000 constitutional amendments introduced in Congress over the past two centuries, only twenty-six have been passed.

The most obvious difference between the European Union and United States mechanisms for constitutional change relates to the nature of the 'amendments' considered. This, in turn, is bound up in the difference between the United States Constitution, which has remained fundamentally unaltered over two centuries, and the European Union Treaties, which are frequently substantially amended. To take a few examples, the thirteenth amendment to the United States Constitution abolished slavery; the seventeenth provided for the direct election of senators; the twentieth changed the date for the start of congressional and presidential terms. By contrast, the Treaty on European Union (the Maastricht Treaty) alone provided for economic and monetary union, created a new legislative procedure, and changed the mechanism for the appointment of the Commission and its President, to take but three substantial examples from a very long list of amendments. Hence, it can be seen that the European Union's mechanism for constitutional change habitually involves not one amendment, but many.

This leads to a second important difference. The fact that any member state or the Commission may table amendments (at virtually any time throughout the intergovernmental conference process, it should be added), together with the fact that an intergovernmental conference will consider and adopt many amendments, opens up the negotiation process in a way unthinkable in the United States. In particular, the European Union's mechanism for constitutional change lends itself to the phenomenon of package deals. Such deals are practised on a vast scale, with concessions in some areas matched by gains in others, and with the deals rendered ever more complex by the increasing number of member states involved and by the developing habit of what one recent newspaper article described as 'special pleading' (*European Voice*, 1997, p. 12).[12] Clearly, the satisfaction of such special concerns can facilitate the agreement of the government concerned to the overall package of constitutional change.

This leads on to a third observation. Although intergovernmental negotiations are mostly carried out by officials, diplomats and junior ministers, they are traditionally completed by the Heads of State or Government, meeting together in special intergovernmental conference summits. Hence, at a very late stage in the process, intergovernmental conferences become tests of the prowess of the politicians involved. Furthermore, once they have initialled an agreement, the participants have a vested interest in selling the result back to their national audiences, since their prestige and authority, as François Mitterrand, Poul Schlüter and John Major all, in different ways, found to their cost, become bound up in the domestic ratification process.

A fourth important difference relates to the fact that, in the case of the European Union, the future of the whole enterprise is increasingly perceived as being predicated upon the success of each exercise in constitutional change. Intergovernmental conferences cannot fail. In this bald statement stalks the shadow of the 1954 European Defence Community débâcle, reflected in the traumatised reactions to the Danish 'no' of 1992.

These four factors – the spread of amendments, the creation of complex package deals, the championing by the Heads of State or Government, and the linkage to the success of the enterprise as a whole – go a long way towards explaining the 100 per cent success rate that the European Union's intergovernmental conferences have enjoyed to date. In terms of the central theme of this chapter, the four factors also explain why intergovernmental conferences rarely achieve ideal results. What intergovernmental conferences produce is not the best possible result in objective terms, but the best possible result given the restraints under which the participants are acting *at the time of the conference.*

This brief comparative analysis of the European Union's mechanism for constitutional change leads to four observations.

CONSTITUTIONAL CHANGE AND THE AVOIDANCE OF EXTINCTION

In neo-Darwinian terms, a capacity for change – above all, adaptation to environmental change – is vital to the survival of organisms. It is commonly held that organisations, like organisms, which fail to adapt to changed circumstances are doomed to extinction. For the European Union, an obvious example of environmental change is enlargement. Indeed, most observers see direct linkage between intergovernmental conferences and successive waves of accession. The 1996–7 Intergovernmental Conference, in particular, was generally seen as a preparatory measure in view of the imminent accession of the central and eastern European countries, together with Cyprus. Seen in this light, the paradoxical ease with which the European Union is able to launch and conduct the process of constitutional change is a considerable organic advantage.

Critics might argue that other constitutional states (like the United States) manage to survive without frequent, and easy, constitutional change. But, by definition, those countries which already enjoy fixed constitutional settlements do not have similarly changing environments. Hence when, following the fall of the Berlin Wall and the collapse of the Soviet Union, the five new Länder of the former GDR were absorbed into the German Federal Republic, it was on the explicit understanding that they would accept the entirety of the Basic Law (and, incidentally, the *acquis communautaire* – Spence, 1991). The absorption of, for example, Alaska (purchased in 1867) and Hawaii (annexed in 1898) into the United States occurred on much the same terms.

In other words, for as long as the European Union remains an evolutionary and organic arrangement, the relative ease with which it is able to bring about constitutional change represents an advantage, enabling it to adapt to frequent environmental change and perhaps even facilitating its survival.

UNINTENDED CONSEQUENCES

The pressure-cooker atmosphere of intergovernmental conferences, particularly in the closing European Council meetings, provides fertile ground for the law of unintended consequences.[13] Compromise solutions are sometimes adopted at a political level so late in the day that it is impossible to think through all of the possible constitutional consequences (for an example from the 1997 Amsterdam European Council, see Smyth, 1997). In any case, it is simply impossible to have a complete picture of how new treaty provisions will 'pan out' in practice. These considerations go some way towards explaining the increasing number – and the increasing importance – of pseudo-constitutional 'inter-institutional agreements' (such as, for example, the 1995 'code of conduct' between the European Parliament and the Commission).[14] It could be argued that the intended effect of inter-institutional agreements is to flesh out the bare bones of treaty provisions and hence to ward off unintended consequences.

The 1987 Single European Act provided good examples of both the types of unintended consequence described above in the form of the assent powers granted to the European Parliament in relation to the conclusion of association agreements (Article 228, **300**). The treaty draftsmen had in mind only association agreements themselves, but it soon became clear that, in legal terms, the Parliament's assent powers applied not only to agreements but also to any revision or addition to such agreements. Moreover, Parliament's powers were further enhanced by the consequences of the collapse of the Communist regimes in Eastern Europe, which soon led to the conclusion of 'European Agreements' with a number of countries. In all, between the entry into force of the Single European Act and the entry into force of the Maastricht Treaty, Parliament was called upon to grant its assent to some fifty-four acts.[15] Thus, what had been intended as a very occasional power became a frequently-used power.

The unintended consequences were not only limited to the quantitative scope of the new power. The European Parliament was swift to realise that it had been given an important lever, both *vis-à-vis* the Union's trade negotiator, the Commission, and with regard to the third state(s) involved, to pursue its own external relations political agenda and in particular in relation to human rights issues. Large financial programmes had to be postponed on several occasions, as the Parliament sought political commitments and concessions on the human rights records of the states concerned. A further unintended consequence was involved, bound up in the Article 228 (**300**) absolute majority requirement. No doubt the treaty draftsmen thought they were underlining the political significance of assent by imposing an absolute majority requirement, but '... it soon became apparent to the Parliament that the absence of an absolute majority was sufficient to bring about delay, whatever the relative size of any simple majority' (Westlake, 1994b, p. 158). The draftsmen of the Maastricht Treaty silently did away with this nuance and considerably weakened Parliament's assent powers by doing away with the absolute majority requirement (in the United States Senate, by contrast, a two-thirds majority is required for advice-and-assent before the President can ratify any treaty). This illustration leads neatly to my next general observation.

CHANGE AND PROGRESS

Change and progress are not necessarily linked, and are certainly not synonymous. Whilst neo-Darwinian theory considers change to be a vital element in evolution and the survival of organisms, change of itself is not necessarily a 'good thing' and, in probability terms, is as likely to lead to decline as progress. Undirected change carries a high risk potential (hence, I would argue, the importance of blueprint draftsmen, of which more below). The picture is further clouded by the fact, already pointed out, that intergovernmental conferences do not result in a single constitutional amendment, but many. Probability alone would lead us to expect that not all of the changes introduced by an intergovernmental conference would represent progress.[16] Hence the torrent of ambiguous judgements regarding the outcome of the June 1997 Amsterdam European Council. As one of the participants in the intergovernmental conference put it, the results were '*entre succès et échec*'; that is, 'between success and failure' (Dehousse, 1997), whilst a former Belgian Prime Minister wittily described the Amsterdam methodology as 'negative positivism' (Eyskens, 1997).

PERCEPTIONS AND PROGRESS

In any case, decline/regression and progress are relative terms. Progress, like beauty, is in the eye of the beholder. In the example of the assent procedure given above, Parliament soon came to see that the absolute majority requirement (probably intended, as in the case of the cooperation procedure, to make it more difficult for the European Parliament to wield its new-found powers effectively) actually enhanced its power. For the Council, on the other hand, the unintended scope of the power was seen as a setback which the Maastricht Treaty duly addressed.

In this context, one of the most potent symbols of progress in integration is the extension to further policy areas of qualified majority voting in the Council – the clarion call of all federalists. Yet, in the longer term, we may look more kindly upon the unanimity principle as a way of combating centrifugal forces and locking us into a quasi-fixed (though perhaps still gently evolving) constitutional settlement. A premonition of this new attitude came already with the 1986 Single European Act, which amended the first paragraph of Article 70[17] so that 'Unanimity shall be required for measures which constitute a step back as regards the liberalization of capital movements'. Hence, unanimity (at least in Article N (**48**), if not in certain key, or core, policy areas) may ultimately come to be seen in a positive light as a constitutional locking device. Unanimity may make it difficult to get anywhere, but it makes it just as difficult to move away.[18]

Two additional observations can be made in the context of the debate about unanimity. The first is that if, as the Parliament has for so long insisted, it were to be given assent powers in relation to Treaty change, then logically agreement would be even more difficult to obtain, since there would be sixteen, rather than fifteen, parties to satisfy (and, including the Commission, seventeen at the negotiating table).[19] This is a classic democratic paradox; enhancing democracy does not necessarily improve efficiency. The second observation is that, even if the unanimity requirement in Article N (**48**) were to be relaxed, the basic equation would not change, since it would still be necessary to put together a package deal over a wide range of issues in order to construct the necessary majority (whether qualified or 'super-qualified').[20]

This leads to a third, general observation. For as long as the European Union remains an evolutionary process rather than a fixed constitutional arrangement, we can expect intergovernmental conferences to remain multi-faceted negotiations covering many issues and resulting in many amendments. Intergovernmental conferences cannot yet be like, say, the co-decision process where, by the third-reading stage, areas of disagreement have been boiled down to just a handful of issues. It will be a very long time before the European Union reaches the stage where, as in the case of the United States, constitutional amendments are singular and infrequent.

THE ROLE AND IMPORTANCE OF BLUEPRINTS – MANIPULATING THE EVOLUTIONARY ENVIRONMENT

Many federalists would find my arguments so far to be uncomfortably deterministic. Many would also object to the idea of permanent flux – apparently excluding the prospect of a fixed constitutional settlement – and to the connected argument that progress may be reversible. I believe that there not only should be, but one day will be, a fixed constitutional settlement. I also believe that Europe's 'blueprint drafters' have a vital role to play in the integration process which will lead to that fixed settlement.

Above all, blueprint drafters have an overall view which determines their short-term tactics. They enable systems to avoid what Dawkins terms 'disadvantageous intermediates' (1986, p. 93). It is they who flag the potential pitfalls and try to steer the integration process away from evolutionary dead-ends. In what might otherwise be the dangerous free-for-all of intergovernmental conference negotiations where, as was explained, any number of amendments may be tabled at any time, the blueprint drafters keep their eyes firmly fixed on the overall objective. Like Europe's cathedral builders, blueprint draftsmen may not live to see the edifice completed, but they will ensure that the part of the construction for which they are responsible is sound and contributes to the whole.

In less subjective terms, the blueprint drafters have an effect on the environment in which constitutional change will take place. For example, the European Parliament may not yet have a place at the negotiating table, but it nevertheless exerts considerable moral and political pressure on the negotiators through its resolutions and reports, particularly when it is able to exploit alliances with sympathetic member states and the Commission.

Blueprint draftsmen also set out the terms of future debate, sometimes with great vision. The mandate which led to the Tindemans Report and, in particular, the aim of reaching agreement 'on an overall concept of European Union', may have been destined not to succeed *in the shorter term*, but as Chapters 6 and 9 demonstrate clearly, the Tindemans Report not only recommended a large number of developments which have since occurred but also flagged the terms of a number of fundamental debates (above all, flexibility) which have since developed and not yet been resolved.

All of the contributors to this book have, in their different ways, acted as blueprint draftsmen. Their previous work has ranged from the pragmatic, incremental approach of the Tindemans Report on European Union, through the regimented precision of the Delors Report on Economic and Monetary Union, to the constant review and examination of the integration process which the Trans-European Policy Studies Association and its members so effectively carry out. The reader may detect notes of impatience and frustration in some of the contributions to this volume, and this brings me on to a final observation based on the evolutionary parallel.

Evolutionary theory is predicated on the effects of gradual change over long periods of time. However, many federalists believe that the European integration process is currently stuck in a dangerous and debilitating 'disadvantageous intermediate'. Citing the confusion surrounding the Amsterdam Treaty, they argue that the evolutionary process described in this chapter is profoundly inefficient and undemocratic. They fervently believe that a European constitution should be drawn up *now*, with the full involvement of the European Union's peoples (for example, Ruffolo, 1997; Leinen, 1997). But as Vandamme points out in Chapter 10, the federalist high tides of the late 1940s and the early 1950s – key moments when popular sentiment might have been tapped – were seen off by British intergovernmentalism and the French *Assemblée Nationale*'s 1954 '*non*'. Nor does there seem any prospect of similar waves of enthusiasm for the integrationist project in the near future; on the contrary, the European Union enjoys largely passive support and more critical attitudes are on the increase.

In the absence of rapid movement to a fixed constitutional settlement, the Union is most likely to continue on a gradual, incremental, organic and evolutionary basis. That means that, to use one of François Mitterrand's favourite sayings, the Union must 'give time to time'. Or, to adapt an Arab proverb, the Union must not so much 'make haste, slowly' as 'act slowly, in haste'. The constant dialectic between these two conflicting expectations – the need for haste on the one hand, the need for time on the other – was graphically illustrated by the contrast between the initial ambitions accompanying the outset of the 1996 intergovernmental conference and the 'disappointing' results achieved at the Amsterdam European Council in June 1997. The dialectic also explains why, as Vandamme points out in Chapter 10, progress in European integration can be perceived at one and the same time as being disappointingly slow and surprisingly fast.

The 'founding fathers' of the 1950s may take pride of place in the European Union's pantheon but, in truth, there have been many generations of 'founding fathers'; Mitterrand, Kohl, Delors, Schmidt, Giscard d'Estaing, Heath, Spinelli, Genscher, Colombo, Jenkins, Tindemans and Hallstein, to name but a few. The list may be long, but all are deserving. And behind them stand the serried ranks of the European Union's blueprint draftsmen. Not a year goes by without some fresh blueprint being drawn up and fed into the continuing debate. Each succeeding blueprint can be likened to the way in which some artists go over their work again and again, gradually building up a deep richness to the emerging picture. Like powerful and tenacious tugboats, each draft constitution, each constitutional proposal, nudges the great mass of the evolutionary integration process forward on a generally coherent and consistent course, even if the final destination is not yet known.

NOTES

1. An early version of this chapter was presented at the Johns Hopkins University School of Advanced International Studies, Bologna Center.
2. Though palaeontology had to await Darwin, the philosopher David Hume had already provided logical disproof of the argument from design a century before the *Origin of Species* was published. Apparent design, Hume argued, was not proof positive of the existence of a creator.
3. The insights of neo-Darwinian evolutionary theory are being exploited in a growing number of disciplines; see, for example, de Gens, 1997, for such insights in relation to business theory. However, see also Jay Gould, 1997, for a critique of what he terms 'Darwinian fundamentalism'. Put simply, the parallels – and they are only parallels – can be overdone.
4. The argument can be put another way. If today the member states were to delegate representatives to a constitutional congress to draw up a 'European constitution', the result would be very different from the current institutional and constitutional arrangements of the EU.
5. '... part of the compromise among the governments was to avoid calling the new provisions the "co-decision procedure". The UK government, which had been vocal in its opposition to co-decision, hoped to camouflage its concession

The process of constitutional change 31

by avoiding the term. The treaty therefore refers only to "the procedure laid down in Article 189B . . . "' (Corbett, 1993, p. 58).
6 SA Roquette Frères v. Council (1980) ECR 3333 Case 138/79 and Maizena GmbH v. Council (1980) ECR 3393 Case 139/79.
7 Welsh (1996, pp. 54–5) maintains that this innovation was inspired by the Anglo-Saxon tradition of building on precedent. A subsequent ruling of the Court (Case 65/93 Parliament v. Council (1995) ECR I-661) has implied strongly that Parliament may not delay indefinitely where the Council requests urgency and where it seems the Parliament is not respecting what the Court sees as a general obligation incumbent upon all the institutions of 'sincere cooperation' among themselves. However, the case concerned tariff preferences. It is still not clear what the Court would decide where Parliament argued it was exerting legitimate legislative powers.
8 For discussions of the cooperation procedure, see Westlake, 1994b, pp. 137–44 and 1994a, pp. 36–9, and for discussions of the co-decision procedure, see 1994b, pp. 144–51 and 1994a, pp. 91–5. For an account of the negotiations which led to the creation of the cooperation procedure, see Corbett, 1989, and for those which led to the creation of the co-decision procedure, see Corbett, 1993.
9 For a more detailed account of the evolution of the Parliament's legislative role, see Westlake, 1997a.
10 For a more detailed account of the evolution of the Parliament's elective function, see Westlake, 1997b.
11 'Almost anything designed will have unintended side-effects and we cannot tell by merely looking at a feature whether it was itself the product of a selective pressure or merely a byproduct' (Brown, 1997). Near to Jacques Vandamme's house in the Ardennes, there is a fencepost which has grown into a tree. The farmer (possibly the same one who intially cut down a tree to make the fence post) now uses the tree to hang electric cables out of the reach of his cattle.
12 *The Economist* wrote of the Amsterdam Treaty 'A further huge rag-bag of other treaty provisions, many of dubious merit, is meant to please individual countries. They include animal rights (to make the British smile); protection of state-owned savings banks (nice for Germany); limiting rights of asylum in other European countries (e.g., for Spain's Basque terrorists); entrenching Strasbourg as the parliament's seat (jam for France)' (21 June 1997). An editorial in *The Times* dubbed the outcome 'Amsterdam soup' (26 June 1997).
13 Or, as a recent work puts it, 'Things Bite Back' (Tenner, 1997). Tenner provides a graphic example from the United States. According to the US National Highway Transportation Safety Administration, the introduction of airbags has saved some 1,500 lives. However, one tragic, entirely unforeseen and unintended consequence has been the accidental deaths of twenty-two infants. Tenner's main recommendation is eternal vigilance and this, I would argue, is an important aspect of the work of Europe's blueprint drafters.
14 See Stacey, 1996, for the only detailed and sustained analysis of interinstitutional agreements known to this author.
15 For a description and list, see Westlake, 1994a, pp. 41–2 and 57–60, and Westlake, 1994b, pp. 157–8.
16 To take one glaring example, the Amsterdam Treaty has now enshrined the Luxembourg Compromise in its provisions on closer cooperation – a clear regression from any pro-integrationist's point of view.
17 On the freedom of capital movements – the Amsterdam Treaty repealed the article, which had been rendered otiose by TEU Article 73b - **56** – as introduced by the Maastricht Treaty.
18 This is distinct from the normative argument that provision for unanimity in areas of great national sensitivity, such as Article 99 and fiscal harmonisation, is

a healthy precaution. The Commission's latest attempt to break the impasse on fiscal harmonisation, with its eschewing of anything similar to the Amsterdam Treaty's enhanced cooperation approach and its exploration of the possibility of a 'code of conduct' or 'gentlemen's agreement', is a clear nod in the direction of this consideration. (*Agence Europe*, 1997, p. 8; Barber, 1997a and b).

19 It would be interesting to speculate on what sort of negotiating mechanism the Parliament might have to establish in order to participate in the IGC. Who would participate? Assuming that it could only be one individual (like the member states and the Commission), would the duty fall to the President? On what basis would he or she negotiate, particularly if negotiations were complex, intense, and very time-consuming (as occurred with the Maastricht and Amsterdam Treaties)? Parliament is a quintessentially pluralistic body. No one individual, or group of individuals, can guarantee Parliament's support, as was demonstrated in the case of the draft directive on biotechnological inventions, where a co-decision third reading draft agreement negotiated by Parliament's conciliation committee was rejected by the plenary! (See Pinter, p. 58, for one suggested mechanism.)

20 What weight, one wonders, would the Parliament's vote be given, and on what basis might this be calculated?

REFERENCES

Agence Europe, 1997, 'The "code of Conduct" meant to limit tax competition between member states takes shape', Monday-Tuesday, 23–24 June

Barber, Lionel, 1997a, 'EU moves towards informal deal on tax levels', *Financial Times*, 30 June

—— 1997b, 'The Big Catch', *Financial Times*, 29 July

Brown, Andrew, 1997, 'Feud for Thought', *The Guardian*, 11 June

Corbett, Richard, 1989, 'The 1985 Intergovernmental Conference and the Single European Act', in Pryce, Roy (ed.), *The Dynamics of European Union*, Routledge, London

—— 1993, *The Treaty of Maastricht*, Longman, Harlow

Cram, Laura, 1996, 'Integration Theory and the Study of the European Policy Process', in Richardson, Jeremy (ed.), *European Union, Power and Policy-making*, Routledge, London and New York

Dawkins, Richard, 1986, *The Blind Watchmaker*, Longman, Harlow

Dehousse, Franklin, 1997, 'Amsterdam entre succès et échec', *La Libre Belgique*, 25 June

de Gens, Arie, 1997, *The Living Company*, Nicholas Brealey Publishing, London

European Voice, 1997, 'Special pleading brings results', 16 May, p. 12

Eyskens, Mark, 1997, 'Amsterdam ou le négativisme positif', *La Libre Belgique*, 26 June

Hesse, Joachim Jens, and Wright, Vincent (eds), 1996, *Federalizing Europe? The Costs, Benefits, and Preconditions of Federal Political Systems*, Oxford University Press, Oxford

Jay Gould, Stephen, 1997, 'Darwinian Fundamentalism', *The New York Review of Books*

Leinen, Jo, 1997, 'Federalists say a European Constitution is necessary', *Agence Europe*, no. 7000, 21 June

Paley, William, 1828 (second edition), *Natural Theology*, J. Vincent, Oxford

Pryce, Roy (ed.), 1989, *The Dynamics of European Union*, Routledge, London

Richardson, Jeremy (ed.), 1996, *European Union. Power and Policy-Making*, Routledge, London and New York

Ruffolo, Giorgio, 1997, 'Beyond the IGC: An Initiative in the European Parliament', *Crocodile*, 'Letter to the Parliaments of Europe', no. 1/2 1996–7, Brussels

Sartori, Giovanni, 1996, *Comparative Constitutional Engineering* (second edition), Macmillan, London
Smyth, Patrick, 1997, 'Schengen dispute reflects final shambolic hours of treaty debate', *The Irish Times*, 7 July
Spence, David, 1991, 'Enlargement Without Accession: The EC's Response to German Unification', Royal Institute of International Affairs, Discussion Paper no. 36, London
Stacey, Jeff, 1996, 'The Impact of Informal Interinstitutional Dynamics in European Policy-making', unpublished paper, Columbia University
Stephens, Philip, 1997, 'The Ragbag Treaty', *Financial Times*, 20 June
Tenner, Edward, 1997, *Why Things Bite Back: New Technology and the Revenge Effect*, Fourth Estate, London
Welsh, Michael, 1996, *Europe United?*, Macmillan, Basingstoke
Westlake, Martin, 1994a, *The Commission and the Parliament. Partners and Rivals in the European Policy-Making Process*, Butterworths, London
—— 1994b, *A Modern Guide to the European Parliament*, Pinter, London
—— 1996–7, 'A Unique Constitutional Experiment', *Talking Politics*, vol. 9, no. 2, Winter 1996–7
—— 1997a, '"The Style and the Machinery": The Role of the European Parliament in the European Union's Legislative Processes', in *Acts of the W G Hart Legal Workshop on Lawmaking in the European Union*, Sweet and Maxwell, Dublin
—— 1997b, 'The European Parliament's "Elective Function"', paper delivered at the 22 April 1997 TEPSA Conference on 'The European Parliament on its way towards becoming an equal partner', Brussels

3 Britain and Europe
The different relationship

Andrew Duff

> There is the United States with all its dependencies; there is the Soviet Union; there is the British Empire and Commonwealth; and there is Europe with which Great Britain is profoundly blended. Here are the four main pillars in the world Temple of Peace.
> Sir Winston Churchill (Churchill, 1950, pp. 79–80)

How different is Britain? Winston Churchill had no doubt that the United Kingdom should be a powerful patron of a united Europe, but he was less clear about how close its own involvement should be. Partisans on both sides of the long quarrel about British European policy have sought to recruit the great man's prestige to their respective causes.

Churchill himself remained a towering figure – a genuine 'founding father' – in Europe for a decade after the end of the Second World War; but his formative years were Victorian; he served the British Empire when it was at its most extended, and was already in his early thirties when he first became a government minister in 1906. So it is not surprising that Churchill's zeal for European unity was qualified by his ambivalence about Britain's role: 'profoundly blended' yes; a pillar of postwar reconstruction, certainly; a guarantor of European security, self-evidently; but different.

Churchill's view of Britain as the centre of a world of English-speaking peoples is a powerful and romantic one. But as a framework within which to adjust British policy to face the realities of the postwar world, it was reactionary. Postwar governments had to cope as best they could with the loss of the Empire, the decline in Britain's economic performance and the social consequences of both. Britain's political system remained unreformed and, in the eyes of many, deservedly so: the image of the defiant prime minister stomping around the blitzed ruins of the House of Commons in 1940 is a striking and durable one. Despite Labour's election victory in 1945, Britain quickly slipped back into the arms of the Conservative party, which governed the country for all but fifteen years of the second half of the century. (The contrast with France, where the prewar political parties and institutions failed to return after Liberation, was marked.)

Only in the field of defence was the UK's status matched with its capability, and its contribution to the security of postwar Europe was never in doubt. Even here, however, Britain's attempt to organise European defence – the Western European Union – was less than whole-hearted and poorly coordinated with the French. And before long, cuts in British military expenditure soon forced unwanted and ill-prepared discontinuities.

To counter the prevailing conservative mood, no alternative intellectual approach gained credibility. John Maynard Keynes died in 1946 and William Beveridge, who had been among the pioneers of British federalist thought, became preoccupied with the welfare state. Ernest Bevin, a radical foreign secretary, was out-gunned in the Labour cabinet of 1945–51. From the Opposition benches, Churchill's follower Anthony Eden continued to inveigh against British participation in moves towards European integration. And it was they, not Bevin, who caught the popular mood, at least until after the imperial débâcle of the Suez invasion in 1956.

That mood was fairly stubborn. British sovereignty was thought to be indissolubly vested within the 'Crown-in-Parliament' at Westminster. There could be no pooling or sharing of sovereignty with others if Britain were to remain a world-class player. British trading instincts were liberal; the UK had world-wide responsibilities that neither France nor Germany enjoyed. European federation, as Churchill asserted, was doubtless a good idea for the others – and seemed to please the Americans – but not for Britain.

Although there were some (mostly Scots) who took exception, such was the overriding British attitude to postwar Europe. The Anglo-French negotiations over the Schuman Plan suggest that had the UK joined the European Coal and Steel Community it would have been a troublesome partner from the start (see Dell, 1995 and Denman, 1996). In the circumstances, the UK government was right to abstain, and Monnet correct in his apprehension about British subversion of pooled sovereignty. Attitudes had clearly not changed much by the time of the Messina conference, and UK participation in the Economic Community (EEC) would have jeopardised the creation of common European institutions, the common tariff and agricultural policy.

ESSENTIAL NATIONAL SOVEREIGNTY

Harold Macmillan, who emerged from the Suez crisis as prime minister, was the first Tory to break free from Churchill's legacy. Macmillan was a moderniser, and saw the dangers of isolation, especially from the United States. His pitch for joining the EEC attempted to reconcile Britain's European and world-wide roles. UK membership, he argued, would rescue the Six from being inward-looking. The UK's special ties and loyalties to the Commonwealth and to the European Free Trade Area would open up the EEC and serve to strengthen the all-important Atlantic partnership.

This general approach survived the rebuff by De Gaulle and the first Labour government of Harold Wilson, and it was essentially the same position as that adopted in the eventually successful accession negotiations in 1971–2. What motivated the UK's European policy was threefold: first, concern for Britain's sharp decline in terms of world security and other developments; second, the need for more financial stability and a higher rate of economic growth; third, the desire to join in shaping the future design of European unity. But it was clear that, despite the friendly rhetoric of Macmillan, Home and Heath, Conservative Britain had not been converted, nor was likely soon to convert, to supporting European federation.

Although genuinely committed to a transformation in British European relations, few of the politicians, officials, lawyers, bankers or businessmen seemed to have more than a sketchy notion about what the European Community was for, how it was run, or about the role of the institutions or the budget. The significance of importing the jurisdiction of the European Court of Justice was neglected. It was hardly noticed that the Treaty of Rome was not an international treaty like any other but possessed a constituent character all of its own. The Commission was thought to be a bossy secretariat rather than an executive body. The European Parliament was seen as most inferior to the incomparable Westminster model. British understanding of the principle of the Community's own financial resources was only partial. The Council was treated like a routine diplomatic negotiation and not as a common institution, and the UK always insisted that it maintained an ultimate, unilateral national veto even where there was no basis for that assertion in law. The Luxembourg Compromise, forced on the Community by De Gaulle in 1966, has had no stronger advocate.

Edward Heath, Tory prime minister from 1970–4 and, earlier, Macmillan's Europe minister, is an exceptionally determined pro-European who has, with Roy Jenkins, shaped British policy to a considerable degree. Even he, however, was reduced to some equivocation over the true nature of the UK's membership. In a statement that has haunted British European policy ever since, his White Paper on EEC accession said:

> There is no question of any erosion of essential national sovereignty. What is proposed is a sharing and an enlargement of individual national sovereignties in the general interest.
>
> White Paper, 1971

Many have found this statement fundamentally ambivalent. While pro-Europeans have focused on the sharing of sovereignty, anti-Europeans have insisted on the preservation of essential national sovereignty. The two camps have never managed to settle the dichotomy. Once Britain had joined the Community in 1973, and had agreed by referendum in 1975 to stay in, opponents of membership came to look increasingly reactionary. But they remained nevertheless powerful, not least because they were able to appeal to the Churchillian notion of British self-esteem, even vanity. Despite their success, pro-Europeans have been on the defensive. It has been especially difficult for the British in these circumstances to welcome the idea that the European Union is a radical departure from the norm, or to see that there are powerful dynamics of integration that drive Europe irrespective of the whims of the governments of the historic nation states. This aspect of the European dimension to British politics is still today overlooked.

Edward Heath has made much of the benefits of membership of the European 'club'. The traditional London club is a superior institution much admired by the English ruling class; it has strict rules and codes of etiquette, and subscription fees; it is comfortable rather than luxurious; and, significantly, members can come and go as they please. Candidates for membership can be vetoed, and guests are tolerated rather than welcomed. What would be intolerable in St James's would be for the club committee to begin to make demands on members' private or professional lives, to insist that members' affinity with the club were to be deepened into a common identity – or, indeed, to effect any radical change at all. London clubs are essentially conservative places, where reform is generally, and reasonably, resisted.

The UK relationship with the European Community is analogous to that of London clubland. The English have difficulty with the notion of the Community as an autonomous representative institution; delegation to a supranational authority is an alien concept; self-government not power-sharing is the norm. The accession negotiations did little to enlighten the British as to the true character of the engagement their government was then pressing. The Paris summit meeting in October 1972, with its far-reaching aspirations for European Union, was dismissed as so much continental rhetoric. In the 1975 referendum campaign on the UK's continued membership, both sides tended to exaggerate the economic benefits and disbenefits. Few pro-Europeans were prepared to engage with the nationalist right-wing, led by Enoch Powell, on the question of essential sovereignty.

A FICKLE POLITICAL SYSTEM

It is hardly surprising that apprehension about British accession has continued to be widespread on both sides of the Channel. The United Kingdom could have taken the lead in Europe promised by Churchill's utterances but not delivered; or it could have acted more or less like France, fully engaged in the EEC, but building a special relationship with Germany. Or Britain could have played a consistently minimalist role, being relied upon to conciliate positions at the level of lowest common denominator. Or, worse, it could have undermined the Community from within.

In the event, what happened was none of these things, but inconsistency. Britain has proved itself to be an entirely unreliable partner, sometimes positive, as in the case of the single market, more often negative, as with monetary and institutional reform. Its partners continue to be suspicious of

UK policy. They watched with amazement as successive British prime ministers sought to undermine the European strategy developed by Macmillan and Heath. Wilson, in 1974-5, made an ill-judged effort to 'renegotiate' the accession treaty. One of his most prominent complaints was that UK membership would undermine its partnership with the United States; and whereas the Conservatives were the 'party of Europe', Labour was the 'party of Commonwealth'. Margaret Thatcher first sought to unpick the budgetary settlement – 'our money back'; she then claimed she had been duped into signing the Single European Act in 1986; and she subsequently fought against the Treaty of Maastricht signed by John Major in 1992. The careers of a long succession of Tory cabinet ministers, including Geoffrey Howe, were wrecked on the reef of European policy. Major, in his turn, later cavilled about the Maastricht settlement, and was particularly sceptical about Economic and Monetary Union (EMU); he now opposes the Treaty of Amsterdam signed by his successor, Tony Blair.

British European policy has been consistent only in the urbanity of its civil servants and in the narrow vision of its politicians. The Westminster system encourages the adversarial and partisan to the detriment of consensus, in contrast to continental parliamentary practice. Hopes, especially strong in Benelux, that the UK would enrich parliamentary democracy within the European Union have been largely unfulfilled. The British have proved to be the single greatest obstacle to the reform of the European Union. Only on rare occasions when cross-party currents have been flowing strongly at Westminster has the UK been decisive in shaping the future of Europe. One such was in October 1971 when Roy Jenkins led 68 other Labour MPs into the Conservative government lobby to support accession; another was in November 1992 when a small contingent of Liberal Democrat MPs, in the most crucial stage of the long drawn-out ratification process, saved the Treaty of Maastricht by three votes.

In Britain, unlike anywhere else, Europe has been the touchstone of domestic politics. Notwithstanding their own unresolved conflict, the Conservatives' domination of British politics since the War was helped because Labour was for years so badly divided on the European question. Wilson's equivocation merely postponed civil war within his party. In 1981 the Jenkinsites broke away from Labour to form the Social Democratic Party (SDP), first allying and later merging with the pro-European Liberals. The electoral appeal of the Liberal Democrats and their predecessor parties effectively kept Labour out of office until 1997, by which time the Labour leadership had managed successfully to reverse the Party's anti-European policies. By that stage, too, the Tories had succumbed to their own internal strife on the matter.

The problem of British-European relations is both cultural and systemic. At the heart of the matter is the British electoral system of single round ballots in single member constituencies. The 'winner-takes-all' electoral procedure has three baleful consequences. First, smaller parties cannot survive unless they have a strong regional basis for support. No party has been more unfairly disadvantaged than the moderate, pro-European Liberals, who have won up to a quarter of the popular vote across the country and yet been left with a handful of seats. A share of the vote that on mainland Europe would carry such a party to participate in government, in Britain has so far condemned it to eternal opposition.

Second, the improbability of having a distinct existence has tended to trap the two opposing sides of the European argument together within both the Labour and Tory parties, rendering those parties brittle and ineffective on Europe. In mainland European politics, right-wing nationalist parties and left-wing socialist parties are separated from the mainstream, and tend to be marginalised. In British politics, the anti-European extremists can capture the centre ground, as they did with Labour in the 1980s and with the Tories in the 1990s.

The third problem about the electoral system is that relatively small swings of support between Labour and Conservatives result in complete reversals of government strategy and personnel. No government – not even that of Blair – wins the votes of a majority of the people. But coalitions between parties in government are thought to be impossible to effect in Britain without the subsequent electoral collapse of the minority party. Mistrust and exaggerated belligerence are embedded in the British political system. Bipartisan agreement is very rare, especially on Europe.

Despite the general respect in which the Westminster 'Mother of Parliaments' is thought to be held, the fact is that the representative capability of the mainly adversarial House of Commons and the mostly hereditary House of Lords has worn thin. The parliamentary elite has not led public opinion on the issue of Europe; nor has it adequately engaged in a dialogue with commerce and industry that is most directly affected by Britain's European partnership.

It has been inevitable, moreover, that such narrowly partisan characteristics have been exported by the British parties to the wider politics of the European Union. In the European Parliament, where until 1999 only the British MEPs were not elected by proportional representation, the British idiosyncrasy has had a particularly deleterious effect.

The poor state of British European policy had its worst effect at the time of the negotiation and ratification of the Treaty of Maastricht. Here UK ministers, divided among themselves, deliberately sought, and won, derogations from central objectives of European integration, having first diluted those objectives. In so doing, the British both undermined the Community system and fuelled popular hostility to the Union at home. The precedent of Maastricht was continued at Amsterdam, in June 1997, when differentiation between the UK and its partners widened further. The new Treaty jettisons the old orthodoxy that all member states of the European Union shall move forward together towards common goals. Political solidarity, the essential element in building the 'ever closer union', has been downgraded in favour of the preservation of unilateral interpretations of essential national sovereignty.

FLEXIBILITY

Maastricht and Amsterdam were the culmination of a differentiation process that had coexisted alongside European integration for years. Even within the original six members of the EEC there were important differences. The Treaty of Rome allows the Benelux trio to complete their regional union. There have been important bilateral arrangements between France and Germany, Britain and Ireland, and within the Nordic Council. Differentiation has always been most marked in the field of defence. Only ten of the fifteen member states have joined (in stages) the Western European Union. Only eleven EU member states have joined Nato.

The variable reception given to the hopes expressed at the summits of The Hague in 1969 and Paris in 1972 served to highlight the differences in approach between member states. These differences were accentuated after UK entry. They were recognised in the Tindemans Report, which suggested that, while the overall concept and principles of European Union had to be agreed by all states, those 'which are able to progress have a duty to forge ahead'. Other states would be helped to catch up (Tindemans, 1976, p. 20). Tindemans insisted that he was not opening the door to '*l'Europe à la carte*'.

The Tindemans Report saw monetary cooperation as the key dynamic of future integration. The European Monetary System was indeed established in 1979 with only six out of eight currencies within the Exchange Rate Mechanism. Differentiation was also regarded as inevitable in the building of the single market. Article 15 of the Single Act said that the Commission would have to take into account 'differences in development' of the member states, and that any derogation from internal market provisions should only be temporary and 'must cause the least possible disturbance to the functioning of the common market'.

The European Community was developing for functional reasons a systematic approach to differentiation. UK accession had increased diversity and heightened the need for cohesion and solidarity. But at this stage differentiation was only a question of variable pace towards common objectives, and both were agreed by all member states according to the principle of 'least possible disturbance'. The Maastricht Treaty made greater use of this multi-speed approach to European integration; but it also added greatly to the disturbance.

It is not an exaggeration to say that the Maastricht Treaty opt-outs for the UK from the single currency and social policy, coupled with similar derogations for Denmark, revolutionised the integration process. These decisions had been anticipated by the signing by only five member states of the Schengen Agreement on the abolition of border controls, and Maastricht regularised this situation by allowing two or more member states to develop closer cooperation on third pillar issues. Maastricht saw the end of the formal consensus between member states about the direction of European integration. Goals were no longer all held in common. Some wished not only to go faster than others, but in different directions. Multi-speed Community Europe was in the process of being replaced by a wider, multi-tier Europe. Institutional differentiation was added to functional differentiation.

THE 1996 IGC

In the Intergovernmental Conference of 1996–7, the majority of member states took the orthodox view that increased solidarity was necessary for an enlarged Union to thrive, and that it would become very much more difficult to manage wider differentiation if the powers of the common institutions, particularly of the Commission and the Court of Justice, were to weaken. Most proposed reforms leant in the federalist direction, and the UK was strongly urged to abandon its Social Protocol.

The problem was that the British government opposed each of these reforms, which, it argued correctly, would take the Union in a more federalist direction. It rapidly became difficult to escape the conclusion that the UK was going to stymie the whole reform programme, a view that was confirmed by the British attitude towards EMU. The UK government sought to avoid the ties that were being designed to associate those without the eurozone with those within. It cast doubt on both the credibility of the project and its timetable; and in doing so, it put itself apart, in a third tier, from those governments, like the Italian, that would participate but could not yet.

To compound matters, the UK engaged in three supplementary battles with its partners during 1996. The first concerned 'mad cow' disease, where the UK reacted to the EU ban on the export of British beef by a systematic policy of non-cooperation which broke Treaty obligations and which caused 117 measures to be blocked in the Council, including the IGC, between 21 May and 24 June (Westlake, 1997). The second battle concerned fish quotas, where the UK threatened to veto all progress at the IGC if it did not get its own way. And, third, the UK sought to undermine the 48 Hour Working Week directive by a futile challenge to the Court on the question of legal base. In all cases, the UK government appeared to be taking a calculated risk that indifference to its interests would be succeeded by discrimination against them.

The other member states seemed inured to the prospect of yet another Conservative election victory. Led by France and Germany, they were quick to draw their own conclusions. It was clear that a successful conclusion of the IGC depended on the skill with which the Fifteen could negotiate a system of differentiated integration, with some member states going further towards unity in various matters than others – and the UK effectively by-passed.

In September 1994 Wolfgang Schäuble and Karl Lamers, on behalf of the CDU/CSU parliamentary party, had set out a deliberately provocative proposal for a 'hard core' of states to exercise a centripetal or magnetic effect on the whole Union (Schäuble and Lamers, 1994). They advanced five mutually dependent proposals that were designed to:

- develop European federal democracy;
- strengthen the hard core;
- deepen Franco-German integration;
- improve the Union's capacity for action in foreign and security policy;
- expand the Union towards the East.

John Major reacted quickly in a speech in Leiden on 7 September 1994. He insisted that 'the way the Union develops must be acceptable to all member states', and that 'no member state should be excluded from an area of policy in which it wants and is qualified to participate'. Major argued against an 'exclusive hard core' of member states as well as 'chaotic non-conformity'. But, he added, 'conformity can never be seen as an automatic principle'.

In November, the French prime minister, Edouard Balladur, contributed a proposal for concentric circles consisting of two tiers of full member states, as well as a third tier of 'partner states', including Russia and Turkey. Alain Juppé, then foreign minister, said that an EU inner core should have '*solidarités renforcées*'. A year later, on 6 December 1995 President Chirac and Chancellor Kohl published a famous letter aimed at Britain, in which they wrote that the 'momentary difficulties of one of the partners in following the move forward should not stand in the way of the Union's ability to take action and advance'. They said that they intended to propose to the IGC a new treaty clause that would allow for '*coopération renforcée*' among those member states that had the will and capacity to go forward.

The Group of Reflection worked to prepare the IGC from June to December 1995 (Reflection Group's Report, 1995). Its conclusion was that flexibility needed to be considered on a case by case basis, observing the following criteria:

- flexibility should serve the Union's objectives, and should only be deployed if all other solutions had been ruled out;
- no one should be excluded from full participation in actions or common policies previously adopted;
- for those who wanted to take part but were temporarily unable to do so, provision should be made for *ad hoc* measures to assist them;
- maintaining the *acquis* must remain a priority;
- a single institutional framework had to be respected.

A large majority of the Reflection Group considered that derogations should not be permanent, and that, while derogations in the Community pillar would jeopardise the internal market, there was greater scope for flexibility in the areas of foreign and security policy and justice and home affairs. There was disagreement about whether an expression of political solidarity would also implicate the minority – possibly the 'neutrals' – in some financial responsibility. It was accepted that some vital national interest might still require the back-stop of a formal veto in security policy, although such an interest would need to be defined and accepted in advance of any decision being taken. From their various individual submissions to the IGC, it was clear that all member states accepted the prospect of differentiated integration.

The emerging strategy of the British government was to cling to *à la carte* flexibility in the hope of preventing the emergence of a federal hard core. The Commission, for its part, firmly rejected the idea of a 'pick-and-choose Europe' (European Commission, 1996, paragraphs 45–6). The President of the European Parliament, Klaus Hänsch, was more blunt. Warning against having resort to 'generalised permanent opt-outs', he said:

> The problem of the British government, with its strong Europhobic, not Eurosceptic element, cannot be resolved by imaginative drafting of Treaty clauses, and by fanciful institutional gadgets. It is a basic political problem ... And we should be wary of writing into the Treaty more permanent exemptions and derogations which weaken the Union's capacity to act in order to deal with a problem and, indeed, a government which may prove to be short-lived.
>
> Hänsch, 1996

A joint declaration on *coopération renforcée* was issued by the French and German foreign ministers, Hervé de Charette and Klaus Kinkel, on 17 October 1996. Stung by the astonishing British tactic of BSE-induced 'non-cooperation', they dropped their previous affirmation that differentiation could only be of a temporary nature. The Irish presidency of the Council followed suit, and proposed that a general clause be added to the Treaty to stipulate the conditions under which differentiation might take place, supplemented by three further articles setting out the arrangements for effecting reinforced cooperation in each pillar.

De Charette and Kinkel proposed that the Commission should have the right to veto potential differentiation arrangements; and the Council would decide by QMV. Under the second and third pillars, the right of initiative would be shared between the Commission and member state governments. In each case a quorum of member states would have to be established. The financing of the administration of reinforced cooperation would be by the EU budget; operational expenditure might be either from the EU budget or from national levies. Flexibility should only be deployed to strengthen and not dilute the *acquis communautaire*, so there would be no flexibility for new entrants to the EU, who would have to make do, like their predecessors, with pre-accession strategies and transitional periods.

The British were clearly suspected of intending to differentiate in order to loosen the ties that bound the member states. A principal British target was the Court of Justice, from which the British Eurosceptics wished to repatriate powers in order to subvert the existing European legal order and breach the principle of 'least possible disturbance'.

The Dutch presidency emphasised therefore that differentiation would need consistent scrutiny and occasional arbitration. It argued that a variegated Europe needed a strong legal order to hold it together: diversity without a powerful Court could lead to anarchy. And the European Commission would have to manage the relationship between the core and the periphery. As far as the institutions were concerned, the IGC agreed to respect the collegiality of the Commission and Court in order to serve the interests of the whole Union. But there was continuing disagreement about how the Council and the European Parliament would have to work in two guises.

THE TREATY OF AMSTERDAM

The negotiations on flexibility became more fraught as the many complexities surfaced during the last stage of the preparations for Amsterdam. The result of the British general election on 1 May prompted some second thoughts about the wisdom of proceeding with flexibility clauses. With the Tories gone, what was the point in constructing an elaborate system of differentiation, with all its attendant risks for the Union? But the negotiations had by now achieved an impetus of their own, and residuary anxieties about British policy, especially in relation to third pillar matters, impelled them forward. Moreover, the Labour government was sticking to its predecessor's position of insisting on being able to veto whether or not flexibility would ever apply.

The Dutch presidency eventually proposed a general clause plus three enabling clauses for each pillar (Dutch Presidency, 1997). The general clause followed the thrust of the earlier debate but established in addition that flexibility would only come into play as a matter of last resort; that a quorum of over half the member states would need to be involved; but that there should be no veto permissible from those not willing to go forward. Within the first pillar, the new Treaty imposed very stringent conditions before flexibility could be triggered, ensuring that existing Community policies would not be affected and that flexibility would not be used as an excuse for discrimination.

At Amsterdam, the general flexibility clause was agreed (Article K.15 – 43). But a major change was agreed to accommodate the British insistence on veto. The new Treaty says that any member state may 'for important and stated reasons of national policy' block the QMV vote to trigger closer cooperation (Article 5a(2) – 11). This enshrines in Treaty form for the first time the notorious Luxembourg Compromise. It makes it virtually impossible, EMU and Schengen aside, for a federal core now to go forward in the first pillar area. The leaders scrubbed altogether the draft clauses on flexibility in the field of Common and Foreign and Security Policy in favour of a form of constructive abstention, where dissenting member states are to agree to waive their objections and not participate in a common policy. Article J.13 (**23**) lays down that only if the constructive abstainers comprise more than one-third of the weighted votes will the decision be blocked. Decisions without military implications will be taken by super QMV – that is, 62 votes in favour cast by at least ten member states – unless Blair's new formulation of the Luxembourg Compromise is invoked. In such circumstances, the Council may vote by QMV to pass the matter up to the European Council for decision by unanimity.

Closer cooperation is, however, allowed for in the third pillar (Article K.12 – **40**). Authorisation will be decided by the Council acting by super QMV unless Blair's caveat is deployed. In which case, the Council may vote by QMV to pass the matter up to the European Council for decision by unanimity.

It was ironic that the new British government at Amsterdam, on whose shoulders many hopes rested in Europe and elsewhere, should have continued to wish to be able to block the emergence of a federal core within the European Union. Churchill would have been unlikely to approve because he would not have wanted to impede the development of a community of strength and stability on the European mainland. He would have been more confident that a successful European federation would have a beneficial effect on Britain too, and on trans-Atlantic relations.

MAKING THE DIFFERENCE

In retrospect, however, and despite the tortuous negotiations on flexibility, the importance of the Treaty of Amsterdam is that it marked the first step in the reconciliation between the UK and its EU partners. The Treaty itself continues the Maastricht process and in some important ways moderates it; it allows enlargement negotiations to begin; and it holds out the promise of more political and institutional reform of the Union in the near future. It is important to recollect that none of these achievements would have been possible under the previous British government.

The United Kingdom, with its new, reforming government, seems now to have decided to take the lead in the process of European reform and is no longer content to play its traditional, reactive role. Thus, the British Presidency of the Council of the European Union from January to June 1998 should be seen as having been a vital test of British leadership, helping to transform the way the Union is generally regarded by the British people.

The Presidency has set the enlargement negotiations in the context of the great issues at stake for the future of Europe. The credibility of the UK government required it to dispel the suspicion that it wanted to widen the Union in order to dilute the authority of the supranational institutions. In addition, the British Government has encouraged a policy of systematic open government in the Council.

Above all, the British government has sought to connect its domestic and its European programme for reform. In July 1997, Mr Blair announced his intention to introduce Proportional Representation for the European Parliamentary elections in 1999. In October, a commission was set up to make a proposal for the electoral reform of the House of Commons. Scotland and Wales voted in referenda for a devolved form of government. In the same month, Chancellor Gordon Brown announced that, although the United Kingdom would not join EMU in the life of the current Parliament, there were no longer any constitutional objections to joining. This statement was widely interpreted as meaning that the British Government would, if re-elected in 2001, seek entry (involving a referendum) in 2002, the year when euro notes and coins are expected to be brought into circulation. Subsequent to this announcement, Chancellor Helmut Kohl promised that a seat would be kept warm for the British Government on the Board of the European Central Bank, a promise re-asserted by President Chirac in a remarkably positive meeting with Mr Blair in November 1997.

Seen in the context of these developments, the Treaty of Amsterdam was not another dreary episode in British differentiation from its European partners, but rather promised a genuine and fresh departure. A settled British European policy, embedded within constitutional change at home, would satisfy the whole Union. A bold British European policy will help to make the difference in the federal construction of Europe.

REFERENCES

Churchill, Randolph (ed.), 1950, *Europe Unite: Speeches 1947 and 1948 by Winston S. Churchill*, Cassell, London

Dell, Edmund, 1995, *The Schuman Plan and the British Abdication of Leadership in Europe*, Oxford University Press, London

Denman, Roy, 1996, *Missed Chances: Britain and Europe in the Twentieth Century*, Cassell, London

Dutch Presidency, 1997, Draft Treaty of 12 June, CONF/4000/97, Brussels

European Commission, 1996, *Reinforcing Political Union and Preparing for Enlargement*, Brussels, February

Hänsch, Klaus, 1996, Robert Schuman Lecture, European University Institute, Florence, 5 July

Reflection Group's Report, 1995, SN 520/95, Brussels, 5 December

Schäuble, Wolfgang, and Lamers, Karl, 1994, *Reflections on European Policy*, 1 September

Tindemans, Leo, 1976, *European Union. Report by Mr Leo Tindemans, Prime Minister of Belgium, to the European Council, EC Bulletin*, Supplement 1/76

Westlake, Martin, 1997, '"Mad Cows and Englishmen" – The Institutional Consequences of the BSE Crisis', *The European Union 1996. Annual Review of Activities, Journal of Common Market Studies*, vol. 35, September

White Paper, 1971, *The United Kingdom and the European Communities*, Cmnd. 4715, HMSO, London, July

4 From closed doors to European democracy
Beyond the intergovernmental conferences

John Pinder

Fame, in contemporary politics, is usually a prelude to debunking or, at best, neglect. Such has been the fate of the famous assertion in the Schuman declaration, that the proposed Community was to be 'the first concrete foundation of a European federation which is indispensable to the preservation of peace'. Europhobes hate such words, the politer Eurosceptics say they are out of date, and for routine politicians they are unfashionable. For Jacques Vandamme, to the contrary, 'la doctrine de fédéralisme . . . répond le mieux aux besoins des citoyens' (cited in Lebohm, 1997). This chapter seeks to build on Vandamme's affirmation: first by showing that a series of Intergovernmental Conferences has brought the Community, now the Union, to a more advanced pre-federal system than most people realise; secondly by arguing that the completion of the federal system is indeed necessary for the citizens; and thirdly by suggesting that this requires a method beyond the conventional IGC.

THROUGH INTERGOVERNMENTAL CONFERENCES TOWARDS A FEDERAL SYSTEM

Vandamme was right, because the citizens need an effective and democratic system that can deal with the profound forces of interdependence which now encompass European states. Two World Wars demonstrated the potential of these states for mutual destruction; and events in the Balkans have provided a terrible reminder that Europeans need to be anchored in a political system which can guarantee they live in peace with one another. Economic integration has, moreover, in stark contrast with the protectionism of the 1930s, shown how much the emergent federal Community means for the welfare of European citizens; and the same can be said of its laws against cross-border pollution.

Powerful interests have responded to these needs. Governments have promoted the pre-federal instruments and institutions that can do much to cope with interdependence in the fields of security, economy and the environment. Business and trade unions have supported economic integration. Green movements, politically influential in several member states, have demanded common action to protect the environment. Federalists such as Jean Monnet, Alcide De Gasperi, Paul-Henri Spaak, Altiero Spinelli and, more recently, Jacques Delors and Helmut Kohl have worked to build a system that would transcend the limits of the traditional nation state.

Much has been achieved through one form or another of intergovernmental conference: in the 1950s, to draw up the founding treaties; then for treaty amendment, notably by the budget treaties of 1970 and 1975, the Single European Act and the Maastricht Treaty; and in parallel with this, by the treaties of accession that brought the number of member states from six to fifteen. Now there is the Amsterdam Treaty produced by the IGC of 1996–7; beyond this, accession treaties for at least ten and perhaps up to twenty or more new member states are sooner or later to come; and, following the Amsterdam Treaty's Protocol on the institutions and enlargement, at least one more IGC before the membership of the EU exceeds twenty. But before the implications of such enlargement are considered, we should see what the IGCs have achieved so far.

FEDERAL POWERS, PRE-FEDERAL INSTITUTIONS

In order to constrain what was then the industrial basis of war potential, the first intergovernmental conference, presided over by Monnet, drew up the treaty that established the European Coal and Steel Community, with its powers of government over those two industries in France, Germany, Italy and Benelux. Monnet insisted that the powers be exercised by an executive independent of the member states' governments. Otherwise, his life experience had taught him, it would be subordinated to too many conflicting pressures and hence ineffective. Since the member states were liberal democracies, the High Authority, as the executive was significantly called, was to be accountable to a European parliamentary assembly and subject to the jurisdiction of a European court; and a ministerial council was set up to facilitate coordination with the governments of the member states. Thus the first Community, though its powers were confined to only two industrial sectors, provided a basis for the institutions that are with us today, in the form of the European Parliament, Council, European Commission and Court of Justice: an extraordinary achievement.

The next intergovernmental conference was a failure. The negotiations for a European Defence Community, starting soon after those for the ECSC and aiming this time directly at the integration of the armed forces of the member states, concluded with an EDC treaty that was signed by all six of them. Meanwhile Spinelli, imbued with federalist thinking, persuaded Prime Minister De Gasperi to insist that a European Army must be controlled by democratic European institutions; the member states agreed that an accompanying treaty for a European Political Community be drafted by the ECSC's assembly, slightly adapted for the task; and the assembly drew up a quasi-federal proposal (see Pistone, 1992, pp. 33–45). But a combination of nationalist and communist opposition gathered strength in France and in August 1954 the Assemblée Nationale buried the project.

The Community then withdrew from its direct attack on the core of national sovereignty and returned to Monnet's approach, putting in place successive building blocks of pre-federal powers and institutions in the less sensitive field of the economy. The next intergovernmental conferences led to the Treaties of Rome, establishing the European Economic Community, together with Euratom as a parallel of the ECSC in the field of atomic energy. Euratom, opposed by De Gaulle after he became President of France, could not flourish. But the EEC, which gave wide powers over both internal and external trade as well as broad responsibilities for economic cooperation to institutions based on those of the ECSC, provided a broad field for the Community's subsequent development.

ECONOMIC POWERS AND INSTRUMENTS

The EEC Treaty and the Single European Act have together given the Community powers over internal and external trade more or less equivalent to those that the commerce clause in the Constitution has, after a couple of centuries of development, given the federal government of the United States. Both the Treaty and the Act were motivated not only by the desire to enhance prosperity within the Community and the ability to compete with those outside it, but also by a determination to continue consolidating the postwar political order in Europe.

Political and economic interests likewise combined to push forward monetary integration. Monetary union was first proposed at the end of the 1960s when Chancellor Brandt wanted to balance his Ostpolitik by embedding Germany yet more firmly in the Western system and President Pompidou sought to deepen the Community as an insurance against the risk that the accession of the insular British, by then in prospect, would weaken it. France in particular also had economic motives for seeking monetary stability through the mutual locking of member states' currencies. That project failed because France would not accept the coordination of economic policy and the strengthening of Community institutions that were German conditions for monetary union. But two decades later, following the success of the European Monetary System in fostering monetary stability on German lines, political and economic motives again converged in the convening in 1990 of the IGC for economic and monetary union. With the advent of the single market, and the integration of financial markets in particular, a single currency was increasingly seen as necessary; and both French and Germans saw it as a means to anchor the newly united Germany irrevocably in the Community. This time, with widespread agreement on the German model of monetary stability, it was not so hard for the IGC to settle on a federal banking system tailored to that end. Here again, there are to be European federal powers equivalent to those of the United States.

Along with trade and money, budgets are a third major field of economic policy. The Union's budget remains small, just below 1.3 per cent of GDP. Yet it is a significant federal instrument of policy, proportionately not much smaller than the US budget up to the 1920s. The origin of its federal characteristics lay in the adoption for the ECSC of the principle that the central authority of a union needs its own sources of revenue if it is not to be rendered powerless by the several governments of the member states; and it became politically significant because of the common agricultural policy, which was a French condition for accepting the EEC Treaty with its common market for industrial products. The accession of Greece, Ireland, Portugal and Spain then expanded the structural funds to become the other major item of expenditure, seen as compensation for the risks they perceived in accepting the programmes for the single market and the single currency, which would open their markets so fully to the more advanced economies.

Thus the negotiations to establish and amend the treaties and to enlarge the Community, as well as the bargains linked with intergovernmental conferences, have given it federal powers similar to those of the US for trade and money and, if on a smaller scale, for the budget. Its powers in the field of the environment, developed incrementally and confirmed in the Single European Act and the Maastricht Treaty, are also significant. Without grasping the nettle of defence integration, the member states have gone far to endow the Community with instruments of economic and, to some extent, environmental policy equivalent to those of a federation.

PRE-FEDERAL INSTITUTIONS

While the economic powers and instruments may be classed as federal, the same cannot be said of the institutions. These remain pre-federal, even if in some respects at a fairly advanced stage.

The High Authority, as the executive of the ECSC, approximated to a government for coal and steel. The EEC Treaty tipped the balance of power from the Commission towards the Council; and the governments have managed to tilt it farther by taking executive decisions in the Council and supervising the Commission's work through hundreds of committees of member states' officials: the phenomenon known as comitology. Yet the role of the Commission has at the same time been enhanced. Its scope has been enlarged by the expansion of the Community's competences. Its effectiveness in promoting legislation has grown along with the replacement of the unanimity procedure by that of qualified majority for voting in the Council on most fields of legislation. The increased authority of the Court and the Parliament has moreover provided a certain counterweight to the Council's predominance. The Commission has, indeed, some of the characteristics of a government. It initiates legislation, having the exclusive right to do so, in matters of Community competence. It has responsibility for executing the Community's acts, though mainly by the uncertain method of trying to ensure that the administrations of the member states play their part in doing so. Only with respect to budgetary expenditure does the treaty give the Commission a full executive mandate, stipulating that it 'shall implement the budget . . . on its own responsibility and within the limits of the appropriations' (EC Article 209 – **279**). A similar provision for implementing other legislation would take it a step closer to becoming a European government. So would an extension of its competence to deal with matters of internal and external security. A European government should also, consonant with the European tradition of parliamentary democracy, have a clearer line of democratic accountability to the legislature, in which the states are represented in the Council and the citizens in the European Parliament.

When the procedure of unanimity applies, the government of each member state can control legislation by the Council, which therefore has little of the character of a house of the states in a federal system such as that of Germany, where the Bundesrat is also composed of representatives of the governments of the component parts. Although the EEC Treaty provided for voting by qualified majority in a number of fields, President de Gaulle's recalcitrance in the mid-1960s presaged two decades in which unanimity remained in practice the rule. It was not until the Single European Act extended the provision for qualified majority voting to most of the single market legislation, and the Council changed its rules of procedure to give effect to this, that it began to become more like a normal legislature, although it retained its extraordinary practice of legislating behind closed doors and still lacks the legislative counterpart of a citizens' house with at least equal powers.

The founding treaties provided for direct elections to the assembly (ECSC Article 21, EC Article 138 – **190**), which could be appropriate only for the Parliament, as it came to be called, of a Community that was seen as an emergent federation. Opposition to this concept delayed the unanimous decision required to hold the elections to the European Parliament until 1976, so that they were held for the first time in 1979. Meanwhile, however, the Parliament had acquired important budgetary powers. The EEC Treaty had stipulated that the Community budget be financed from its 'own resources' and the French government, concerned to secure the financing of the common agricultural policy, insisted that the necessary decision be taken. But this also required unanimity; and the Dutch parliament and government for their part insisted that public expenditure, at the European as at the national level, must be subject to parliamentary control. Since the European budget could not be controlled by six separate national parliaments, the Dutch argued, the power of control would have to be given to the European Parliament. The Dutch were supported by the Belgians, Germans and Italians, and although the French, in defence of their national sovereignty and agricultural interests, managed to keep the agricultural expenditure out of the Parliament's control, the amending treaties of 1970 and 1975 have enabled the Parliament's budgetary power to grow until it equals or exceeds that of the Council over a large part of the Community's expenditure. This and the direct elections may be seen historically to have been crucial first steps in what has been called the 'third democratic transformation': the first such transformation having been the introduction of direct democracy into the Athenian city-state, the second carrying democracy through representative government to the level of the nation state, and the third taking it up to the level of a group of interdependent nation states (see Dahl, 1989, pp. 2, 318–20).

These steps have been followed by the attribution to the Parliament of substantial legislative powers, again in an attempt to apply the principles of parliamentary democracy as new powers are transferred from the member states to the Community. Thus when the scope for legislation by majority voting in the Council was extended by the Single European Act and the possibility for the member states' parliaments to control Community legislation was thereby diminished, some member states, in particular those that had supported giving the Parliament its budgetary powers, wanted to give it similar powers over other legislation. Others, notably Britain, Denmark and France, resisted, but settled for the 'cooperation procedure', giving the Parliament substantial influence though not full power over single market legislation, together with the power of assent over treaties of accession and association. The Maastricht Treaty, following the IGC on political union that went in parallel with that on economic and monetary union, took the process farther, extending the scope of assent and introducing the procedure of co-decision, which puts the Parliament on a more or less equal footing with the Council in fields of legislation that have so far accounted for about a quarter of the laws enacted since the Treaty came into effect; and the Amsterdam Treaty more than doubles the number of articles to which co-decision applies.

The Maastricht Treaty also gave the Parliament the power to approve – or not – the appointment of each new Commission, and the Amsterdam Treaty extended it to the appointment of the Commission's President. This could, if used in conjunction with the power that the founding treaties gave it to dismiss the Commission by a two-thirds majority, as well as its more recently acquired budgetary and legislative powers, lead to a form of parliamentary government in which the executive is responsible, if not to the Parliament alone, at least to the two chambers of the legislature.

While the Council is still the dominant legislative institution, the Parliament has, then, moved a substantial part of the way towards becoming an equal legislative partner, to which the Commission is also at least in part accountable.

Like the direct elections, the mission of the Court of Justice was stipulated in the founding treaties, which provided that the Court 'shall ensure that in the interpretation and application of this Treaty . . . the law is observed' (ECSC Article 31, EC Article 164 – **220**). In order to fulfil this obligation, the Court established that Community law must prevail should the law of a member state conflict with it. The Court also concluded that, since the treaties accord rights to individuals, these rights must be enforceable in the member states' courts. On the basis of these two principles, of primacy and direct effect, the Court has developed a legal system that has 'most of the characteristics of a federation' (Hartley, 1994, p. 55).

It was the Court also, without explicit authorisation from the treaties, which introduced into Community law the principle that the citizens must be protected against infringements of human rights by the Community institutions. The Court's grounds were that it could not ensure the observance of Community law if a member state could argue that this infringed its citizens' rights. So the Court had to ensure that the rights were respected. The Maastricht Treaty went part of the way to confirm this by providing explicitly for the respect of fundamental rights and the Amsterdam Treaty gives the Court jurisdiction for ensuring that the rights are indeed respected by the Union's institutions.

If the legal system, thanks to the founding treaties and the Court that they established, has most of the characteristics of a federation, the same cannot yet be said of the political institutions, though they are at an advanced pre-federal stage. The Parliament is midway between a consultative assembly and a federal house of the citizens, with its substantial legislative and budgetary powers and degree of control over the Commission. The procedure of qualified majority applicable to the bulk of legislation gives the Council a federal characteristic, but its encroachment on the powers of the executive, the retention of the unanimity rule for the remainder of legislation and the lack of an equal partner representing the citizens still preclude it from becoming a federal house of the states. The Commission is likewise not yet a federal executive. Thus the federal rule of law is not complemented by a federal system of representative government.

This pre-federal system applies, moreover, only to the Union's central, Community pillar, not to the flanking pillars concerned with external and internal security, which remain organised on more intergovernmental lines, even if the Amsterdam Treaty provides for all the member states save Britain and Ireland to transfer to the Community the powers required to ensure that people can move freely across the frontiers between them. Reform of the Community institutions to make them federal might, given its existing federal powers, be said to create a federal union. But it would not be a federal state. For that, the federal institutions would have to dispose also of powers in the field of security, including control over armed force. (In his chapter in this book, Jacques Vandamme distinguishes federal union and federal state in this way.)

CITIZENS NEED A FEDERAL EUROPE

Citizens have gained greatly from the pre-federal Community. France and Germany have been reconciled and Western Europe has enjoyed half a century of stable peace. United Germany remains anchored within the system. The European economy has made enormous progress. In all this, the Community has played a central part.

But the Community remains inadequate, and the arrangements for external security more so. The Community needs to be able to provide the European framework for a dynamic economy that can conquer unemployment, not only by completing the single market and single currency but also by creating a Europe-wide infrastructure for the next century and sponsoring an ambitious programme of research and development. The single currency is an instrument of great potential, but its consequences cannot be fully foreseen. Powers of government will surely be needed at Community level to deal with them. Stronger institutions will also be required to deal with the strains of accommodating the economies of the Central and East Europeans when they accede, and some of them will also bring new political and security problems. The Union as a whole is likely to have to shoulder more of the responsibility for European security and for its own defence, hitherto largely assumed by the United States. As one of the richest regions of the world, it should also, in the interests of its own citizens, be capable of making a powerful contribution to the development of a decent world system.

Underlying all these specific needs of the citizens are the principles of democracy, including representative government and the rule of law based on fundamental rights. These principles are, by and large, applied in each member state. But, apart from the rule of Community law, they are not properly applied by the Union, or even by the Community. Since democracy is the stronger system, the centrifugal forces within the Union are stronger than the centripetal: a built-in bias towards disintegration. That risk will escalate in geometrical progression as the number of member states rises from fifteen to twenty, twenty-five, then thirty or more, and at the same time they become increasingly diverse. Proceedings in the Council and the comitology process will become ever more complicated. Decisions for which unanimity is required, already hard to take, will be virtually unattainable. The treaties, unamendable because of the unanimity rule, will become a political straitjacket. Many forecast that the Union will then degenerate into a free trade area. They are too optimistic. Free trade, which in a modern economy means little without single market legislation, will become impossible. Disintegration will bring with it economic fragmentation and international anarchy. Not only will the Union's emergent multi-national democracy be destroyed. The political problems that stem from interdependence, which crucially affect the citizens' welfare, will become insoluble; and the democracies of the member states, unable to cope either jointly or severally, will themselves be at risk.

So the citizens need a democratic and effective Union: democratic, with the European Parliament as fully empowered co-legislator with the Council and principal institution to which the Commission is responsible; effective, with majority voting the general rule in the Council and with the Commission as a responsible government.

Should the aim be a federal union or a federal state? Here federalists face a dilemma. Without a federal state, there is the danger that discord in the field of security, or even conflict between member states, will overcome the centripetal power of integration within a federal union. Yet it would be risky to entrust control over preponderant armed force to newly democratic Union institutions. The dilemma will probably be resolved by real politics: member states are not likely to agree to transfer such responsibility at least until the institutions have been well and truly tested. Federalists will be wise to settle meanwhile for the aim of a fully democratic federal union, accompanied by partial integration in the field of security. Such a federal union, in effect a fully democratic and effective European Community, flanked by increasingly effective security arrangements, should provide enough benefits for the citizens and be a sufficiently powerful attractive force until such time as the federal principle can also be applied to defence.

BEYOND INTERGOVERNMENTAL CONFERENCES TO CONSTITUTIONAL REFORM

From the intergovernmental conference that designed the ECSC up to the Maastricht and Amsterdam Treaties, IGCs have faced increasing difficulties. The conference for the ECSC was a matter strictly between governments, with parliamentary approvals taken for granted. After the EDC Treaty was rejected by the Assemblée Nationale in 1954, parliaments could no longer be ignored. Monnet then created the Action Committee for the United States of Europe in order to ensure that the main democratic political forces would approve the Treaties of Rome and go on to promote further integration. But it was not until British accession to the Community that citizens began to be consulted directly about the results of intergovernmental negotiations: first in France, before ratification of the Treaty of Accession in 1972, then in Britain in 1975 after accession had been followed by a change of government. The results of both these referenda were positive, in the British case by a massive majority of two to one. The Danes then held a referendum on the Single European Act, which was approved by 56 per cent of the votes. Some weeks earlier, few had expected a yes vote. But the Danes derived much economic benefit from the Community and the government worked to persuade them that a vote against the Act would be a first step towards withdrawal from it (Corbett, 1987, pp. 266–7).

That referendum, with its less than wholehearted endorsement, was the forerunner of the Danish referendum on the Maastricht Treaty in June 1992 in which, after the mainstream political parties had ensured a massively favourable vote in the Folketing, the noes had it by 50.7 to 49.3 per cent. Citizens had evidently not been impressed by the copies of the Treaty distributed to each household in all its byzantine complexity, rendered yet more incomprehensible through not being accompanied by the treaties that it was to amend. Whatever their motives, the forty thousand Danes who swung the vote, though they changed their minds in the repeat referendum in 1993, initiated a fraught year of ratification debates, from the '*petit oui*' of only 51 to 49 per cent in the French referendum, through the long months of trench warfare in the House of Commons, to the ambiguities of the guardedly favourable judgement of the Karlsruhe Constitutional Court. It was evidently a treaty too far for many citizens, although governments in Germany, Italy, Belgium and the Netherlands in particular, judging it too weak to meet the challenges that lie ahead, insisted that a new IGC be convened without delay.

While the single currency is a most powerful instrument, the institutional reforms introduced by the Maastricht Treaty were relatively modest. Nor has the Amsterdam Treaty made them sufficiently effective or democratic to meet the needs of enlargement, or, for that matter, of the economic and monetary union; and the arrangements for flexibility, though understandable given the frustration evoked by the obstructionism of Britain's former Conservative government, give rise to fears of future disintegration as much as to hopes that a hard core will take the lead towards a federal Europe. Despite the modesty of its results, moreover, there is no guarantee that they will meet with the approval of the citizens in each of the several referenda that will ensue. More decisive reform will in any case be needed if the Union is to survive and flourish after its future enlargement. But how can the citizens be persuaded to accept it?

DEMOCRATIC AIM, DEMOCRATIC PROCESS

If the Union is to survive, let alone flourish, the democracies of the member states must be balanced by a democracy of the Union itself, even if only, in the first instance, of its central, Community pillar.

This cannot be brought about without the support of the citizens. Hard decisions have to be taken: removing the veto from Council procedures on Community matters; giving the citizens' representatives in the Parliament equal status with the states' representatives in the Council; transferring executive powers from the Council to the Commission. These will be resisted by many of the political and bureaucratic interests that are vested in the status quo; and the citizens will support the devils they know unless they realise that great principles are at stake, on which their future and that of Europe as a whole depend: that both the ability of democracy to master the forces which affect their lives, and their rights to control political power and be protected against its abuse, require that their national democracies be complemented by a European democracy, based on the double legitimacy of both states and citizens (Louis, 1995, pp. 332–3). Particularly in those countries where democracy is most deep-rooted, citizens have to be persuaded that the necessary reforms are not just one more turn of the wheel in a bureaucratic game that erodes sovereignty through incomprehensible treaties, but that such reforms will, as a proper constitution requires, lay down the 'principles and rules that identify the sources, purposes, uses and restraints of public power' (Duchacek, 1987, p. 142).

Although the incremental way in which the Union has developed, through a succession of intergovernmental negotiations and conferences, has made it so complex and hard for citizens to understand, it has nevertheless endowed the Community not only with federal powers that are essential to master the modern economy and environment, but also with pre-federal institutions that require limited, though crucial, reforms to make them democratic. But the increasing difficulties which have confronted IGCs as they have come closer to these reforms, and as citizens' resistance to their outcomes has grown, have suggested that a more democratic process is necessary if the establishment of a European democracy is to be accomplished. The process as well as the end will have to reflect the double legitimacy of states' and citizens' representatives. The result will be more surely democratic, because the citizens' representatives and the parliamentary or party officials who work with them have a more direct interest in democratic institutions than the officials and diplomats who do most of the negotiating for the states. It will for similar reasons be more understandable to the citizens; and the process, which will inevitably be more open, will be more attractive to them. A process based on citizens' as well as states' representatives is better designed both to produce a democratic result and to secure for it the citizens' support.

But how could such a conference be convened, given that some governments would oppose the inclusion of citizens' representatives and others would be unwilling to press for it? The European Parliament has the right of assent over the action of the Council with respect to accession of applicant states; and it could justifiably insist that accession must be preceded or accompanied by a sufficient strengthening and democratisation of the institutions. The Parliament could also point to the inadequacy of the present, intergovernmental procedure for treaty revision whereby unanimity is required and at least one member state will surely resist some of the reforms that will become increasingly essential as the Union is progressively enlarged. A majority of the member states could surely accept the force of this argument and, if they are confronted by an evident necessity to do so, vote to convene a conference as TEU Article N (**48**) entitles them to do. The Parliament, for its part, could so confront them by making its assent for accession conditional on the convening of a reform conference designed to result in a democratic and effective Community.

One such condition should be the participation in the conference of representatives of the European Parliament, equal in number to those of the member states, who should include in their delegations members of their own parliaments. Other conditions could include acceptance, as a basis for the work of the conference, of the principles of voting by qualified majority as the general rule in the Council, of full legislative co-decision with the Parliament and of accountability of the Commission to the Parliament on a basis of at least equality with the Council. In order to avoid the risk that a small minority of member states could prevent the others from making the institutions democratic and effective, moreover, a final condition could be that the amended treaty – or, to describe it more accurately, constitution – would be presented for ratification as a whole, so that the alternatives would be either membership of a reformed Community that was accepted by a large majority of the existing member states or, for those that reject ratification, a new relationship that would as far as possible preserve for them the benefits of the single market.

POTENTIAL SUPPORT FOR THE PROJECT

The European Parliament would not be likely to embark on such a project without a fair chance of success. A threat to hold up accession would be seen as obstructionism unless there was enough support among governments and citizens to make the project credible.

The Eurobarometer surveys have shown substantial majorities of EU citizens in favour of co-decision and of 'a European government responsible to the European Parliament', as well as common defence, military and foreign policies. There are also more citizens in favour than against in all member states, including the supposedly anti-Union British, with only some Scandinavian exceptions (European Commission, 1996, Table 3.13). While citizens' responses to survey questions may fluctuate from time to time, and may not be reflected in votes in referenda, it is evident that citizens' minds are open to proposals for reform, even when couched in such forthright words as 'European government', and even in a country such as Britain after both the government and most of the media had been militantly hostile for a number of years.

The balance of opinion among member states' governments was demonstrated in the report of their representatives in the Reflection Group that prepared the ground for the 1996–7 IGC and, though with some backtracking, in the negotiations themselves. Most were in favour of making qualified majority voting and co-decision a general rule. A majority also favoured a step towards defence integration through the incorporation of WEU into the Union (Reflection Group's Report, 1995, paragraphs 34, 86, 100, 117, 119, and European Policy Centre, 1997, pp. 8 and 9). The strength of Europhobes and sceptics in the Conservative Party had by the time of the IGC turned the British government against all such proposals for strengthening and democratising the Union. But the new Labour government that concluded the negotiations favoured a significant extension of qualified majority voting and of co-decision. Although its policy remained closer to that of the Conservative government with respect to internal and external security, its approach to the Community institutions was closer to that generally adopted by the Germans and others in favour of reform. With British citizens as favourable, or at least open to persuasion, as Eurobarometer has shown them to be, the Labour government could well move towards accepting the necessary institutional reforms; and given the importance for France of retaining its partnership with Germany, it is not likely that a French government would let itself be overtaken by the British in a matter of such concern to the German government, mainstream parties and political class.

Nor are these attitudes on the part of member states matters merely of political conjuncture. The motives that have sustained the pre-federal development of the Community so far remain rooted in the profound interests of interdependent European states: the anchorage, for stability and security, of all the member states, including Germany, within strong European institutions; the economic strength derived from the single market and single currency, together with the joint management of the integrated economy; the defence of common interests in an increasingly uncertain and potentially dangerous world. These motives still prevail among a majority of the member states. Britain, among the larger ones, has been the sole exception hitherto. If a negative British stance were to persist, the alternatives for Europe would be to accept the failure of the Union or to develop a federal core. This stance has, however, severely damaged British interests and it is reasonable to hope that the Labour government will carry Britain into the European mainstream and towards readiness to accept the necessary reforms.

The chance of success for an initiative by the European Parliament should, then, encourage it to act, in conjunction with the parliaments and governments of the more supportive member states, along the lines suggested above. With citizens throughout most of the Union largely favourable, the process of a reform conference could gather momentum to the point where a large enough majority of the member states would be able to accept the results of the conference, in accordance with the conditions originally set by the Parliament. Since the Community institutions already possess an advanced pre-federal structure, this would not be a leap in the dark, so any minority of reluctant states might well decide to fall in with the majority; and even if they did not, they too would benefit from the stability and security that would be brought to Europe by a democratic and effective Community covering the greater part of the continent.

Those who are not convinced that the support will be wide and deep enough would do well to reflect on the words of William the Silent, cited by Jacques Vandamme at the conclusion of his own chapter in this book: 'Point n'est besoin d'espérer pour entreprendre ni de réussir pour persévérer.' Or, more crudely, in the parlance of the British army in which Jacques once served: 'press on regardless'. Or, most succinctly, following the motto of the House of Orange, which the Dutch Resistance used as the name of its principal newspaper: 'Je maintiendrai'.

REFERENCES

Bogdanor, Vernon (ed.), 1987, *The Blackwell Encyclopaedia of Political Institutions*, Basil Blackwell, Oxford

Corbett, Richard, 1987, 'The Intergovernmental Conference and the Single European Act', in Pryce, Roy (ed.), *The Dynamics of European Union*, Croom Helm, London

Dahl, Robert A., 1989, *Democracy and its Critics*, Yale University Press, New Haven

Duchacek, Ivo D., 1987, 'constitution/constitutionalism', in Bogdanor, Vernon (ed.), op. cit.

European Commission, 1996, *Eurobarometer: Public Opinion in the European Union*, no. 45, Brussels, December

European Policy Centre, 1997, 'The IGC state of play', in *Challenge Europe*, no. 12, Brussels, January–February

Hartley, T.C., 1994, (First edn 1981) *The Foundations of Community Law*, Clarendon Press, Oxford

Lebohm, Hans H.J., 1997, *The Netherlands Presidency of the European Union*, (Report on Clingendael/ISEI/TEPSA Conference, 15–16 November 1996), Clingendael Institute, The Hague

Louis, Jean-Victor, 1995, '*La constitution de l'Union Européenne*', in Telò, Mario (ed.), infra

Pistone, Sergio, 1992, 'La lotta del movimento federalista europea dalla resistenza alla caduta della Comunità Europea di Difesa nel 1954', in *I Movimenti per l'Unità Europea dal 1945 al 1954*, Jaca Books, Milan

Pryce, Roy (ed.), 1987, *The Dynamics of European Union*, Croom Helm, London

Reflection Group's Report, 1995, SN 520/95, Brussels, 5 December

Telò, Mario (ed.), 1995, *Démocratie et construction européenne*, Editions de l'Université de Bruxelles, Brussels

5 Making European foreign policy work

Gianni Bonvicini

THE ORIGIN OF 'EUROPEAN FOREIGN POLICY'

The ambition to create a European foreign and security policy is a goal that runs parallel to the entire history of the integration process, from the European Coal and Steel Community (ECSC, 1952) to our own day, marked by the fourth major revision of the Treaty of Rome, which instituted the European Economic Community (EEC, 1957).

But, contrary to the history of the Community, which can boast an extraordinary continuity, attempts to cooperate in the foreign policy field have suffered a series of setbacks and resurrections. This chequered history has made the prospects of arriving, sooner or later, at a genuinely 'common' policy, rather than a simple coordination of national foreign policies, much more precarious.

Only with the Treaty of Maastricht (7 February 1992) was the first serious attempt made to 'communitarise' European Foreign and Security Policy (CFSP). In the intentions of the framers of the Treaty this attempt should have been completed in the space of five years (Article N – **48**) in what has come to be known as the Amsterdam Intergovernmental Conference (16–17 June 1997). As we will see, this process has remained incomplete, and today it is still difficult to speak of a common foreign policy in the strict sense.

After so many years of experience and numerous treaty reforms, we must ask ourselves why CFSP has had such a difficult history compared to the undoubted progress made in the Community sector (Hill, 1993, pp. 305–28). The pat answer having to do with the deeper roots of foreign policy in national sovereignty explains nothing, except, perhaps, the fact that in this sector the process began much later than in the economic sector. National foreign and security policies are subject to processes of globalisation analogous to those we experience in the economic sphere. And today, in particular, with the emergence of concepts such as that of 'comprehensive security', their bond with economic policies is even more obvious and direct. All the same, the resistance of governments to relinquishing their residual sovereignty in this sector is still extremely strong.

The real reason, probably, is tied to contingent historic factors which have set European foreign policy in one given ideological context of integration rather than another. In fact, European foreign policy has traditionally been viewed as an expression of the 'cooperative', as opposed to the 'integrative', ideology and, for this reason, it has become the involuntary object of the battle over the type of Europe to be built that has divided entire generations of politicians and intellectuals.

These differences were manifested from the very start in formal terms, as well. European Political Cooperation (EPC) was conceived in 1970 by a protocol of agreement among the member governments, at a level, in other words, far inferior to that of a simple international treaty. For this reason, EPC lacked authentic legal status. Its quite circumspect appearance on the European scene was also, in political terms, very different from that of the EEC. Beyond diplomatic circles and a narrow group of scholars, no one was actually aware that a first attempt to coordinate national foreign policies had begun. In the first draft of the Davignon Report the organs of EPC represented little more than the organisational structures of a club of willing people. There was no autonomous executive, no assembly, no voting procedure. To avoid confusion with Community institutions, the Council of Foreign Ministers was initially called 'Conference', while remaining identical in composition. A Political Committee had the task of preparing the ministers' meetings and implementing their 'directives', which were not, however, binding in nature (Nuttal, 1992).

The EEC, on the contrary, has a far more solid and complex structure. It is the fruit of an international treaty and has a unique binding and legitimate character. More precisely, the Treaty of Rome, which to a large extent was anticipated by the ECSC Treaty of 1952, was traditionally defined as an international treaty of a type all its own – ad hoc or supranational – and, therefore, even more intensive in character. In fact, the Treaty of Rome expressed a capacity to 'govern' that was virtually unknown in traditional international organisations, and its political ambition was to gradually transform the Community into the 'United States of Europe', as was often repeated at the time of its foundation (Lindberg and Scheingold, 1970). This capacity to govern was based not only on the binding nature of the laws approved, which were directly applicable in the member countries (by means of their 'compulsory' transformation into ordinary legislation), but also, and primarily, on the presence of an executive, the Commission, representing the common interest and with exclusive power of initiative, and on qualified majority voting within the Council of Ministers. Moreover, beyond the formal 'legitimation' it possessed through national ratification processes (which were also valid for other international agreements), the Treaty of Rome contained a provision of substantive legitimation through the passage of an electoral law (Article 138 – **190**) for the Strasbourg Assembly, which would allow the future European Parliament to come directly into contact with its citizens. In short, these are all elements familiar today, but worth mentioning to stress once again their revolutionary character in the context of the international relations represented by the birth of the EEC.

From the institutional and legal standpoint, the two structures are totally different from each other. The first structure is 'rigid' while the second has the flexibility typical of intergovernmental agreements. From the outset, it was apparent that any sort of 'linkage' between them would prove difficult. In fact, over the years, the question of the bond between them has proved to be one of the thorniest sticking points.

As pointed out above, the political origin accounts for the structural differences. The EC was born out of a compromise between the federal and confederal philosophies termed 'neo-functionalism'. For EPC the question never even arose. From its inception EPC has represented the confederal approach at its most radical. In effect, the different birth dates (the first in the early 1950s, the second in the early 1970s), not to mention the traumatic historical experiences arising from the European integration process in that span of time, underlie these two profoundly different conceptions (Kirchner, 1992, pp. 1–38).

If, for the EC, the basic goals are to overcome nationalism and to achieve a convergence of interests for the joint reconstruction of the European economy, for EPC these issues count little or not at all. EPC only answers to the need to enhance the visibility of Europe's role in the world and to complement economic integration with political integration, without running the risk of traumatic ruptures, such as the 1966 'empty chair' crisis provoked by French suspicions over the excessively supranational character of the EC, or the fracture experienced in 1954 in the field of political integration with the shelving of the European Defence Community by the French Assemblée Nationale. This is why the painless and infinitely less challenging road of the intergovernmental approach, in its softest version, was chosen.

THE EVOLUTION OF EPC AND THE DEVELOPMENT OF COOPERATION WITH THE EC

In functional terms, EPC was based on a pragmatic method of the incremental development of its organs and activities. EPC followed the technique of 'Chinese boxes', adding from time to time, on the basis of its experiences, new procedures and new organs to make its external action more effective (Bonvicini, 1988, pp. 49–70).

Thus, there was a transition from the first Davignon Report to the second, in 1973, marked by the addition of the Group of European Correspondents (a sort of Coreper, but with officials sitting in their respective ministries rather than in Brussels) and by the doubling of the annual number of meetings of the Conference from two to four. The 1981 London Report introduced other improvements, both within the Presidency, with the inauguration of the 'troika' system, and procedurally, with the possibility of convening an emergency meeting within forty-eight hours. For the first time, the political aspects of security were listed among the issues to be dealt with. After the failure of the Genscher–Colombo plan in 1983, which had sought to introduce voting mechanisms into EPC, a new step forward was achieved with the inclusion of the protocols relative to EPC in Article 30 of the Single European Act (SEA) in 1986. SEA Article 30 sought to bring order to EPC procedures and added a permanent secretariat (in its 'lightest' version) to the pre-existing organs. Despite its insertion into an international treaty, EPC once again remained strictly intergovernmental, and with no binding provisions (Dehousse and Weiler, 1990).

Nevertheless, as already noted, EPC's primary problem was that of its relations with the pre-existing structures of the EEC. The rapprochement between the two 'legs' of Europe's external activity, the economic and the political, was achieved very gradually and with a significant dose of mutual suspicion.

The key point in dispute was the role of the Commission. Initially, the Commission was excluded from consultation to avoid interference in the delicate mechanism of diplomatic cooperation. It was only from 1973 onwards that the Commission was partially associated for issues of economic competence. But it was actually the Commission itself which viewed the birth of EPC with misgivings, seeing in it a challenge to its own external economic competences. The positive collaborative experience between the services of the Commission and the working groups of EPC in preparing the 1975 Helsinki Conference on CSCE was the turning point for better mutual relations. In the 1981 London Report and, subsequently, in the SEA, the Commission is 'fully associated' with EPC (SEA Article 30.3.b).

A similar fear of 'contamination' was, at the outset, also felt by the Council, which kept Community issues strictly segregated from political issues. The physical limit was reached in the notorious case of the splitting (geographical and otherwise) of a meeting of the foreign ministers, who were obliged to meet in Brussels in the morning on Community questions and in Copenhagen in the afternoon on foreign policy matters (Danish Presidency, 1973).

All the same, the force of events and the pressures exerted by third countries obliged the Europeans to advance along the road of progressive cooperation between the two decision-making structures (Bonvicini, 1978). The concept of 'consistency' introduced in the SEA (Article 30.5) was born of this experience. There was a growing conviction that the Community's external relations could not be based on the distinction between the commercial/economic and political spheres much longer. The interrelations between the two spheres have always been extremely powerful, especially from the perspective of third countries, who struggled to, and were sometimes vexed by having to distinguish between, EC and EPC. The concept of 'consistency' proved to be the precursor for the subsequent adoption of the principle of 'comprehensive security', through which the potent bond between the various aspects of international, political, economic and military relations is underscored.

The application of the 'consistency' concept and, subsequently, the addition of an increasingly clearer security dimension to foreign policy created the dilemma of whether EPC was drawing nearer to the EC, in institutional terms, as well, or whether the EC was advancing towards EPC. This question loomed large, particularly after the signing of the Maastricht Treaty and remains topical to this day.

In effect, the Treaty of Maastricht attempted to translate into institutional terms this drawing together of the two structures, which under the reign of the old EPC had seen only practical progress, but no institutional progress. From this perspective, and in the light of the experiences which followed the signing of the Treaty, the key elements in this rapprochement between the procedures of the two pillars were qualified majority voting, the partial power of initiative of the Commission and the possibility of recourse to the Community budget.

The results of this operation have often been questioned, especially in regard to the four basic requirements of European foreign policy: effectiveness, representation, legitimation and, not least, the security dimension.

INITIATIVES FOR A MORE EFFECTIVE EUROPEAN FOREIGN POLICY

This is perhaps the oldest problem of European foreign policy. Many accusations of ineffectiveness have been voiced over the years. Today, in the light of the Balkan experience, the critical voices are louder still (Smith, 1996, pp. 2–21).

The first aspect of effectiveness is represented by the capacity rapidly to respond to crises, as was decided in London in 1981, with the introduction of the clause enabling the convening of emergency meetings within forty-eight hours.

But the key problem has always been the need to pass from the 'declaratory' phase, a typical result of the experiences in European foreign policy, to the action phase. In short, to make the shift from words to deeds. For many years, the deeds were those represented by the economic tools at the disposal of the EC, in both the positive sense, through cooperation and association agreements, and the negative sense, with the application of economic sanctions. A number of significant case studies, such as one on the 1982 Falklands crisis, revealed the importance of Community tools used in support of EPC positions.

The third, and last, aspect of effectiveness has centred around voting procedures. It seemed rather absurd that on the same issue or in regard to the same third country unanimity had to be reached in EPC, a factor which also slowed the taking of any action, while the EC could decide on the basis of qualified majority voting, at least for certain issues such as those relative to trade policy (Nuttal, 1992, pp. 55–76).

Maastricht offered the occasion to respond to the accusations voiced by EPC critics that the organ was, in essence, declaratory. The few examples of 'active' policy were entrusted to fact-finding missions, which began after the establishment of the troika in 1981, and the use of the Community's economic tools, basically economic sanctions, during episodes of international crisis. But there was certainly no appropriate formula to favour the passage from words to deeds. For this reason, the Treaty of Maastricht created an elaborate procedure that would permit a very gradual transition from the 'principle' of a joint action to the 'execution' of that same action in a decision-making continuum that would directly link the various phases of the emerging European foreign policy. At least theoretically, a step was taken towards the definition of European 'foreign policy' as being made up of positions and consequent actions, which was certainly not the case for the old EPC (Edwards and Nuttal, 1994, pp. 84–103).

When considering the issue of joint actions, we must also deal with the problem of their credibility. From this to the introduction of the qualified majority vote was, in theory, only a short step. In fact, however, since this was traditionally an intergovernmental area, the introduction of qualified majority voting was beset by serious obstacles, such as, for example, overcoming the prior requirement of double unanimity. Faced with the prospect of a substantial 'communitarisation' of CFSP, the reaction of the governments was to reiterate the priority of 'consensus', even at the cost of undermining the principle of effectiveness which, logically, would have led to the introduction of majority voting.

To make the adoption of joint action and its continuity over time more palatable, an 'opting out' clause was inserted for those countries which found it difficult to continue the action. This clause also had another purpose: to reiterate the primacy of the national interest in CFSP. Thus, joint action was diluted by the addition of further cautions, such as, precisely, the freedom of a member country to withdraw from a common commitment in the course of its application, although this in itself did not hinder continuation of the objective by the other parties. But this clause contributed to the jeopardising of other important aspects of foreign policy action, such as continuity over time and overall credibility.

In the same perspective of making CFSP more effective, the concession of a partial right of initiative granted to the Commission, which at the time of EPC was kept on the sidelines of the decision-making process, should be noted. This concession was considered by the institutional experts of CFSP as constituting another small revolution. In political terms, as mentioned above, the Commission was long considered a 'foreign body' in diplomatic activity and, as such, was for years even excluded from COREU, the telex network connecting the offices of the member states' European Correspondents. Thus, the decision to divide the power of initiative between the

Council of Ministers and the Commission marked the end of the great formal exclusion. Moreover, the recognition of a function such as the power of initiative, typical of the first, Community, pillar, was of great symbolic significance. The sole difference, and not a trifling one, lay in the fact that the exercise of initiative was not exclusive but concurrent. Still, this held promise of a gradual assumption of responsibility by the Commission in CFSP, which, in theory, left open the option of a future 'communitarisation' of the intergovernmental structure.

THE EXTERNAL REPRESENTATION OF THE UNION: SPEAKING WITH 'ONE VOICE'

Another important question had to do with the external representation of the Community through a so-called 'single voice'. Attempts made over the years to strengthen the role of the rotating Presidency responded to this need by proposing EPC as the 'sole interface' with the rest of the world. The troika formula, launched in London in 1981, was formulated for this purpose, but its success has been limited. In the eyes of a third government it was virtually impossible to understand why, for Community matters, it could turn to a single interlocutor, the Commission in Brussels, with a good chance of receiving credible answers, while for EPC matters it had to address itself to the rotating Presidency in its respective capital with very slim prospects of receiving competent and exhaustive answers. The great 'external' limitation of EPC was the lack of a fixed representative with ongoing competences. Instead, it relied on a structure based solely on the concept of rotation and the national origin of the organs (from the Political Committee to the Correspondents Group). The 1986 Single European Act attempted to resolve this by creating a permanent secretariat, but in its lightest and most innocuous version, to the point that the famous and oft-repeated Henry Kissinger comment about the lack of a single telephone number for the Union's foreign policy has remained valid (Lak, 1992, pp. 41–51).

The possibility of entrusting mandates to the Presidency (TEU Article J. 5.2 – **15**) runs along the same lines. The idea of bestowing greater visibility and autonomy on the Presidency is reflected in the proposal to charge it with the task of representing 'in principle' the Union's position on a specific common action. Besides meeting a general need for the 'personalisation' of CFSP, the message in this article was aimed, within the Union, at avoiding, by anticipation, individual national initiatives and, outside the Union, at bolstering the image of a 'single' negotiator. This competence was also to be exercised in international organisations or conferences, venues in which the matter of the 'representation' of the Union was an old and unsolved problem.

Finally, there is the matter of the Secretariat. With the Maastricht Treaty, the old EPC secretariat was merged with that of the Presidency of the Council. This decision was also a step towards the greater rationalisation of

CFSP tools and the enhancement of the role of the rotating Presidency, which has always remained the true engine of European foreign policy. This measure also gives an indication of a certain significance on the need to make the organisational structure of CFSP permanent. It further consolidated the first initiative of a 'light secretariat' launched by the SEA. Clearly, this was a transitional solution that left the door open to more serious institutional choices, such as a 'heavy secretariat' or a 'Mr. CFSP', as became clear immediately after ratification of the Treaty of Maastricht.

THE DIFFICULT PROCESS OF LEGITIMATION

This is a much neglected issue in the history of EPC. The institutional mechanism was in the hands of the diplomatic world, which was more inclined to engage in confidential negotiations than political debate. The foreign ministers themselves, by limiting the activity of EPC solely to the declaratory phase, rarely felt the direct consequences of national parliamentary control.

For its part, the European Parliament played only a marginal role in the decision-making process. Only with the London Report was it placed in more direct contact with the political summit of EPC, through the six-monthly reports of the rotating Presidency and the hearings of the ministers before the Political Affairs Committee. Despite the fact that EPC limited itself to little more than 'cosmetic' initiatives with regard to the European Parliament, the latter had, since the mid-Seventies, made emphatic efforts to present itself as the true political interface with EPC. The Parliament did this by initiating debates and passing resolutions on all the major foreign policy issues, including security and defence policy, then still quite distant on the horizons of EPC itself. The resolutions on the deployment of Euromissiles in Europe, and the backing of Europe's action in support of the United Kingdom in the first phase of the Falklands War were particularly noteworthy. Both these resolutions acted as useful cover for a number of national parliaments in a quandary about what they should do.

Furthermore, the European Parliament sought to conduct an authentic foreign policy of its own, inviting the major leaders of the day, among them Sadat, Gorbachev and Reagan, to speak before the plenary assembly. But, almost unnoticed, the Parliament gained a real foot inside the mechanisms of Community foreign policy with the SEA, through the 'power of assent' in relation to association and enlargement agreements. When initially granted, these powers seemed quite modest, but now, with the new geopolitical scenario in Europe, they have grown in stature. In short, the question of legitimation and democratic control has been an issue that gradually and laboriously made headway during the development of EPC. Today it has assumed a far more direct and urgent character than in the past.

Along the same line, the Treaty of Maastricht provided for the possibility of recourse to the Community budget. Since the old EPC involved intergovernmental activity, the financial contributions were always national and the European Parliament was held at bay from the decision-making processes. This new norm was another significant innovation in the final draft of the Maastricht Treaty because, on the one hand, it introduced the concept of financial 'solidarity' for foreign policy actions and, on the other, it paved the way for a more effective role for the European Parliament in defining European foreign policy.

Partially linked to the issue of legitimation is another innovation introduced by the Treaty of Maastricht, which conferred upon CFSP the competence of protecting the rights of Community citizens in third countries (TEU Article J.2 – 12) (Obradovic, 1996, pp. 191–221). Beyond the substantive importance of this provision, it could be seen in political terms as a way of gaining legitimation in the eyes of the citizen. EPC had never before sought direct contact with the 'European' citizen, since the concept of citizenship enjoyed validity only nationally. The sole interlocutors of EPC were the governments and, in part, the European Parliament, which, theoretically, could have acted as an indirect intermediary between the citizens and EPC. But the Parliament's lack of substantive competences in relation to EPC weakened this theoretical link. The decision reached at Maastricht to insert into the Treaty articles on European citizenship (Article 8 c – 20) revealed a first tangible possibility of linking CFSP activity to the direct interests of European citizens, by making the embassies of the EU member states in third countries work on behalf of their rights and safety, regardless of their nationality.

THE SECURITY AND DEFENCE DIMENSION OF THE UNION

Security and defence policy formally entered the Treaty framework through the Maastricht Treaty. At least in formal terms, this too represented a significant step forward, particularly if it is recalled that security, and then only its political aspects, had been mentioned in the Community/Union context for the first time in the London Report (1981). The economic aspects were added in the Solemn Declaration of Stuttgart (1983), and entered in this double sense in the SEA (Article 30.6 a).

In the span of the next five years (1986 to 1991) even defence, and not just security, became an issue, if only as a future prospect. The overcoming of traditional Irish opposition (because of neutrality) and Danish misgivings (because of general suspicions about integration) was clearly the result of the new climate that emerged in 1989. This climate was less favourable to Irish-type neutralist positions and was rooted in the conviction that, sooner or later, the Americans would delegate to Europe a greater share of the responsibilities for its own defence, placing in doubt the role of NATO. These fears proved ungrounded, and NATO became an indispensable element in Europe's new security framework. The debate thus returned to its starting point, as the drawn-out negotiations about what role to confer on the Western European Union (WEU) on the eve of the Amsterdam Intergovernmental Conference in 1997 attested (Wohlfeld, 1997, pp. 63–70).

In effect, the introduction of defence and security policy into the Treaty of Maastricht proved to be little more than a cosmetic operation. Although the WEU got off to a quick start (in 1992, even before ratification of the Treaty was completed, the WEU approved in Petersberg the main lines of its own recovery, from the planning cell to peacekeeping operations), the facts soon exposed the limits of the decision-making process in the defence field. Even more than in the field of foreign policy, where defence was concerned the very strict rules of the intergovernmental method applied, beginning with unanimity. The consequence of this was the gradual disappearance of the WEU in crisis areas as soon as the spectre of military intervention loomed.

At the beginning of the Bosnian crisis the WEU succeeded in playing a relatively effective role beside the UN, patrolling the Adriatic and the Danube. But as the military confrontation intensified, the WEU was forced to give ground to NATO, which was better organised and more determined in military and decision-making terms. The disappearance of the WEU was even more glaring in Albania, in which responsibility was essentially handed over to the OSCE.

Hence the issue of security turned out to be the major failure in the initiative to reform the old EPC as embodied in the new, but incomplete, CFSP incorporated into the Treaty on European Union at Maastricht (Taylor, 1994, pp. 1–16).

THE LIMITS OF AMSTERDAM AND THE FUTURE OF CFSP

The overall experience of CFSP in the short period between the Maastricht and Amsterdam IGCs was, therefore, unsatisfactory, not only because of limited effectiveness, but also because of the incomplete nature of the experiment being conducted. This certainly weakened the prospects for reform as the Amsterdam Intergovernmental Conference drew nearer (Regelsberger and Wessels, 1996, pp. 29–54).

In the first place, the trial period of the new policies and new procedures had been too short to be able to judge its effectiveness thoroughly. The Treaty of Maastricht officially came into effect in October 1993, after an extenuated and agonising period of ratification in the member states. Negotiations for its revision officially got underway on 29 March 1996, at the European Council of Turin. But unofficially they had actually begun much earlier, in the summer of 1995, with the creation of the Westendorp Reflection Group. For a subject such as foreign and security policy, so deeply ingrained in national sovereignties, such a short period to test the will to 'communitarise' the few innovative procedures introduced by the

Maastricht Treaty was certainly an obstacle to the sort of subtle yet substantive reform which might have been possible had the trial period been longer.

As noted, the negotiations leading to the Amsterdam Treaty effectively began in 1995. They were carried out in an atmosphere of deep disappointment over the functioning of CFSP, felt not only by the experts, but also by public opinion. There was a widespread perception that the Union was not in a position to assume the role and the responsibilities that the proliferation in serious border conflicts necessitated. The call to do more, better was echoed in much of the European press. The Reflection Group and, subsequently, the personal representatives of the foreign ministers, found themselves in the uncomfortable position of having to answer mounting criticism and, concurrently, acting as custodians of national sovereignty, which was still strongly felt in the CFSP field. This long-standing ambiguity can be traced back to the origins of EPC and is reflected in the difficulty of following a precise path in dealing with the institutional changes to be made to CFSP.

In the second place, certain key regulations, such as qualified majority voting for common actions, were never properly experimented with. It proved impossible to construct a united front on this issue. Even though several valid compromise proposals were made, it was quite clear that a decisive 'communitarisation' of CFSP on voting procedures was still, and remains, inconceivable. Even a country such as Italy, notoriously enthusiastic about making the whole structure of the European Union more *communautaire*, adopted a very conservative stance on the qualified majority voting issue in CFSP, ultimately accepting the continuation of unanimity at least in the sphere of general principles and strategies. The intergovernmental approach and the instinct to protect national sovereignty are still deeply ingrained.

The same prudence marked the approach to the Commission's right of initiative. The Commission moved very cautiously, knowing perfectly well that in the history of EPC it itself had been a key factor in the member states' fear of losing control over common foreign policy and security. The Commission was thus able to dodge the accusation of activism which, in the past, had haunted it when it had dared to anticipate the Council's slow reaction to certain international crises.

Furthermore, the Commission stayed on the defensive so as to protect its 'foreign policy' competences, derived from the power attributed to it in the Treaty to promote the Union's external economic policy. As always, there was fear about possible 'contamination' by the intergovernmental method (characteristic of the second pillar) of the first, Community, pillar, in which the Commission enjoys an especially prominent role. For example, humanitarian actions were a matter of dispute between proponents of Community jurisdiction and their opponents, who believed that CFSP should enjoy the right of initiative in this field. The same objection was made with regard to the new article 228.a (**301**) of the Treaty of Maastricht relative to the use of economic sanctions. On one hand, this article was hailed as a remedy for the defects of the Treaty of Rome on the matter. In the past, beginning with the Falklands crisis in 1982, EC Articles 113 (trade policy) and 224 (measures in derogation of trade agreements) (**133 and 297**) had been used in a very ambiguous and controversial manner. In fact, the two articles were 'bent' to the needs of European foreign policy to adopt sanctions, while never mentioning this possibility (Holland, 1991). Article 228.a sought to remedy this anomaly by providing explicitly for recourse to economic sanctions. But the way in which the procedure was formulated and the vocabulary used created a suspicion that intergovernmental procedure was surreptitiously besting Community procedure, even on a matter, such as trade policy, traditionally considered to be one of the Community's core competences. The mention of 'common positions' or 'actions' as the starting element of a decision-making procedure in the area of sanctions conjured up visions of the obstacle of prior double unanimity (TEU Article J.3 – **13**) and, therefore, the 'dominance' of CFSP over the EC. In other words, the positive effect achieved in terms of the link between CFSP and EC was counteracted by suspicions of the 'intergovernmentalisation' of the first pillar by the second. This was, in short, exactly the opposite of everyone's expectations for cooperation between foreign policy and Community activities on the eve of the signing of the Maastricht Treaty.

The provision for recourse to the Community budget was also the object of numerous disputes and diverging interpretations between the Council and the European Parliament. The former was reluctant to acknowledge control over foreign policy actions, while the latter was eager to play a more active role in CFSP. Requests by the European Parliament for expenses relative to joint actions to be classified as being 'non-obligatory' expenditure, which gave the Parliament the power of veto, were not frequently accepted by the Council of Ministers, since the Council preferred to maintain total control over the management of foreign policy. What had been considered an indirect path for the intervention of Parliament on CFSP questions and an interesting gambit for a greater legitimation of common foreign policy proved to be more a hotbed of procedural contention between Parliament and Council than a mechanism leading to enhanced and substantive democratic control.

Nor was progress made on the front of 'external representation', mentioned by the Maastricht Treaty through the instrument of 'mandates' to be entrusted to the Presidency. With Amsterdam on the horizon, all sorts of proposals were made, from a 'Mr. CFSP' to a Secretary General (Bonvicini and Merlini, 1994, pp. 1–10). This point was hotly debated and could have been an important signal of the will to make a qualitative leap forward in the conception of CFSP. The lack of an internal and external 'reference point' for CFSP was from the very start one of the basic snags in augmenting its overall credibility. The light secretariat of EPC and of the

Council of CFSP certainly both fell short of solving the problem. What might have been expected was a decisive upgrading of the competences of the organ (not the person) in charge of CFSP. In other words, either a Mr CFSP or a Secretary General would have been fine, as long as he/she possessed certain powers, particularly the right of initiative, had a budget at his/her disposal and was generally accountable before the European Parliament. This would have amounted, in short, to a sort of hybrid Commission for CFSP. This approach was never accepted, and the focus was placed more on the 'level' of the organ (or person) than on its competences. But a telephone number without power does not solve the identity problem of CFSP as an international actor.

The great paradox of this entire matter is that in order to enable the Union to fulfil its international role in a more credible manner almost all the governments of the Union recognised the necessity of further improving the CFSP mechanisms (Van den Broek, 1996, pp. 1–5). The negotiators for the Amsterdam Intergovernmental Conference moved in this direction. But, once again, the need to mediate between divergent positions prevailed, and the changes enacted did not substantially alter the nature of CFSP. The problem of a European foreign policy has remained largely unresolved, and the march towards a more convincing 'consistency' among the Union's old pillars requires additional progress along the road of effectiveness, representation, and legitimation. In short, neither the Treaty of Maastricht nor that of Amsterdam solved the problem of the persistent imbalance between the tools at the disposal of the EC and those in the hands of CFSP. In carrying forward common foreign policy, the Fifteen possess an impressive array of economic tools, from association agreements to sanctions, a certain number of diplomatic tools, from declarations to joint actions, and no truly military device. In this incomplete condition, it is genuinely hard for the Union to deal with the emerging policy of 'comprehensive security', which requires the combined use of economic, diplomatic and military means in a continuing and effective manner. For as long as this proves impossible, the overall credibility of the Union will continue to suffer in the eyes of third countries. In short, the activities of conflict prevention and conflict resolution which current geo-strategic circumstances require of the Union cannot be performed (Robins *et al.*, 1997, pp. 65–179).

In the future, this imbalance is destined to grow. With the introduction of the euro, the European Union will inevitably be forced to play a bigger international role. As a 'global currency', the euro will require a policy towards the dollar and the yen, with unavoidable repercussions for the Union's foreign policy. But with a 'European government' for the economy, it will be even more difficult to count on a 'government' for foreign policy, should foreign policy remain as it is currently formulated in the Treaties. The two main pillars of the Union will continue to support a dangerously inclined roof, making the voice of the Union in the world precarious and scarcely credible, and with possibly negative results for the affirmation of the euro as a global currency in competition with the dollar. In today's world, the bonds between the economy and foreign policy are growing ever tighter, and both contribute to the general credibility of the system.

The debate on the role of CFSP *vis-à-vis* the EC must be explored in depth. The simple introduction of constructive abstention, as provided by the Amsterdam Treaty, will certainly act to shrink the area of dissension between governments in a sector in which national interests are still deeply rooted. But this will not be enough to solve the basic question regarding the consistency between the two main pillars of the Union. Abstention without clear mechanisms linking the EC and CFSP is destined to generate confusion and competition between the two. The single voice of the Union should be represented in both the foreign (and security) policy dimension and the economic dimension, and coordination between the two must be close and automatic. Another Amsterdam is needed to solve this crucial question. The next intergovernmental conference must concentrate on this vital horizontal link and on the institutional mechanisms that are needed to make it effective. Otherwise, the Union will be unable to perform its role as the international actor that recent history has assigned it.

REFERENCES

Bonvicini, Gianni, 1978, 'Der Dualismus zwischen EPZ und Gemeinschaft', in R. Rummel and W. Wessels (eds), *Die Europäische Politische Zusammenarbeit*, Europa Union Verlag

—— 1988, 'Mechanisms and Procedures of EPC: More than Traditional Diplomacy?', in A. Pijpers, E. Regelsberger and W. Wessels, *A Common Foreign Policy for Western Europe?*, M. Nijthoff Publishers, The Netherlands

Bonvicini, Gianni and Merlini, C., 1994, Merlini, 'Il futuro della Pesc', Doc. IAI9436, Rome

Dehousse, Renaud and Weiler, Joseph H.H., 1990, *EPC and the Single Act: From Soft Law to Hard Law?*, European University Institute, Working Paper EPU no. 90/1, Florence

Edwards, Geoffrey and Nuttal, Simon, 1994, 'Common Foreign and Security Policy', in A. Duff *et al.* (eds), *Maastricht and Beyond*, Routledge, London

Hill, C., 1993, 'The Capability Expectations Gap, or Conceptualising Europe's International Role', *Journal of Common Market Studies*, no. 3, September

Holland, M., 1991, 'Sanctions as an EPC Instrument', in M. Holland (ed.), *The Future of European Political Cooperation*, Macmillan, London

Kirchner, Emil J., 1992, *Decision Making in the European Community*, Manchester University Press, Manchester

Lak, M.W.J., 1992, 'The Constitutional Foundation. Comparison of EC and ECP: the Two Components of a CFSP', in R. Rummel (ed.), *Toward Political Union. Planning CFSP in the European Community*, Westview Press, Boulder, Colorado

Lindberg, C., and Scheingold, S., 1970, *Europe's Would-Be Policy. Patterns of Change in the European Community*, Prentice-Hall, New Jersey

Nuttal, Simon J., 1992, *European Political Cooperation*, Clarendon Press, Oxford

—— 1992, 'The Institutional Network and the Instruments of Action. The Interaction of EC and EPC in Common Frameworks', in R. Rummel (ed.), *Toward Political Union. Planning CFSP in the European Community*, Westview Press, Boulder, Colorado

Obradovic, D., 1996, 'Policy Legitimacy and the European Union', *Journal of Common Market Studies*, no. 2, June

Regelsberger, Elfie and Wessels, Wolfgang, 1996, 'The CFSP Institutions and Procedures: A Third Way for the Second Pillar', *European Foreign Affairs Review*, no. 1

Robins, P. *et al.*, 1997, 'European Foreign Policy: Europe The Peace Maker?', *Cambridge Review of International Affairs*, no. 2, Spring

Smith, C.J., 1996, 'Conflict in the Balkans and the Possibility of a European Union Common Foreign and Security Policy', *International Relations*, no. 2, August

Taylor, T., 1994, 'West European Security and Defence Cooperation', *International Affairs*, no. 1

Van Den Broek, H., 1996, 'Why Europe Needs a Common Foreign and Security Policy', *European Foreign Affairs Review*, no. 1

Wohlfeld, M., 1997, 'CFSP Reform Debate and the IGC: a WEU Perspective', in *CFSP Reform Debate and the IGC. National Interests and Policy Preferences*, Working Paper, Research Group on European Affairs, Bertelsmann Foundation, Munich, March

6 Flexibility, differentiation and closer cooperation
The Amsterdam provisions in the light of the Tindemans Report

Wolfgang Wessels[1]

THE '*ACQUIS ACADÉMIQUE*' ON FLEXIBILITY

A number of themes reoccur in the political and public debate about Europe's future. In critical periods, these are unearthed from academic ivory towers or from dusty diplomatic archives. Debates often seem to reinvent the wheel rather than using an old concept adapted to today's challenges. Exploiting the rich patrimony of integration debates and studies, or what might be called, in analogy to the *acquis communautaire*, the *acquis académique*, is surely the duty of all academics. Such sunken reflections provide valuable opportunities to enrich the conceptual and strategic debate, particularly in political circles, where political actors under short-term pressures tend to neglect the insights gained from past experience.

The vast body of reflection related to the concept of 'flexibility' is surely a case in point: differentiation, *coopération renforcée, abgestufte Integration, Europe à plusieurs vitesses*, multi-speed Europe, *Europe à la carte, Kerneuropa* (hardcore Europe), *géométrie variable*, opting out, opting in (Schneider and Wessels, 1977, Stubb, 1996, Wallace and Wallace, 1995 – see also general references at the end of this chapter). The issues which were so prominent during the 1996–7 Intergovernmental Conference – revising the Treaties and preparing for further enlargement – have surely been vital topics from the very inception of the integration process. Monnet (1976, p. 371) and Spaak (1969, pp. 284–91) argued strongly for a 'small' supranational Europe of the Six – what we might today call a 'core Europe' – and against a larger, inter-governmental Europe along the lines of the Council of Europe. Over the decades, the debate about deepening and widening has evolved into several schools.

The 1976 Tindemans Report on European Union (Tindemans, 1976) and the 'new approach' it proposed provided a significant input into the ongoing discussion. In fact, some of the basic principles of the relevant chapter of the Tindemans Report to the European Council (see Box 6.1) are still being debated and remain valid arguments. They can be identified in major provisions of the Maastricht Treaty, particularly in the rules for the third stage of Economic and Monetary Union, and in the new provisions as formulated by the 1996–7 Amsterdam Intergovernmental Conference.

Box 6.1 Excerpts from the 1975 Tindemans Report

'**A new approach**

It is impossible at the present time to submit a credible programme of action if it is deemed absolutely necessary that in every case all stages should be reached by all the States at the same time. The divergence of their economic and financial situations is such that, were we to insist on this progress would be impossible and Europe would continue to crumble away. It must be possible to allow that:
– within the Community framework of an overall concept of European Union as defined in this report and accepted by the Nine;
– and on the basis of an action programme drawn up in a field decided upon by the common institutions, whose principles are accepted by all,
1 those States which are able to progress have a duty to forge ahead,
2 those States which have reasons for not progressing which the Council, on a proposal from the Commission, acknowledges as valid do not do so,
– but will at the same time receive from the other States any aid and assistance that can be given them to enable them to catch the others up,
– and will take part, within the joint institutions, in assessing the results obtained in the field in question.
This does not mean Europe *à la carte*: each country will be bound by the agreement of all as to the final objective to be achieved in common; it is only the timescales for achievement that vary . . .
This system could, as matters turn out, be of great assistance in enabling the process of development of the Union to regain its momentum . . .'

Tindemans, 1976, pp. 20–1

In order better to understand today's debate it is useful to return to the conceptual roots, particularly those of the 1970s, and hence to see what can be learnt from the past in understanding and applying the Amsterdam Treaty's provisions for closer cooperation. There is a vast literature (see the select references at the end of this chapter), but I propose simply to compare the 1975 Tindemans text with the provisions of the 1997 Amsterdam Treaty.

This chapter is not so much a contribution to the history of integration concepts as an attempt to interpret and evaluate the various provisions for flexibility as these have evolved, and to see how these might illuminate the current debate on closer cooperation.

INTEGRATION OR DISINTEGRATION STRATEGY?

The fundamental dilemma

The 1975 Tindemans Report began with an analysis that could just as easily have been plucked from today's debate, and which will be of even greater relevance after eastern enlargement; 'It is impossible to submit a credible programme of action if it is deemed absolutely necessary that in every case all stages should be reached by all States at the same time.' Since 'progress would be impossible and Europe would continue to crumble away, . . . those States that are able to progress have a duty to forge ahead'. Tindemans thus neatly summed up the fundamental dialectic between the Union's capacity to deal effectively with impending problems and the principle that all member states should dispose of the same right to participate in all of the Union's activities (and hence be subject to all of the incumbent obligations).

Article 43 (K. 15) TEU does not beat about the bush but, rather, pithily declares that 'Member States which intend to establish closer cooperation between themselves may make use of the institutions, procedures, and mechanisms laid down in the Treaties . . .' Common to both the Tindemans and the Amsterdam Treaty concepts is a strategy of either integrating member states and their policies or, failing that, of keeping them tied into the common framework. Indeed, both documents are based on a similar cost-benefit analysis. Imperfect integration within the Community is to be preferred – for the sake of the stability of the overall framework – to over-dogmatic adherence to first principles. According to this analysis, an over-rigid insistence on respect for the Community orthodoxy would risk encouraging some member states to pursue common ventures outside the single institutional framework (a term emphasised by the Maastricht Treaty) and hence weaken the judicial system and political and economic solidarity. Both approaches embody similar pro-integration logic. The alternatives are not so much between perfect and imperfect integration as between some kind of Union-based flexibility (facilitated by derogations) on the one hand, and activity wholly outside the Union's legal and institutional framework on the other. The second-best option is preferred to exclusion.

Second-best integration strategy; or a general principle for the Union

The different formulations of the Tindemans and Amsterdam Treaty versions of flexibility are indicative of the differing perspectives on integration adopted by their authors. From the perspective of the Treaty on European Union, flexibility is not so much a major step necessary for further integration (as Tindemans saw it) as a mechanism which can take into account the political will, interests and perceptions of the member states. The difference is even more telling in terms of the scope of the two formulations. For the Tindemans Report, the field of application was clearly delimited to the economic, fiscal and monetary policy areas; in effect, at that time, Tindemans was implicitly arguing for the *communautarisation* of the currency 'snake'. In this sense, Tindemans' approach was a conceptual forerunner of the Maastricht Treaty's provisions on Economic and Monetary Union.

But as time went by and the discussion continued the terms of the debate were gradually extended. From being an exceptional approach for one particular policy area with very specific characteristics, the flexibility concept increasingly came to be seen as a more general strategy for the Community and the Union as a whole. Thus, the new Amsterdam Treaty provisions are a clear step towards constitutionalising the concept of closer cooperation as a permanent and Union-wide principle. The fundamental nature of the step taken is reflected in the new Treaty provisions, with the basic rules set out in the general provisions of the Treaty on European Union being complemented by specific rules in two of the three pillars.

Perhaps it is just as indicative of the way in which the concept has evolved since the mid-1970s that the first pillar clause (EC Article 5a – **11**) lists certain inviolable principles and *domaines reservés*. The impression given is of a fortress being built around what is thought to be the *acquis communautaire* – core areas considered sacrosanct. In the third pillar (cooperation in the fields of Justice and Home Affairs), the new Amsterdam provisions (TEU Article K.12 – **40**) make it difficult to discern the limits of closer cooperation. In the second pillar (the Common Foreign and Security Policy) the provision for 'constructive abstention' (new TEU Article J.13(1) – **23**) is seen as a functional equivalent of closer cooperation, and this view makes the line between normal and exceptional procedure even fainter.

Another crucial difference between the Tindemans and Amsterdam Treaty approaches to the concept concerns timing. For Tindemans, the second-best option was only an intermediary step which would, ultimately, lead all member states to full integration. The Amsterdam Treaty's provisions on closer cooperation are less assertive on this point. Tindemans was more 'pro-active' in pursuing a certain '*finalité politique*' (European Union), whereas the new provisions seem reactive and defensive. While they include the possibility of opting in, they do not necessarily expect that all other member states will follow according to a fixed plan and within a fixed period. The old underlying understanding, that all 'ships in the convoy' will reach the harbour, only at different times, is no longer so dominant.

Respecting the Community orthodoxy

The two approaches – Tindemans and Amsterdam – share perhaps more similarities when the rules governing compatibility with the Community's and the Union's principles are considered. Indeed, the clear and regularly repeated warning against any violation of the Community's and the Union's rules and spirit is a trademark of both texts. There is, as there has always been, fundamental opposition to concepts such as *Europe à la carte*, in which political or functional interests are not obliged to take into account overall integration objectives and fundamental principles.

The Tindemans Report addressed this issue when setting the terms of reference for any kind of flexibility 'within the Community framework of an overall concept of European Union'. Article 43 **TEC** requires that closer cooperation should be aimed at 'furthering the objectives of the Union and at protecting and serving its interests', and that it: 'respects the principles of the Treaties and the single institutional framework'; 'concerns at least a majority of Member States'; and does not affect the '*acquis communautaire*'.

This *leitmotif* is repeated in the clauses specific to the EC Treaty. TEU Article 5a (**11**) elaborates on the conditions for applying the closer cooperation clause in the first pillar by stressing the basic principles and policy fields of the *acquis communautaire*. Thus, Article 5a (**11**) declares that closer cooperation may be established provided that the cooperation proposed: 'does not concern areas which fall within the exclusive competence of the Community'; 'does not affect Community policies, actions or programmes'; 'does not concern the citizenship of the Union or discriminate between nationals of Member States'; 'remains within the limits of the powers conferred upon the Community by this Treaty'; and 'does not constitute a discrimination or a restriction of trade between Member States and does not distort the conditions of competition between the latter'. Specific safeguard clauses are also set out in the more intergovernmental third pillar.

Both the Tindemans and the Amsterdam Treaty approaches reveal bad consciences in the context of respect for the fundamental principle of equal rights and obligations for each member state. Their answers to this fundamental dilemma must be seen as sub-optimal solutions. In this sense, the Amsterdam text of the late 1990s does not signify any decline in the understanding of the Union as a community of equal partners. Both the Amsterdam Treaty (explicitly) and the Tindemans Report (implicitly) stress that use of the provision should be exceptional; in the words of the new Article 43 TEU, the provisions on closer cooperation should be resorted to 'only . . . as a last resort where the objectives of the Treaty could not be attained by applying the relevant articles laid down therein'. Both, but particularly the Amsterdam Treaty, establish precautionary rules designed to prevent use of the fall-back position, or second-best option, from undermining the basic properties and characteristics of the Union. The draftsmen of the Amsterdam Treaty clearly had a pro-integration strategy in mind and, whilst seeking flexibility, did not wish to create an opening for gradual disintegration or a *Europe à la carte*.

Perhaps more than in the 1970s, those possibilities have been at the backs of the minds of those who propose closer cooperation. It is not only a matter

Box 6.2 Excerpts from TEU Title VII

'**Provisions on Closer Cooperation**

Article 43

1   Member States which intend to establish closer cooperation between themselves may make use of the institutions, procedures and mechanisms laid down by this Treaty and the Treaty establishing the European Community provided that the cooperation:

a   is aimed at furthering the objectives of the Union and at protecting and serving its interests;
b   respects the principles of the said Treaties and the single institutional framework of the Union;
c   is only used as a last resort, where the objectives of the said Treaties could not be attained by applying the relevant procedures laid down therein;
d   concerns at least a majority of the Member States;
e   does not affect the *acquis communautaire* and the measures adopted under the other provisions of the said Treaties;
f   does not affect the competences, rights, obligations and interests of those Member States which do not participate therein;
g   is open to all Member States and allows them to become parties to the cooperation at any time, provided that they comply with the basic decision and with the decisions taken within that framework;
h   complies with the specific additional criteria laid down in Article 11 of the Treaty establishing the European Community and Article 40 of this Treaty, depending on the area concerned, and is authorised by the Council in accordance with the procedures laid down therein.

2   Member States shall apply, as far as they are concerned, the acts and decisions adopted for the implementation of the cooperation in which they participate. Member States not participating in such cooperation shall not impede the implementation thereof by the participating Member States.'

of *Europe à la carte*, which was already ruled out by the Tindemans Report (and has been ever since), but also the concept of a 'hardcore Europe' composed of the economically more successful states, as the Schäuble/Lamers paper was, outside Germany, widely understood to have proposed. The Schengen agreement has also been seen as a case of outside cooperation weakening coherence among the European Union's member states, and even threatening the *acquis communautaire*. Other commentators have noted the trend towards a *directoire* of the larger member states in the field of the Common Foreign and Security Policy (for example, the contact group for Bosnia). Clearly, such trends could considerably reduce the saliency of the Union.

'INS' AND 'OUTS': CENTRIPETAL DYNAMICS

Ability and willingness – criteria for distinguishing between members

The Tindemans Report assumed that macroeconomic performance would offer clear and definite criteria for distinguishing potential 'ins' from potential 'outs' and that it would demonstrate the 'divergence of their economic and financial situations'. The procedure for distinguishing between the two categories seemed simple and plausible; 'Those States which have reasons for not progressing which the Council, on a proposal from the Commission, acknowledges as valid do not do so.' TEC Article 109k (**122**), as introduced by the Maastricht Treaty, on 'derogations' for member states not fulfilling the criteria for the third stage of Economic and Monetary Union, was apparently based on this philosophy. The Tindemans approach thus stressed objective economic indicators. Member states were supposed to be willing, but temporarily unable, to take up additional obligations.

The Amsterdam Treaty's provisions do not refer to reasons, whether objective or subjective, and ability and willingness are not mentioned. It is apparently left up to the member states, as a function of their political circumstances and interests, to decide whether or not to participate. Whereas the Tindemans approach assumed a fundamental obligation and interest of each member state to be fully involved and to make progress when possible, the Amsterdam Treaty's approach is more agnostic. From the viewpoint of the 1990s, the categorisations and procedural mechanisms of the Tindemans Report seem simplistic. Several experiences have highlighted the flaws in the approach which was proposed by Tindemans, but also in the similar approach espoused by the Maastricht Treaty. Member states and their governments do not like having to admit that their countries are only second rate. As important, they are very reluctant to apply for the relatively junior status of invited guest, a status which would involve losing their rights to full and equal participation. In effect, the Tindemans approach requires a high degree of modesty and self-restraint on the part of the member states and their representatives. But it is surely against the instincts of politicians to limit their own rights to a mere seat without a vote at a table in the knowledge that, in so volunteering, they may also be creating additional hurdles to their full participation at a future date.

The debate over the Maastricht criteria has shown that the emphasis on economic criteria is not mainly in the interest of the weaker countries, as the Tindemans Report had supposed, but seems in practice to reflect the preference of the stronger countries to keep the less competitive out. At issue is not so much the danger of over-charging the underperforming countries, as the risk of over-loading the joint venture and hence increasing the burden of the more successful countries. The debate has thus been completely turned on its head; the requests of the less able countries for derogations from the common obligations – which are then accorded on the basis of objective criteria – has been replaced by the claims of the potential outsiders that it is against the basic principles of the Union to exclude any state which is willing and declares itself fit for further progress. Moreover, the supposedly objective criteria involved have also become the subject of major controversy. The basic assumption of the Tindemans Report – that divergences in economic and fiscal performance are objectively self-evident and simply a matter of statistical clarification – has been beset by political and academic doubt.

It is surprising that, at least at a first reading, the Amsterdam Treaty's provisions do not address this issue at all. No rules or procedures are formulated for distinguishing between advanced and non-participating member states, at least as far as the initial establishment of closer cooperation is concerned. On the other hand, the procedures for opting in later are more specific. If member states want to 'establish or develop closer cooperation', no state willing to join this group can be excluded, as no additional criteria for becoming a founder member are enumerated. The point can be put more starkly in the form of a question. Could an advance group, perhaps after secret deliberations, simply 'out' itself as a group for closer cooperation, or would the Commission be required, in its 'opinion to the Council' (Articles 5a and K.12(2) – **11 TEC** and **40 TEU**), to develop its own criteria for the exclusion of willing member states? Since the new provisions offer no clarification on this point, it would seem to be a simple matter of a unilateral declaration of intent to join the closer cooperation by each interested member state. Given the difficulty of joining later, member states would presumably think twice before turning down the right to become a founder member of closer cooperation.

If such an interpretation of the Amsterdam Treaty is valid, then the new provisions ignore the simple fact that there might be objective reasons – however vague – for forming advanced subgroups. Eastern enlargement might further increase the gaps between the differing capacities of the member states, gaps which subsequently might not be easy to diminish. Thus, if all member states want to participate and none can be excluded, the more advanced, larger or stronger member states might be inclined to opt for closer cooperation outside the European Union framework; by forming, for example, a leading *directoire* based on size, or a core group. Furthermore, the 'outs' might additionally demand compensation or further safeguards before allowing the 'ins' to move ahead. These potential temptations need also to be considered in view of the rules granting the right to advance. If this identification of the Amsterdam Treaty's shortcomings is correct then, in effect, a vital reason for any kind of closer cooperation is undermined by the very provisions themselves.

In conclusion, whilst the Tindemans Report was simplistic in its assumptions about objective categorisations, simple procedures and the self-effacing nature of member state governments, the new Amsterdam Treaty provisions are completely blind to the whole *problematique* of objective differences among member states and how they should be handled.

Procedures for establishing closer cooperation: a qualified majority in the Council and the Luxembourg Formula re-stated

Close examination of the procedure for the establishment of an advance group is also important because it highlights another key issue. The Tindemans Report insisted that, in order to keep flexibility compatible with a shared understanding of the Union, and in view of the avowed objective – the so-called '*finalité politique*' – of a European Union, the proposed new approach should only be pursued 'within the Community framework of an overall concept of the European Union as defined in this report and accepted by the nine (*Member States of that period*), and on the basis of an action programme drawn up in a field decided upon by the common institutions, whose principles are accepted by all'. Though this safeguard clause was clearly open to interpretation (for example, what exactly did 'principles' mean in this context?), the basic message was unequivocal; differentiation had to be based on consensus among all members.

The absorption *expressis verbis* of the Amsterdam Treaty's provisions for closer cooperation into the common provisions of the Treaty on European Union and into EC Treaty Article 5 and TEU Article K.12 (**11 TEC** and **40 TEU**) strongly implies that the general principle of flexibility and the provisions fixing the respective rules have been agreed upon by all the member states, both through unanimity among the Heads of States or Government at the European Council in Amsterdam and through the member states' respective ratification procedures.

But the provisions for making a specific decision to establish an advance group of closer cooperation in a given case seem to be potentially conflictual. Two opposing positions are implicit in the provisions. On the one hand, some member states might consider it inappropriate that their more rapid progress should be blocked by other member states unwilling (though perhaps able) or unable to take up additional obligations. The possession of such a potential veto right by non-participating member states could be perceived as disproportionate and might encourage the creation outside the European Union framework of a 'hard core' of progressive states. On the other hand, one could imagine that some member states would demand that each case should be accepted by all, including those opting out or requiring a derogation, either of their own wish or – to borrow from the Tindemans approach – because of their objective situation.

The analysis implicit in the Tindemans Report demonstrates clearly that there is more to the discussion than a simple dispute between the 'British' point of view and other, more pro-integration, forces. Agreement among all of the member states about the areas and the modalities of closer cooperation can be understood as a fundamental prerequisite in maintaining shared responsibility for the overall framework of the Union. Seen from this perspective, the safeguard clauses in the Tindemans Report are a crucial factor in upholding the Union's coherence and stability.

A further line of argument is hidden in the Tindemans Report's insistence on safeguard clauses. Such clauses may guarantee minority protection for weaker member states, but on the understanding that those states which are unable to take up additional obligations will resort to the safeguard provisions wisely and responsibly. Mutual trust and solidarity are strongly implicit in the Tindemans Report's proposals.

In the late 1990s, this interpretation of the safeguard clauses has been dramatically reversed. Many now see insistence on the consensus principle as the creation of the possibility for a veto to be exercised by one or a few states unwilling to pursue the path of further integration and prepared to abuse the rule in order to block the progress of other, more progressive, states. The suspicion goes even deeper: the prerequisite of consensus is perceived as being an instrument of procedural power directed against the Union and, even more importantly, against a majority of the member states who want to use the Union to continue to pursue their – perhaps vital – interests. This attitude includes the fear that agreement with the non-participating countries will have to be paid for by concessions made on the part of the advancing countries. In other words, from the point of view of a majority of member states wishing to move further forward, the power of minority states to force concessions in this way would amount to a situation of 'representation without taxation'.

Such fears are echoed among those states who might not want to, or will not be able to, follow a more progressive group. They are afraid that the *avant garde* might take decisions affecting their own interests at the initial moment of establishing the closer cooperation, but also, and perhaps even more importantly, in subsequent decisions of the advance group. According to this view, the power to set the scene for those who might wish to follow would effectively amount to a situation of 'taxation without representation'.

The Tindemans Report's provisions reflected a spirit of mutual loyalty *vis-à-vis* the Community/Union and its participating states. The late 1990s, on the other hand, have been characterised by a lack of confidence and a degree of mutual distrust. The accumulated negative experiences of the past twenty years have led to second thoughts and the search for more procedural safeguards.

These difficulties are reflected in the Amsterdam Treaty's specific provisions for the establishment of closer cooperation in the first and third pillars. In EC Treaty Article 5a (**11**), the granting of authorisations is governed by several steps; 'Member States which intend to establish closer cooperation as referred to in paragraph 1 may address a request to the Commission, which may submit a proposal to the Council to that effect. In the event of the Commission not submitting a proposal, it shall inform the Member States of the reasons for not doing so.' Thus the provisions give the Commission considerable responsibility as the guardian of the EC *acquis* and of the principles it embodies. Should closer cooperation be seen by some member states as a hostile move, the Commission might find itself subject to considerable pressure to resist the request to draft a proposal. This line, identical to that of the Tindemans Report, stresses that the Commission has the right not to present a proposal to the Council, even if urged by the necessary quorum of member states. Thus the Amsterdam Treaty, like the Tindemans Report, acknowledges and confirms the Commission's traditional sole right of initiative.

However, the basic political and institutional problem concerns the decision-making method of the Council itself. Four alternative scenarios illustrate the fundamental dilemma of the 1990s and in so doing reflect the mixture of trust and mistrust among the member states.

Under the first scenario, the decision authorising closer cooperation would be taken by 'a qualified majority comprising the votes of the Member States concerned.' This version, present in several drafts considered by the 1996–7 Intergovernmental Conference, would have led to considerable flexibility, because not all participating states would have needed to agree. Did this formula imply that the Commission would be the only institution legally able to prevent the establishment of closer cooperation by a group of states?

Under the second scenario, the decision would be taken by 'a qualified majority comprising the votes of the representatives of the Member States concerned in the cases referred to and in a list of cases, and unanimously in other cases'. Thus the areas in which the mechanism for establishing closer cooperation might apply would have been clearly delimited.

Under the third scenario, decisions would be taken 'unanimously'. Thus each member state, including those who had clear intentions of not participating, would have had a say and, at the end of the day, the right of veto.

Under the fourth scenario, which was the solution adopted in the Amsterdam Treaty, decisions are to be taken by states 'acting by qualified majority on a proposal from the Commission and after consulting the European Parliament. If a member of the Council declares that, for important and stated reasons of national policy, it intends to oppose the granting of an authorization by qualified majority, a vote shall not be taken. The Council may, acting by a qualified majority, request that the matter be referred to the Council, meeting in the composition of the Heads of State or Government, for decision by unanimity.'

This formula combines two safeguard clauses. Protection of the supranational element is derived from the fact that the Council can only decide on the basis of a proposal made by the Commission, which will in turn be bound by the extensive criteria for closer cooperation. Safeguard for the intergovernmental element is derived from the explicit insertion, for the first time, of a modified version of the 'Luxembourg Compromise' into the Treaty. The potential role of the Court of Justice requires fuller consideration, as its jurisdiction will extend to closer cooperation (see Jean-Victor Louis's chapter below). The Council, meeting in the composition of the Heads of State or Government, is to be the final arbiter.

The right to block closer cooperation is slightly discouraged by the requirement to enumerate 'important and stated reasons of national policy'.

In the third pillar, 'authorization ... shall be granted by the Council, acting by a qualified majority of the Member States concerned and after inviting the Commision to present its opinion; ... If a member of the Council declares that, for important and stated reasons of national policy, it intends to oppose the granting of an authorization by a qualified majority, a vote shall not be taken. The Council may, acting by a qualified majority, request that the matter be referred to the European Council[2] for decision by unanimity' (Article K.12(2) – **40**). In this procedure, the safeguard mechanism for the EC element, as required by Article K.12.1(a), that closer cooperation should respect 'the powers of the European Community and the objectives laid down by this Treaty', is weaker. The intergovernmental check is again based on a version of the Luxembourg Compromise.

In this debate about the decision-making rules, some consideration should be given to the regime under which they will be applied. Where there is sufficient trust in the behaviour of the partners and the European Union institutions, even provisions which are geared to a more restrictive interpretation of flexibility might operate smoothly. The Union's culture of working consensually will be of utmost importance.

An additional restraint is imposed by the provisions about the minimum number of member states which must participate. According to the provisions of Article K.15(1d) (**43**), such a decision should concern 'at least a majority of Member States'. This criterion takes no account of the potential desire of potential core countries – for example, the founding member states, or the larger member states – to try to advance with a smaller number than half of a Union of 20 or 25 member states. The provision for a quota for participating states might thus counteract the original intentions of the Amsterdam Treaty's draftsmen, and might in the end have dysfunctional effects.

Closer cooperation at work: 'decision-takers' and 'free-riders'?

The Tindemans Report did not overlook the problems associated with the non-participating states; they were to 'take part, within the joint institutions, in assessing the results obtained in the fields in question'. Similarly, TEU

Article K.16(1) (**44**), as introduced by the Amsterdam Treaty, stipulates that 'all members of the Council shall be able to take part in the deliberations', but that 'only those representing participating Member States shall take part in the adoption of decisions'. Thus the aim in both cases is full transparency for the 'outs'. The non-participating states' problems can at least be put on the table. Members of the advance group, together with the European Union institutions, are also obliged to respect an additional provision; Article K.15(1F) (**43**) stipulates that closer cooperation should not 'affect the competences, rights, obligations and interests of those Member States which do not participate therein'.

Both formulas seem somewhat simplistic. Given the extended degree of mutual inter-dependencies among the economic, social and political systems of the member states within what is already a highly-integrated Union, the decisions of a closer circle will almost inevitably affect the non-participating countries in one way or another. At the same time, the granting of observer status and the loyal attitudes of the EU institutions involved cannot constitute any kind of guarantee for the non-participating states. Experience would suggest that, at the end of the negotiating day, decisions will only – or at the least mainly – take the interests of the participating states into account. Thus, even if the non-participating states are granted a veto in the creation of the closer circle, their influence on decisions taken thereafter would tend to be minimal. Even with all the safeguard clauses set out in the provisions of the Amsterdam Treaty, it is difficult to imagine how the interests of the states outside the closer circle could be sufficiently respected. The non-participating states would run the risk of being down-graded to 'decision-takers', instead of being co-decision makers like the participating states.[3]

It would however be one-sided just to mention the problems of the 'outs' with the 'ins'. Difficulties might also arise the other way around. The problem, which was apparently not considered by the Tindemans Report, concerns the behaviour of the non-participating states once the closer circle has started to operate. The Tindemans approach assumed and required that those unable to participate would be prepared to stay within the set framework and that they would take whatever steps were necessary to achieve the pre-agreed objectives: 'each country will be bound by the agreement of all as to the final objective to be achieved in common; it is only the timescales for achievement which vary'.

Such an unequivocal and virtually automatic process can no longer be guaranteed. If they were to feel excluded from common policies, the non-participating states might not see the need or the obligation to respect those policies nor, indeed, share the loyalty of the closer group. They might even take steps to profit from not being part of the agreement (take, for example, the perennial debate about the possibility of social or environmental dumping), or draw free-rider profits from the actions of the participating states. The debate about the protocol on the exchange rate mechanism for member states not participating in the first wave of Economic and Monetary Union is illustrative of this sort of concern.

The new Amsterdam Treaty provisions will not be sufficient to prevent such attitudes. TEU Article K.15(2) (**43**) declares that 'Member States not participating in such cooperation shall not impede the implementation thereof by the participating Member States.' It is not clear whether this provision could be made to apply to member states profiting indirectly from the actions of others; it would in any case be difficult to implement. Participating states would have difficulty in convincing those with no say in the decision-making process to behave in the desired way. It might also be difficult to resort to the Court of Justice in such cases.

Given this analysis, it would seem that not only the non-participating states might have burdens imposed upon them without proper participation; members of the closer circle might find themselves confronted with actions which they might not perceive as being compatible with their own policies. Members of the inner circle might therefore prefer to see the outer circle on board. Thus, the hidden centripetal dynamics of the provisions on closer cooperation might encourage the participating and non-participating states to employ the normal European Union framework, involving all member states.

Opting in: obstacles for the 'outs'

Non-participating states could face another set of difficulties of greater potential importance; the procedures, conditions and timing for joining an advance group. The Tindemans Report implied that whenever such states were able to catch up with the others, they would join the advance group without more ado. Article K.15(1g) (**43**) (TEU) declares that closer cooperation 'is open to all Member States and allows them to become parties to the cooperation at any time, provided that they comply with the basic decisions and with decisions taken within that framework'. These provisions are seriously flawed. To give an example, the advance group might take decisions going beyond the initial concept. The non-participating states would then be confronted with a moving target which would be outside their own control. Their passive role ('provided that they comply') is strongly implicit in the second half of Article K.15(1g) (**43**) TEU.

To make life even more difficult for the non-participating states, Article 5a(3) (**11**) sets out rather laborious procedures for opting in; 'Any Member State which wishes to become a party to cooperation set up in accordance with this Article shall notify its intention to the Council and the Commission, which shall give an opinion to the Council within three months of the receipt of that notification. Within four months of the date of that notification, the Commission shall decide on it and on possible specific arrangements as it may deem necessary.' This provision underlines that opting in depends not only on a declaration of intent by the member state wishing so to do; certain rules would have to be followed. Applicant states would be scrutinised by the Commission and their applications would face rejection by this avowedly supranational body. In an earlier draft considered by the 1996–7 Intergovernmental Conference, it was proposed to give this power of rejection to a majority of the states participating in closer cooperation. Under the final draft, participating member states are excluded from the ultimate decision about the members they would have to work with. The risks for the non-participating states are evident.

In the third pillar, the Treaty states in Article K.12(3) (**40**) that 'Any member which wishes to become a party to cooperation set up in accordance with this Article shall notify its intention to the Council and the Commission, which shall give an opinion to the Council within three months of receipt of that notification, possibly accompanied by a recommendation for specific arrangements as it may deem necessary for that Member State to become a party to the cooperation in question. Within four months of the date of that notification, the Council shall decide on the request and on possible specific arrangements as it may deem necessary. The decision shall be deemed to be taken unless the Council, acting by a qualified majority, decides to hold it in abeyance; in this case, the Council shall state the reasons for its decision and set a deadline for reexamining it. For the purposes of this paragraph, the Council shall act under the conditions set out in Article K.16 (**44**) of the TEU.' This provision seems more logical in terms of the original intention for closer cooperation.

The procedures for the 'outs' and the procedures for opting in thus imply considerable disadvantages for those states not participating in the original agreement for closer cooperation. Such cost-benefit analyses will also create strong centripetal pressure to join the first wave. Aware of all the potential disadvantages of non-participant status, each member state would presumably make intensive efforts to be part of the initial closer circle. The lessons of the Messina experience for the United Kingdom are clear: early self-exclusion imposes a high price, as joining later is only possible on the terms of the founding states. The new provisions of the Amsterdam Treaty are therefore more likely to serve as an incentive – or even 'whip' – encouraging the potential 'outs' to search for inclusive solutions within the normal European Union framework. Thus, without even being applied, the provision might induce an increased tendency to employ the usual rules for all. Another potential effect of the opting-in difficulties considered here might thus be to promote negative attitudes which would discourage any and all closer cooperation.

Solidarity – a neglected principle

A major element of the Tindemans Report concerned support for the non-participating states; 'those States which have reasons for not progressing . . . will at the same time receive from the other States any aid and assistance that can be given them to enable them to catch the others up'. Thus, the Tindemans version of differentiation implied that the objective difficulties of certain states would be tackled with the solidarity of the Union itself, much as the cohesion fund provides in relation to Economic and Monetary Union.

Such a consideration is absent from the new Amsterdam Treaty articles. One reason – a hidden version of the free-rider paradox – is obvious. If non-participation is not only a matter of ability but also a matter of will, it would be counter-productive to offer support for countries which were simply unwilling to go ahead, since such a provision would pay handsome dividends for staying outside. Another reason might have been the hidden assumption that closer cooperation should serve as a step towards a core Europe or a Europe *à géométrie variable* consisting only of some members who – especially in the light of eastern enlargement – might no longer be too interested in the participation of all members. Over the past twenty years, the unequivocal assertion of the Tindemans Report, that 'it is only the timescales for achievement which vary', has apparently fallen by the wayside.

The role of EU institutions and procedures: complexity and ambiguity

The Tindemans Report proposed that its envisaged action programme should be 'decided upon by the common institutions', although an appropriate procedure for the Council was not suggested. In reflection of the general logic behind what was then considered to be a new approach, the Report's provisions emphasised the pre-eminent role of the Community institutions.

Article K.16 (**44**) TEU is more general in this context. It states that 'for the institutional purposes of the adoption of the acts and decisions necessary for the implementation ... the relevant institutional provisions of the Treaties shall apply'. Two controversial and confusing conditions are added: 'However, while all the members of the Council shall be able to take part in the deliberations, only those representing participating Member States shall take part in the adoption of decisions; the qualified majority shall be defined as the same proportion of votes of the Council members concerned weighted in accordance with Article 148(2) (**205**) of the Treaty establishing the European Community; unanimity shall be constituted by only those Council members concerned.' A similar proportional formula for voting in the European Parliament was only dropped at the last moment.

These provisions raise a number of questions. For the Council and its administrative substructure (Coreper, the other preparatory committees, the working parties) the implementation of these procedures would necessarily be complex and would require a review of traditional procedures; for example, could a member state occupying the Presidency of the Council preside over the Council, Coreper and the working parties in a normal way even if the state in question was not a participant in the policy area in question? How would 'comitology' (the committees involved in the adoption of delegated legislation) work? Such practical issues highlight the fundamental problems which could easily split the institutions into sub-bodies. It might subsequently prove impossible to talk any more about a 'single institutional framework' (TEU Article C – 3).

Where closer cooperation has been established, the Amsterdam Treaty provides that all 'acts and decisions necessary for the implementation of cooperation activities shall be subject to all the relevant provisions of the Treaty, including those regarding the role of the Commission and the Court of Justice' (Article 5a(4) – 11). These provisions imply that, in line with normal procedures and practices, and irrespective of the potential difficulties mentioned above, the Commission and its services will present draft proposals, and that the Council, Coreper and its working parties will prepare and take decisions with the votes of the participating states. The Commission and the 'comitology' committees would be responsible for follow-up decisions. The compliance of the member states with legislation adopted in the context of closer cooperation would be adjudicated by the Court.

The potential role of the European Parliament is less clearly defined. The overall role of the Parliament is mentioned in both the Tindemans Report and in the Amsterdam Treaty's new provisions. Article K.17 (**45**) TEU states that 'The Council and the Commission shall regularly inform the European Parliament of the development of closer cooperation established on the basis of this Title.' Under TEC Article 5a (**11**), authorisations for closer cooperation shall be granted by the Council 'after consulting the European Parliament'. Under the third pillar, 'the request shall also be forwarded to the European Parliament' (Article K.12.2 – **40**). Would this weak role for the European Parliament include those policy areas where the Amsterdam Treaty has otherwise granted the Parliament enhanced powers – for example, in the field of environmental policy? Would closer cooperation thus automatically reduce the European Parliament's role and powers? Does the Parliament's exclusion explain why the draft provisions concerning the voting rights of members of the European Parliament were dropped at the last minute?

Article K.16.2 (**44**) TEU provides that 'Expenditure resulting from the implementation of the cooperation, other than administrative costs entailed for the institutions, shall be borne by the participating Member States, unless the Council, acting unanimously, decides otherwise'. This rule clearly reduces the burdens on the operational budget of the EC and reflects the general principle of 'no taxation without representation'. However, it also ensures that the Parliament – twin arm of the Union's budgetary authority – has no role to play.

This observation aside, the provision is unlikely to create major problems where acts of a legislative nature are concerned. But the propensity to use the Union's procedures will be drastically reduced if actions are envisaged which would need additional financing. Past experience demonstrates that participating member states would have great difficulty in agreeing among themselves on additional financing. Further problems would occur where the non-participating states could also profit as free riders from the actions of the closer circle; for example, if some countries are prepared to take up a peacekeeping operation in line with the Petersberg tasks which would also benefit other member states. Burden sharing through the EC budget could be an important incentive for those more active states to proceed via the European Union's institutions. Otherwise, core countries, or a *directoire* of larger member states, might wonder why they should offer access and information to the rest of the member states if they do not themselves profit from using the more cumbersome and complex procedures. In such cases, direct action outside the Union framework might prove more rational.

If closer cooperation is to be kept within the EC's jurisdiction, it will be of the utmost importance that the Court should take up cases of conflicts and play its traditional role of interpreting ambiguous procedures. This would normally imply that the Court should also deal with the complaints of non-participating states, where they feel that their interests may have been violated (TEU Article K.15(1f) – **43**). By the same token, 'Member States not participating in such a cooperation shall not impede the implementation thereof by the participating states' (TEU Article K.15(2) – **43**). Given the complexity and potential difficulties involved in implementing these provisions, the Court may well find itself pushed into a major role in making the procedures function on the basis of agreed interpretations. Although the provisions fall under the Court's jurisdiction (Article (1c) – **46**), a set of crucial terms ('important reasons' – Article 5a(2); no effect on the 'interests of non-participating Member States' – Article K.15(1f) or of 'Community policies' – Article 5a(1b)) seem so vague that the Court might be reluctant to give rulings on them.

While the European Parliament's role has apparently been weakened, and while the Court's role has yet to be defined, the Commission has not lost any of its traditional rights (despite some of the proposals considered by the Intergovernmental Conference). In particular, it has retained its sole right of making proposals to the Council and of presenting its opinion under the third pillar. Its role has even been significantly strengthened through its authority to decide on applications for opting in. Given these new-found powers, the Commission could easily find itself involved in controversial situations as broker among the conflicting interests of a growing number of member states.

FIVE THESES AS CONCLUSIONS: CENTRIPETAL DYNAMICS

The Tindemans Report is a useful point of reference in highlighting the costs and benefits of any kind of flexibility. The analysis in this chapter leads to five conclusions concerning the Amsterdam provisions.

The first is that both the 'new approach' of the Tindemans Report and the Amsterdam Treaty's provisions for closer cooperation are responses to the dilemma between, on the one hand, the European Union's capacity to deal with impending problems and, on the other, the Union's coherence, stability and solidarity. Assuming differences in the willingness and ability of member states to take up the same rights and obligations, any cost-benefit analysis has to compare imperfect solutions within the European Union with the costs of policy set-ups outside the Union framework, or the benefits of some kind of joint approach to the costs of a reduced relevance of the Union in some policy fields. In this sense, the Tindemans Report is not a yellowing document collecting dust on library shelves but a valuable input to the present debate. The need to reflect further on the problems highlighted by Tindemans and partly answered by the Amsterdam Treaty's provisions will almost certainly grow with the next waves of enlargement.

The second conclusion is that, given the twenty-year period between the Tindemans Report and the Amsterdam Treaty, and given the experiences gathered during that period, the provisions for closer cooperation represent surprisingly limited progress. The architects of the rules for closer cooperation have certainly taken into account some of the lessons resulting from the debate about the Tindemans approach, some of the subsequent reflections, and other experiments with the flexibility concept over the past two decades. But some clear progress on the procedural side is counterbalanced by the creation of new problems, where the Tindemans approach was more convincing. Other difficulties, where the Tindemans Report could offer only tentative solutions, remain unsolved. Taken altogether, the Amsterdam Treaty provisions have even complicated the mechanism for establishing closer cooperation. From this perspective, the new provisions are little improvement on the Tindemans approach.

A third conclusion is that both approaches offer only second-best options for getting out of the dilemma. The Tindemans Report proposed an approach which, at least at first sight, was attractive and based on an apparently logical dynamic. The Amsterdam Treaty's rules on closer cooperation have the 'merit' of highlighting the problems involved in creating, managing and implementing this second-best option. A comparison of TEU Articles K.15(**43**) and K.12(**40**) and TEC Article 5a(**11**) with the over-simplistic assumptions of the Tindemans Report about how differentiation might function illustrates the stark fact that there are no easy solutions for reconciling the differing demands and needs of the Union and its member states. It is a version of the prisoners' dilemma writ large. In effect, if differentiation is to work, all member states must behave in a benevolent way (this was Tindemans' assumption). A political regime of mutual trust must first be established.

My fourth conclusion is that the new Amsterdam Treaty provisions will increase the complexity, opaqueness and lack of accountability of the European Union without guaranteeing more effective and efficient policy solutions. Given conflicting demands and preferences, the Amsterdam Treaty's provisions have created procedures which do not live up to the norms and the standards generally set by the architects of the Treaties. Further lengthy and detailed debate will be necessary to establish when and how the rules may be applied. The issue of democratic accountability raises even greater difficulties. And, if these are the costs, the benefits are not clearly visible. Will the procedures for the establishment and management of closer cooperation prove efficient? Given the high level of interdependency within the Union and all the problems considered above for the 'ins' and the 'outs', each potential case will require detailed examination to establish whether closer cooperation would really create more effective policy in the interests of the Union. Normal European Union provisions, including some new rules for differentiation within the Treaty (like the new paragraphs 3–9 of Article 100a TEC – **95**), or perhaps less cumbersome procedures outside the Treaty framework, might prove more attractive than the complex and time-consuming rules for closer cooperation. Even once established, closer cooperation may not fulfil its objectives.

My last conclusion is – to take a 'best case' scenario – that the very existence of the provisions for closer cooperation might lead to them not being applied. The provisions might work as a negative incentive, to encourage reluctant member states to resort to the Union's normal provisions. Despite the intentions of some of its authors, the concept might thus reinforce the Union's centripetal dynamics. As the analysis in this chapter demonstrated, the in-built logic of power and influence will push both the 'outs' and the 'ins' to resort to the provisions only in exceptional circumstances. It is not only the complexity and top-heavy nature of the procedures but also their potential consequences for the outer and inner circle which will make member states think long and hard before considering use of the closer cooperation provisions as a realistic option.

Paradoxically, this conclusion is in direct contradiction to the assumption that the European Union is becoming increasingly dominated by centrifugal forces and, indeed, with the logic whereby the closer cooperation formula might provide a Union-based exit. As this chapter has shown, member states will have reason to fear that the provisions on closer cooperation will strengthen the tendency towards a Europe *à la carte* or a core Europe. Closer cooperation might thus be seen not as a safeguard against these deviations but as disguised legitimation for moving away from the Community orthodoxy.

In conclusion, this comparison of the approaches of the Tindemans Report and the Amsterdam Treaty's provisions has demonstrated that much more thought needs to be devoted to the various concepts of flexibility and how they might work in practice. Ultimately, however, it is clear that only more fundamental constitutional reform would render these second-best options superfluous.

NOTES

1 The author would like to thank Alexandra Habot for her help in the drafting of this chapter.
2 It is not clear why this article should refer to the 'European Council' whilst Article 5a.2 refers to 'the Council, meeting in the composition of Heads of State or Government'. The most probable explanation is a straightforward drafting oversight. The Maastricht Treaty formally introduced the European Council into the pantheon of the Union's institutions. TEU Article D (4) describes it as being composed of the Heads of State or Government and the President of the Commission, assisted by the Ministers for Foreign Affairs and by another member of the Commission. Article K.12 has now introduced the concept of European Council 'decisions' – it previously acted through resolutions and Presidency conclusions. Did the draftsmen of Article K.12 really intend that two Commissioners and the Ministers for Foreign Affairs should also be involved in such decisions? (Westlake, 1995, pp. 25–31).
3 The 'decision-takers/decision-makers' dichotomy is borrowed from the old debate among EFTA member states about the relative benefits of membership of the European Economic Area and of the European Union itself.

REFERENCES

Bonvincini, Gianni, Louis, Jean-Victor, Vasconcelos, Alvaro and Wessels, Wolfgang, 1996, 'The Revision of Maastricht', TEPSA, Brussels

Boulanges, Jean-Louis and Martin, David, 1995, 'Resolution on the functioning of the Treaty on European Union with a view to the 1996 Intergovernmental Conference – Implementation and development of the Union' (A4–0102/95) 17 May

Club de Florence, 1996, *Europe: l'impossible Statu Quo*, Bruxelles

Commissariat au Plan,1979, *La France dans les années quatre-vingt*, Paris

Dahrendorf, Ralph,1979, 'A Third Europe?', Third Jean Monnet Lecture, European University Institute, Florence

De Charette, Hervé, 1996, 'Noyau Dur ou Avant-Garde Européenne? Que Doit-On Faire Ensemble, Que Peut-On Faire a Quelques-Uns?' (speech of the French foreign minister before the European Movement), Paris

Deubner, Christian, 1995, *Deutsche Europapolitik: Von Maastricht nach Kerneuropa?*, Nomos, Baden-Baden

Deubner, Christian and Ehlermann, Claus Dieter, 1995, 'Increased Differentiation or Stronger Uniformity', Paper delivered to the 1995 Conference on European Law, The Hague

Duff, Andrew, 1997, *The Treaty of Amsterdam. Text and Commentary*, The Federal Trust, London

Ehlermann, Claus-Dieter, 1984, 'How Flexible is Community Law? An Unusual Approach to the Concept of "Two Speeds"', *Michigan Law Review*, 83, pp. 1274–93

Europäische Kommission, 1996, Stellungnahme der Kommission: Stärkung der Politischen Union und Vorbereitung der Erweiterung, 2/96

Europäisches Parlament, 1995, 'Bericht über die Funktionsweise des Vertrags über die Europäische Union im Hinblick auf die Regierungskonferenz 1996', *Verwirklichung und Entwicklung der Union*, 4/95

European Parliament (Intergovernmental Conference Task Force), 1996, White Paper on the 1996 Intergovernmental Conference, vol. I, Official Texts of the European Union Institutions, September

GEPE, 1995, Etude sur l'intégration différenciée, TEPSA, Brussels

Grabitz, Eberhard (ed.),1984, *Abgestufte Integration. Eine Alternative zum herkömmlichen Integrationskonzept?* Kehl am Rhein, Strasbourg

Hasse, Rolf H., 1994, 'Kerneuropa: Variable Geometrie – zwischen Integrationsdynamik und Spaltung', *Wirtschaftsdienst* X, pp. 503–6.

IEE, GEPE, 1995, *La Différenciation dans l'Union Européenne*, Université Libre de Bruxelles, Institut d'Etudes Européennes, Brussels

Kohl, Helmut and Chirac, Jacques, 1995, Gemeinsamer Brief an den Präsidenten des Europäischen Rates (Joint letter to the President of the European Council), 12 December

Lamers, Karl, 1994, 'Kerneuropa – flexible Methode der europäischen Integration', *Wirtschaftsdienst* X, pp. 495–7

Lamers, Karl and Schäuble, Wolfgang, 1994, 'Reflections on European Foreign Policy' – Document by the CDU/CSU Group in the German Bundestag, Bonn, 1 September (CDU/CSU Fraktion des Deutschen Bundestages, Überlegungen zur europäischen Politik)

Maillet, Pierre and Velo, Dario, 1994, *L'Europe à géométrie variable*, L'Harmattan, Paris

Major, John, 1994, William and Mary Lecture, Leiden, 7 September

Monnet, Jean, 1976, *Mémoires*, Fayard, Paris

Müller-Brandeck-Bocquet, Gisela, 1997, 'Flexible Integration – Eine Chance für die europäische Umweltpolitik', *Integration* 4, pp. 292–305

Picht, Robert and Wessels, Wolfgang (eds), 1990, *Motor für Europa?, Deutschfranzösischer Bilateralismus und europäische Integration*, Europa-Union Verlag, Bonn

Piepenschneider, Melanie, 1996, 'Regierungskonferenz 1996. Synopse der Reformvorschläge zur Europäischen Union' (Working paper of the Konrad-Adenauer-Foundation), 2nd Edition, Sankt Augustin

Quermonne, Jean-Louis, 1995, 'La Différenciation dans l'Union Européenne: l'Europe à géométrie variable', in *La Différenciation dans l'Union Européenne*, Université Libre de Bruxelles, Institut d'Etudes Européennes, Brussels

Reflection Group Report (1995a) Brussels, SN 520/95 (REFLEX 21) 5 December

Reflection Group Report (1995b) Brussels, SN 509/95 (REFLEX 10) 20 August

Remacle, Eric, 1995, 'L'intégration différenciée dans la PESC, la Politique de Défense Commune et la Défense commune', in GEPE, Etude sur l'intégration différenciée, TEPSA, Brussels

Rodriques, Stephane, 1995, 'L'intégration différenciée dans les domaines de la justice et des affaires intérieures', in GEPE, Etude sur l'intégration différenciée, TEPSA, Brussels

Scharrer, Hanz-Eckart, 1977, 'Differenzierte Integration im Zeichen der Schlange', in Wessels, Wolfgang and Schneider, Heinrich (eds), *Auf dem Weg zur Europäischen Union?*, Bonn, pp. 143–65

Schneider, Heinrich, 1992, 'Europäische Integration. Die Leitbilder und die Politik', in Kreile, Michael (ed.), *Die Integration Europas*, PVS-Sonderheft 23, Opladen, pp. 3–35

Schneider, Heinrich and Wessels, Wolfgang (eds), 1977, *Auf dem Weg zur Europäischen Union?*, Europa-Union Verlag, Bonn

Spaak, Paul-Henri, 1969, *Memoiren eines Europäers*, Hoffman and Campe, Hamburg

Rifkind, Malcolm, 1996, Speech by the Foreign Secretary, Mr. Malcolm Rifkind, at the Churchill Commemoration (1996), University of Zurich, Switzerland, 18 September

Szukala, Andrea and Wessels, Wolfgang, 1997, 'The Franco-German Tandem and the '96 Agenda: Back to a smaller Europe?', in Edwards, Geoffrey and Pijpers, Alfred (eds), *The Politics of European Treaty Reform: The 1996 Intergovernmental Conference and Beyond*, Pinter, London, pp. 74–9

Tindemans, Leo, 1976, Report by Leo Tindemans, Prime Minister of Belgium to the European Council, Bulletin of the European Communities, Supplement 1

Vandamme, Jacques and Mouton, Jean-Denis (eds), 1995, *L'avenir de l'Union européenne: Enlargir et Approfondir*, Presses Interuniversitaires Européennes, Bruxelles

Wallace, Helen and Riley, Adam, 1985, 'Europe: The Challenge of Diversity', Chatham House Papers 29, The Royal Institute of International Affairs, Routledge, London

Wallace, Helen and Wallace, William, 1995, 'Flying together in a larger and more diverse European Union', Working Documents (W87) of the Netherlands Scientific Council for Government Policy, The Hague

Wessels, Wolfgang, 1994, 'Integrationspolitische Konzepte im Realitätstest', *Wirtschaftsdienst* X, pp. 499–503

Wessels, Wolfgang, 1997, 'Der Amsterdamer Vertrag – Durch Stückwerksreformen zu einer effizienteren, erweiterten und föderalen Union?', *Integration*, 3, pp. 117–35.

Westlake, Martin, 1995, *The Council of the European Union*, Cartermill, London

Wimmer, Per T., 1993, 'Les Dérogations de l'acquis de l'Union. Vers une Europe à la Carte après Maastricht?', in Monar, Joerg, Ungerer, Werner and Wessels, Wolfgang (eds), *The Maastricht Treaty on European Union: Legal Complexity and Political Dynamic*, European Interuniversity Press, Brussels

7 The rule of law

Jean-Victor Louis

> The gentle, but powerful influence of laws and manners had gradually cemented the union of the provinces
>
> Edward Gibbon,
> *The History of the Decline and Fall of the Roman Empire*, p. 27

I have been asked to provide a (necessarily short) reflection on the role of the Court of Justice of the European Communities in the context of an increasingly differentiated integration process. No doubt I owe this assignment to my training and profession as a lawyer or, at least, a jurist. As everyone knows, jurists are not keen on futurology. But I imagine this subject is one which Jacques Vandamme would appreciate, for he has long been engaged in interdisciplinary research on the future of the process of European integration and indeed was responsible for some of my prospective studies in the field.

In order better to understand the future role of the Court in an enlarged and possibly diversified Union it is useful to recall the reasons which led to the establishment of judicial remedies in the Paris Treaty and their elaboration in the Rome Treaties. I will then consider – very briefly, for the facts are well known – the achievements of the Court in affirming the rule of law in the Community. The next section will identify certain developments dating from Maastricht or before and look at the way the 1996–7 Intergovernmental Conference considered the Court, thereby taking a closer look at some of the trends which characterise enduring governmental attitudes towards the Court. In conclusion, I will sketch what I see as being some of the salient features of the Court as a cornerstone of integration in the next century.

THE ROLE OF THE COURT UNDER THE TREATIES OF PARIS AND ROME

There is no mention of a Court of Justice in the 9 May 1950 Schuman Declaration. The Declaration mentions only the need to provide some sort of mechanism for the settlement of disputes. Such a mechanism could have been based on arbitration rather than a permanent court of law. The negotiators made provision for the creation of a Court of Justice for three reasons.

The first was of a constitutional nature. The argument, based on the need for so-called 'structural convergence' ('*Strukturelle Kongruenz*'), was advanced by the West Germans, who had recently inaugurated a new constitution ('*Grundgesetz*') which strictly limited the powers of the Authority at every level through the organisation of a comprehensive network of jurisdictions. In retrospect, it seems remarkable that the constitutional problems of the time were solved at European level and did not fall prey to the pretensions of the national courts to control Community legislation.[1]

The second reason was inherent in an integration process which included the attribution of competences, as does a federal system, to a common authority. Legal remedies are indispensable if political solutions to disputes – otherwise reached, for example, by negotiations among unequal partners – about the respective powers of the states and the institutions are to be avoided. Only a court can provide uniform interpretation and application of the law.

The choice demonstrates the wisdom of the founding fathers, and their understanding that the relations between the member states and their institutions were not to be governed by international law but by a kind of new system of law, much nearer to internal law. Under traditional international law, litigation among states is almost exclusively a process of declaratory interpretations of the rules, whereas Community jurisdiction is about the legality of the action of both the states and the institutions. It is not by chance that the model for the appeal procedure before the Court of the ECSC was the organisation of redress as it evolved in the nineteenth century case law of the French *Conseil d'Etat*, an administrative law court.

The third reason for the creation of the Court was to be found in the need for legal protection for the addressees of the acts adopted by the High Authority; that is to say, coal and steel companies and, in some specific cases, other legal and natural persons. It is well known that the Court gave a relatively extensive interpretation to the possibility for appeal by private persons against acts of the High Authority, and that the over-restrictive wording of Articles 173 (**230**) and 175 (**232**) of the 1957 EEC Treaty concerning appeals for annulment and for inaction was a direct reflection of governments' reaction to the possibility for such plaintiffs to appeal against regulations.

These three reasons remain today valid justifications for the intervention of the Court of Justice in guaranteeing respect for the law under the treaties. Jurisdictional control is inherent in a Community based on the rule of law. Our democratic and law-abiding societies could not countenance granting real powers affecting their essential interests and those of their citizens to bodies uncontrolled by law. The intervention of the Court guarantees uniformity in the application of the rules by avoiding purely political solutions to legal difficulties and it protects the interests of the citizen and other private persons concerned by the rules.

The ECSC system was based on the centralisation of appeals at the level of the European Court of Justice. This centralisation was possible due to the sectoral nature of the Coal and Steel Community. Few private addressees were involved. The system changed with the transition to so-called general integration under the Treaty of Rome. This treaty made of the national judge the Community judge '*de droit commun*' and the system of preliminary rulings by the Court, allowing it to preserve uniformity of interpretation, developed. In the Community legal order, the Court[2] on the one hand, and the national courts on the other, are the two pillars of the legal system. Community law was to be characterised by three '*Gleich*' concepts, as succinctly formulated in 1965 by Professor Leontin Constantinesco: Community law must be '*Gleichbindend, gleichbleibend und gleichbedeutend*', meaning that the binding content of the law is the same for everybody, that it cannot be changed by the member states, and that it is to have the same meaning in every member state (pp. 29–30). Exceptions, if made, result from specific protocols annexed to the treaty (for example, the protocols on Luxembourg and agriculture, or on intra-German trade), or from physical or other objective differences.

The principle of equality must take into consideration objective differences. No reservations or exceptions to the treaties are admitted except those accepted at the time of signature by the partners and duly registered as such. These seem sound and obvious principles, given the political objectives of the integration process. But it is remarkable that the rules of direct effect and primacy, as well as basic concepts such as those concerning the distribution of competences between the Community and the member states (implied powers, exclusive competences, pre-emption, joint competences) are all part of judge-made law.

THE COURT AND THE DEFINITION OF THE COMMUNITY'S LEGAL ORDER

Without the case law of the Court, the Community system would have been completely different. Both the concept and the practical reality of a law of integration would have been missed. In the justly famous 1963 *Van Gend & Loos* case (26/62 [1963] ECR 1), the Court affirmed that individuals were subject to Community law and that this law directly conferred rights and imposed obligations upon them. The Court went on to affirm the primacy of Community law over national law, based on the Treaty itself and conceived as an obligation derived from it for the national judge. The landmark decision in that context was *Costa/Enel* (Case 6/64 [1964] ECR 585), though many others followed; *Internationale Handelgesellschaft* (Case 11/70 [1970] ECR 1125), *Simmenthal* (Case 106/77 [1978] ECR 629), and *Factortame* (Case 213 [1990] ECR I-243), to name but a few of these truly historical judgements. More than thirty years later, there are still some jurisdictions, such as the French higher courts, and still some authors who are convinced that this primacy is based not on the Treaty, but on the Constitution. Perhaps this is not so surprising. Some jurisdictions in the United States apparently still pretend that state law is superior to federal law.

The *AETR* doctrine on implied powers to conclude international treaties was created by the Court in 1971 (Case 22/70 [1971] ECR 263), and the standing of this doctrine was still such that, during the Maastricht Treaty negotiations, the member states appended a declaration (no. 10) to the Treaty stating that, in some specifically-mentioned articles, no derogation from the *AETR* doctrine was intended.

The case law on the exclusiveness of the common commercial policy has been well-illustrated by opinions 1–75 (on export credits – opinion of 11 November 1975 [1975] ECR 1355) and 1–78 (natural rubber – opinion of 4 October 1979 [1979] ECR 2871). The disappointing Uruguay Round opinion (1–94 – opinion of 15 November 1994 [1994] ECR I-5267), which was based on a restrictive vision of what trade policy really signifies, did not change the basic orientation. It is remarkable and worthwhile recalling, particularly for those who are tempted to confuse the member states, as authors of the treaties, and the Governments, who were their negotiators, that all of the achievements of the Court mentioned so far were obtained in the face of opposition by some, a majority, or even all, of the member states (expressing themselves through the Council). Thus the Court has played a precious role in stating what the basic necessities of the system are, through reference to the objectives and the spirit of the treaties.

Usher (1977) has demonstrated the importance of the interpretation given by the Court to Article 5 (**10**) of the EC Treaty (the so-called 'loyalty clause') in encouraging reciprocal cooperation between the member states and the institutions.

In its more recent jurisprudence, starting with *Francovich* (Cases C-6/90 and C-9/90 [1991] ECR I-5357), the Court has developed the concept of the liability of the member states for failure to implement Community law. So great has been the impact of this case law that the British Government tabled a proposal to the 1996–7 Intergovernmental Conference which was designed to limit liability for damages where there had been a manifest and serious breach of an EC obligation by the member state concerned.

In short, the Community's legal order would be inconceivable without the European Court of Justice. This simple fact was starkly illustrated by the second and third pillars of the Maastricht Treaty, which characterised the intergovernmental method. These stressed the unanimity principle in the Council and the prominent role of the Council in comparison with the role of the supranational bodies (the Commission and the Parliament), and provided for the exclusion – sometimes partial, sometimes total – of the Court of Justice.

INTERGOVERNMENTAL TRENDS VERSUS THE COMMUNITY SYSTEM

Intergovernmentalism has always been present in the history of the Community, from its very inception. The Treaties were not only based on supranational features. If it had been otherwise, we would long since have been living in a kind of federation. The European Coal and Steel Community was paralysed by the unanimity required in the Special Council of Ministers for the declaration of a manifest crisis, and in practice the High Authority used its powers more through intergovernmental negotiations and compromises than through simple consultation of the Special Council. The Rome Treaty (the EEC Treaty more than the ill-fated Euratom Treaty), strengthened the role of the Council as legislator, while the Commission failed to impose itself as the executive branch, let alone as an embryonic government. The story of the so-called 'Luxembourg Compromise' is well known. The subsequent reluctance to vote emphasised the intergovernmental nature of the Council and weakened the supranational Commission.

But it was the development of political cooperation – meaning foreign policy cooperation – at the beginning of the 1970s which constituted, notwithstanding its achievements, the main threat to the Community system. An intergovernmental procedure was set in place, assigning a weaker role to the institutions than was the case in the Community system and, of course, excluding any intervention by the Court.

The duality of these procedures was rendered official by the 1986 Single European Act, which juxtaposed SEA Article 30 on European Political Cooperation with the provisions amending the Community treaties (hence the 'Single' Act). Through the creation of the so-called third pillar, the Maastricht Treaty extended the intergovernmental methods of European Political Cooperation (which itself was re-dubbed, with some pretension, the Common Foreign and Security Policy – CFSP) to cooperation in the fields of Justice and Home Affairs. Intervention by the Court in these new fields was excluded by Article L (**46**) of the Treaty on European Union.[3] The important but limited improvements concerning the role of the Court of First Instance (TEU Article 168a – **225**), the attribution to the Court of Justice of a power of sanction against member states in cases of non-respect of infringement rulings (TEU Article 171(2) – **228**), the codification of the case law of the Court on the admissibility of appeals brought by or against the European Parliament, and the legal control provided over the acts both of the European Monetary Institute and of the European Central Bank (TEU Articles 173 and 175 – **230** and **232**), were but little compensation for these blows to the Court, particularly as far as the third pillar was concerned.

In parallel, some member states organised, through the Schengen agreements, a form of cooperation among themselves which was designed to compensate for their partners' lack of political will. Naturally, no role was assigned to the Court of Justice. As Labaye, writing on the Intergovernmental Conference and the third pillar observed, these developments denoted a denial not only of the judge but also of effective rules (1997, pp. 137–8). The two go hand-in-hand. Immediately after the signing of the Single European Act, discussions started on the exact extent of the binding nature of commitments reached under SEA Article 30. The compulsory nature of common positions and joint actions under Articles J.2 (**12**) and J.3 (**13**) of the Maastricht Treaty has been questioned less but, since access to the Court of Justice is denied, only very theoretical appeals based on international law are open to the member states. On the other hand, the binding nature of common positions and joint actions under Article K.3(2) (**31**) in the third pillar has created controversy in a field where legal certainty should be paramount.

It should also be noted that the possible option of granting the Court competence in the Article K.3 (**31**) field has been used only sparingly and restrictively. In its May 1995 report on certain aspects of the application of the Treaty on European Union, the Court observed that, at that time, the only convention concluded in the field of justice and home affairs – the convention on a simplified extradition procedure between the member states of the European Union, drawn up by a Council Act of 10 March 1995 – did not 'give any jurisdiction to the Court of Justice' (European Court of Justice, 1995). Since then, three conventions have been negotiated under Article K.3 (**31**), concerning respectively the use of informatics in the customs field, Europol, and the protection of the financial interests of the European Communities (for a precise list, see Sauron, 1997, pp. 91–2). All of these conventions or specific protocols recognised some role for – or the possibility of the member states to grant a role to – the Court of Justice, but as far as the preliminary rulings procedure is concerned, they all provide for a less binding mechanism than the one created by EC Treaty Article 177 (**234**), and two of the conventions provided a dispute settlement role for the Council.

These developments are hardly surprising. Every time the member states have decided to create what Sauron has described as a '177 *conventionnel*' (meaning the attribution by conventions to the Court of the task of interpreting those same conventions), they have always changed and weakened the system as it was formulated by the Rome Treaty.[4] This is why, in its 1995 report, the Court described the preliminary ruling system as being 'the veritable cornerstone of the operation of the single market' and emphasised the consequent need to avoid limiting access to the Court.

A number of reasons have been evoked for 'correcting' the 177 (**234**) system in specific conventions: the complexity or the technical nature of the matter, the need for a rapid solution, the wish to avoid over-burdening the Court, and so on. The results, and possibly the intentions, of these 'corrections' are always the same; to limit the role of judicial intervention at the Community level. Thus when, at the 1996–7 Intergovernmental Conference, the so-called '*communautarisation*' of some parts of the third pillar was said to include an 'adaptation' of the role of the Court of Justice, it came as no surprise.

Other parts of the Amsterdam Treaty are also indicative of the restrictive attitude of national administrations towards the case law of the Court. Labaye has written in this context of the states' 'revenge' for a 'thirty year guarantee of Community obligations', and of a clear preference for political rather than judicial settlements (Labaye, 1997, p. 137). How otherwise to understand the fact that in 1994, for the first time in the history of the Community, the Council considered it opportune expressly to exclude, in the preamble of the decision of approbation, the direct effect of the provisions of the 'GATS' and 'TRIPS' resulting from the Uruguay Round of GATT negotiations?[5] Moreover, at one stage the 1996–7 Intergovernmental Conference considered a proposal for an Article 113a which, in the view of its promotors, would have 'corrected' the difficulties of limiting the common commercial policy as the Court had partly done in its opinion 1–94 (cited above). The draft text provided that international agreements concluded under the article would have no direct effect. In other words, what had not been possible for some member states to achieve as far as directives were concerned would have been achieved for certain categories of international agreements. The proposal was not adopted. But in the new Amsterdam Treaty provisions regarding Title VI (the third pillar) of the TEU, direct effect has been excluded for both 'decisions' and 'framework decisions' (new Article K.6 – **34**).

The same Intergovernmental Conference refused to grant the Court of Justice the autonomy it had requested for the adoption of its rules of procedure; changes to them will still require the unanimous approval of the Council, in accordance with the provisions of EEC Treaty Article 188(3) (**245**). Nor was another, rather modest, proposal of the Court concerning the participation of Advocates General in the election of the President accepted. Another suggested proposal, for the Council to be able to adapt, not only Title III of the Statute (procedure), as is presently possible under the terms of Article 188(2), but the whole of the Statute itself (including Titles I and II, on the Judges and Organisation), was rejected, although no change to the amending procedure (unanimous Council decision at the request of the Court after consultation of both the Commission and the Parliament) was suggested.

With the Court itself opposed to any role for the European Parliament in the appointment of judges, the procedure remains unchanged, with the consequence that governments will continue the tradition of accepting without any discussion the nominees of their partners. The arguments advanced by the Court itself and by the literature (see, for example, Club de Florence, 1996, p. 132) in favour of a reduction in the number of judges had no chance of being heard by the Intergovernmental Conference. Proposals to prolong the mandates of the judges to one non-renewable term of ten or twelve years were also ignored.

The maintenance of the status quo in regard to the Court was probably also due to the lack of support around the conference table for the British Government's proposals, generally considered as being unduly hostile towards it. (United Kingdom, 1996. See Duff, 1997, p. 152; the government's most radical ideas were never tabled, so hotly were they criticised by the British legal profession.) Given the circumstances, the absence of amendments to the Treaty Title concerning the Courts might be considered in a positive light. It could be argued that the lack of substantial change denoted confidence in and respect for the institution concerned.

I would profoundly disagree. Maintaining things as they are necessarily makes it impossible to prepare the Court for the challenge of enlargement. As Duff puts it, 'for reasons of geographical size, linguistic and cultural differences and disparities in legal traditions and structures in an enlarged Union, it would already be a significant achievement to secure the full transposition and enforcement of the present *acquis communautaire* under the current system of judicial control'. And, he continues, 'the principal problem is overload, faced with the prospect of enlargement' (Duff, 1997, p. 153).

In 1990, before the beginning of the Maastricht Treaty negotiations, Jacqué and Weiler made a series of innovative proposals for reforming the European Union's judicial system (Jacqué and Weiler, 1990). Their idea, of creating regional courts, with suggestions as to the composition and working of the courts, was dismissed, notably in the reports of the Court of First Instance for both the 1991 and the 1996 Intergovernmental Conferences. The Court of First Instance's preferred solution to the problem would be the creation of specialised chambers within the Court itself. But this would not solve the geographical problem in an enlarged Community. There is already – as there indeed has been for many years – a problem of the average length of proceedings before the Court of Justice. In its 1995 report, the Court observed that there had been some progress in this regard, both for direct appeals and for preliminary rulings. This progress was due to the reform of the competences of the Court of First Instance and other rationalisation measures, but the delays nevertheless remain excessive. Although undue haste in regard to questions of a constitutional nature could prove counter-productive, it is surely inadmissible that judges or potential plaintiffs should refrain from referring questions or bringing cases before the Court of Justice through fear of the delays implied for the settlement of cases.

Since future demand for judicial intervention, although foreseeable, is not entirely and precisely predictable, I believe that the best way to proceed would be to introduce into the Treaty a legal basis which would allow for possible changes to the organisation of the judicial system. Such a measure would, in other words, deconstitutionalise the issue by creating a flexible way to cope with future problems. The procedure would have to be democratic – that is, based on co-decision with the European Parliament –

and efficient – that is, provide for majority voting in the Council. Neither of these two characteristics, it should be noted, is met by the current Article 188 (**245**) provisions in relation to the modification of the Court's statutes. The procedure would also have to preserve the prerogatives of the Courts, which would enjoy sole right of initiative and/or assent powers. Such a suggestion has, alas, little chance of being accepted since member states would not wish to lose their control in relation to such an important aspect of the balance of power within the Union.

There is a recurrent trend towards intergovernmentalism in the European Union. The classification of competences according to the 'pillars' system exacerbated the trend, but it is also discernible in the Community pillar of the Union. Supranational institutions like the Court are, if not precisely under attack, at least under close scrutiny. The more the Community intervenes in 'what really matters', the more the member states are jealous of their prerogatives. Furthermore, intergovernmental procedures inevitably exert a contagious effect on Community procedures, despite all the precautions taken by the authors of the Treaty (see especially TEU Article M – **47**). This is particularly the case when actions under both procedures are complementary, as is the case, for example, with foreign policy and external relations. Thus diplomatic settlements based on informal procedures tend to be preferred to judicial remedies and strict legal rules.

DIFFERENTIATION AND THE COURTS

As already observed, it was not the Maastricht Treaty which created mechanisms of diversified integration; they existed long before that. The Single European Act introduced the concept explicitly into the Treaty, especially in the field of environmental protection, but also in the internal market itself (Articles 100a(4) and 8c, renumbered 7c by the Maastricht Treaty – these have now become Articles **95** and **15** respectively under the Amsterdam Treaty). But it was the Treaty on European Union which gave differentiated integration its *lettres de noblesse* by providing for derogations (Article 109k – **122**) and possible exemptions (British and Danish protocols) in the context of Economic and Monetary Union, and by exonerating the United Kingdom from the agreement annexed to the Social Protocol.

The Treaty on European Union did not make differentiation an all-purpose solution. It was intended to solve specific difficulties. On the one hand, it recognised the different stages of economic convergence of the member states and allowed for temporary derogations. On the other hand, it had to cope with the political difficulties bound up in the attitudes of two member states. Under the provisions of TEU Article N (**48**), revision of the Treaties still requires the unanimous assent of the member states. Without the special solutions found for the United Kingdom and Denmark, a revision would not have been possible at Maastricht, since the other member states were not willing to break off negotiations with the two isolated countries. Politically, if not legally, the exemptions were granted on an implicit understanding that they were, *de facto*, temporary. The general conviction was that both countries would join Economic and Monetary Union once it had become a reality, and that the incongruous situation created by the Social Protocol would last only as long as the governing majority in the United Kingdom – so far the latter has proved to be a correct assumption. Neither solution, it was understood, could be invoked in favour of the possibility of permanent derogations nor serve as precedents applicable for accession candidates.

The Amsterdam Intergovernmental Conference considered at length the possibility of adopting general and specific (by pillar) clauses for what was dubbed 'flexibility – strengthened cooperation'. Most governments, together with the Commission, presented proposals in this context. For some, the provisions were to provide for well-structured flexibility allowing for wide diversity. For others, the provisions were to constitute an element of self-defence against the blocking attitudes of a minority of member states. The reading of the texts which resulted from the negotiations, especially the general clause of Title VIa – Title VII of the TEU (Articles K.15–17 – **43–45**) and the clause related to the so-called Community pillar (Article 5a – **11**), gives the impression that the insertion of such provisions was more important than their potential effectiveness. Given the widespread and entirely legitimate concerns about preserving the Community *acquis*, the unity of the institutional system and the cohesion of the Union, recourse to the use of such clauses would in practice prove very difficult. Moreover, both articles include the possibility for a member state to invoke 'important and stated reasons of national policy' to oppose the granting of an authorisation by qualified majority for closer cooperation. Where a member state chooses to invoke such reasons, a vote shall not be taken. The Council may, by a qualified majority, consequently decide to refer the matter up to the Council, meeting in the composition of Heads of State or Government, where a decision would in turn have to be taken by unanimity. This top-heavy procedure only further confirms my initial diagnosis.

In my opinion, the Amsterdam Treaty's flexibility provisions should be greeted with scepticism, perhaps particularly where the first pillar is concerned. In the Community field, 'different levels of commitment for different groups of states' could result in a situation very similar to that of the 'flexible Europe' or *Europe à la carte* which John Major wanted, as he made clear in his 1994 Leiden speech (Major, 1994; see also Duff, 1997, p. 153). I believe, in line with the European Movement, that differentiation should be organised on the basis of commitment to and participation in Economic and Monetary Union. Participating member states along with those willing to participate should be allowed to develop the accompanying policies and necessary political complements to the current provisions. Furthermore, non-participating member states should ultimately not be able to participate in the Community (Union). To this end, a timetable should be established. The same possibility of going ahead with internal and external security should be open to the same member states which are participating or willing to participate in Economic and Monetary Union, with its political complements, and a timetable should be established, if needed, for the participation of the others.

Duff and Wessels give detailed analyses of the differentiation concept in their contributions to this volume. Having made my position on the issue clear, I would like to return to a consideration of the role of the Court in this context.

In the Amsterdam Intergovernmental Conference the need was felt to include an explicit provision in the draft new EC Article 5a (**11**) allowing the Court to control respect for the conditions enumerated for recourse to strengthened cooperation. Perhaps the authors of the draft article had in mind the controversies about the 'justiciability' of the subsidiarity principle in Article 3b(2) (**5**), as introduced by the Maastricht Treaty. But surely, within the framework of the EC Treaty, there should have been no hesitation about the possibility for the Court to control the acts of the institutions. In this case, the act (of authorisation) has to be taken by the Council, and its possible submission to legal control is not in doubt, as the final version of Article 5a(4) (**11**) soberly confirms.

In the Amsterdam Treaty's Article K.7 (**35** – cooperation in the field of Justice and Home Affairs), control powers for the Court have also been provided in order to ensure respect in particular for the powers of the Community, and for the intended aim of establishing 'an area of freedom, security and justice'. As in the first pillar, explicit provision is made for the powers of the Court to apply in cases of closer cooperation in this field (Amsterdam Treaty Article K.12(4) – **40**).

Another question raised by differentiated integration concerns the possibility for non-participating member states to appear before the Court where a case concerns an act adopted in the framework of differentiated integration. Such hypotheses are, it should be stressed, far from being purely theoretical. Under the EC Treaty, there are already provisions enabling the Council to adopt regulations or other acts from the beginning of the third stage of monetary union with the vote only of participating member states (EC Article 109k.3 – **111** – enumerates these articles). Protocol no. 11 to the Treaty on European Union, on 'certain provisions relating to the United Kingdom of Great Britain and Northern Ireland', includes a much larger list of provisions which would not apply to it were it to decide not to move to the third stage of Economic and Monetary Union.

Numerous articles of Protocol no. 2 annexed to the Maastricht Treaty, on the Statute of the European System of Central Banks and the European Central Bank 'shall not confer any rights or impose any obligations' on a member state with a derogation (Article 43.1 of the Protocol). Among those articles is Article 34, which provides different categories of acts to be adopted by the European Central Bank.

Under the former Protocol no. 14 on social policy, the United Kingdom 'shall not take part in the deliberations and the adoption by the Council of Commission proposals made on the basis of this Protocol and the above-mentioned Agreement'.

Article K.6(2) (**34**), as amended by the Amsterdam Treaty, provides that conventions in the field of Justice and Home Affairs cooperation should be unanimously adopted by the Council, but that, once adopted by at least half of the member states, they may enter into force for those member states.

Usher (1997) identified an interesting precedent concerning a case heard by the Court in 1976, involving the 1968 Brussels Convention (on the recognition and execution of judgements in civil and commercial affairs). The case was heard by the Court before those member states which had joined the Community in 1973 had signed the Accession Convention to the Brussels Convention. The question arose as to 'whether the United Kingdom and Ireland could exercise the right to submit observations in regard to the interpretation of a convention to which they were not parties?' (A right granted to any member state under Article 20 of the Court's statute.) The answer given by the Court was that 'under the 1972 Act of Accession, the new member states were *legally obliged* to accede to the 1968 Convention, and that they therefore had an interest in expressing their views when the Court was called upon to interpret a convention to which they were required to become parties' (Case 12/76, *Tessili Como v. Dunlop*, [1976] ECR 1473).

Extrapolating from this ruling, one might have thought that a member state should not be allowed to present observations in a preliminary ruling procedure if the act to be interpreted is a convention which could not be part of the *acquis communautaire* to be taken over by the member state concerned; for example, in the case provided by the envisaged addition to Article K.3(2) – that is, the hypothetical case of a member state which is not part of the majority where a convention adopted under the terms of Article K.3(2) (**31**) has been applied. In a system where not only the acceptance of the convention itself but also the acceptance of the jurisdiction of the Court is optional, such a consequence seems logical.

The situation is in principle different when the acts adopted are clearly part of the *acquis communautaire*. This was the case, for example, for directives based on the Social Protocol. These directives are an integral part of Community law and the Article 177 (**234**) procedure (setting out the Court's jurisdiction with regard to preliminary rulings) applies fully to them. A United Kingdom court may ask the Court for an interpretation of a provision of such a directive (not applicable in the UK) where the provision is relevant to the judgement it has to make.

The Amsterdam-amended version of Article K.7 (**35**), relating to jurisdiction in Title VI (the third pillar) of the Treaty on European Union, provides the possibility for member states to accept by a declaration the competence of the Court to give preliminary rulings on conventions concluded under the Title. It is expressly provided that *any* member state shall be entitled to submit statements of case or written observations to the Court in cases which arise under paragraph 2 of the Article (on preliminary rulings), no matter whether they have or have not made such a prior declaration of acceptance of the Court's jurisdiction.

This possibility is based on the open nature of the conventions and on the possibility for the member states to make, at any time after the entry into force of the convention, a declaration accepting the competence of the Court to interpret the convention or to interpret and decide on the validity of application measures.

The process of differentiation in relation to the establishment of Economic and Monetary Union also has some incidence on the competence of the Court.

The question of the so-called 'territorial application' of Economic and Monetary Union regulations adopted either by the Council or the European Central Bank has already been raised during the preparatory works related, on the one hand, to the draft euro regulation based on Article 109l(4) (**123**)[6] and, on the other, to the draft complementary legislation to be adopted by the Council under EC Treaty Article 106.6 – **107** (Article 42 of the Statute of the European System of Central Banks and of the European Central Bank). A similar problem will arise in relation to European Central Bank regulations, which will be adopted for the euro area.

I share the view that there is no problem of 'territorial application' involved in those acts concerning the Economic and Monetary Union. They are part of Community law and the limitation imposed on their field of application is related to the material field of application, not to the territorial one. Any judge within the Community will have to consider these acts as Community law and will thus be able to request an interpretation of the Court.

The question is more complex where direct appeals for annulment by non-participating member states are concerned. Are they to be regarded as privileged applicants under Article 173(2) (**230**) in their quality as member states, or should they have to demonstrate an interest as prescribed, by Article 173(4), for any natural or legal person? I agree with Usher that such a delicate question could better have been expressly resolved by the Treaty itself, but I would be inclined to admit the possibility for the non-participating member state to act under Article 173(2). After all, such non-participating member states have a vocation ultimately to participate. The case of a member state steadily refusing the move to the third stage of Economic and Monetary Union should, I believe, be resolved by the transformation of its link of participation in the Union. It is, in effect, a question which goes beyond the technical problem of admissibility of appeals before the Court.

TRENDS FOR THE FUTURE

What should be the trends discernible in the actions of the Court(s) in the run-up to the new century? In the first place, I would like to see greater emphasis put within the Community legal order on the place of the citizen or, more generally, the private person. Consequently, the accent should be – as has been the case, with some exceptions, for more than thirty years – on the direct effect of Community law, enabling private persons to invoke direct effect before their national jurisdictions. At the same time, private actors' access to the European Court(s) should be enhanced and extended (Duff, 1997, pp. 144–5). This doesn't mean that the institutions and the member states should not have privileged access. But it does mean that the limitations currently imposed by the Treaty, as interpreted by the Court, on appeals by private persons are unacceptable.

If there is no revision of the Treaty on this point, the Courts should do their best regardless. Admittedly, the introduction into the Treaty of a hierarchy of norms, and the implications of such a hierarchy for judicial control, would have simplified the Courts' task. In the absence of such a reform, progress will, I fear, be limited. The possibility of an appeal for violation of human rights – an explicit list of which should be inserted in the Treaty – against any Community act would be another important reform. More than ever, the actions taken by private parties before the Court are a necessary complement to the actions of the member states and the institutions, which could be very reluctant to take appeals before the Court themselves. Preliminary rulings and direct actions are complementary and the one cannot substitute for the other.

In the second place, the successive revisions of the Treaties have resulted in growing complexity and a multiplicity of regimes and exceptions. Simplification of the Treaties – a declared objective of the 1996–7 Intergovernmental Conference – was not achieved. As a result, the legal panorama will be less transparent than ever. There are many reasons for this situation. Among them are the need to take into account in the Treaty the very diverse preoccupations of an ever-increasing number of member states; the remarkable intricacy of the differentiation clauses, special regimes, derogations and exceptions; the adoption of political resolutions by the European Council when, as has been the case for Economic and Monetary Union, changing the rules is either impossible or dangerous; not to mention the existence of the pillars, straightforward jargon, and problems bound up in a multi-lingual system. These heterogeneous factors are a source of obscurity and confusion which not only make texts illegible and incomprehensible for the citizen but endanger the founding principles of integration. This may make the role of the Court more complicated and delicate, but it also imposes on judges the duty of ensuring that principles triumph over the confused or restrictive letter of the texts. Constructive interpretation, inherent in the law of integration, is becoming increasingly necessary.

In the third place, faced with a trend which leads governments to prefer political acts of unspecified binding value to legal rules, or diplomatic negotiations to legal remedies, the role of the Court must be to defend the idea of a 'Community based on law'.[7] It is not only in the matters covered by the second and third pillars that the preference of governments for informal or unspecified instruments and procedures exists; there are examples in the Community sphere as well. The Stability Pact and the Exchange Rate Mechanism II (governing the relations between the euro area and non-participating currencies) will be primarily based on European Council resolutions. On the other hand, the differences of status of the member states in relation to the single currency will necessarily make the unitary representation of the Community in monetary affairs towards the external world very difficult. Pragmatism will be the *leitmotif*, obscuring the transfer of competences of the member states in favour of the Community (respectively, the Council and the European Central Bank).

The Court of Justice will have to ensure respect for competences and obligations deriving especially from the 'loyalty clause' (EC Treaty Article 5 – 10) in order to enable the rule of law to prevail. If not, the risk for the system would not be limited to a 'constitutional order of states' (Duff again, 1997, p. 137), but the prospect of regressing slowly but surely into a process of purely intergovernmental cooperation, the supranational elements dwindling to mere vestiges of a more dynamic past.

I believe that, if the basic features of the law of integration are to be maintained, then the enlarged European Union of the twenty-first century must preserve the full capacity of action of its Courts of Justice. This supposes an in-depth reflection which should ideally involve the Courts themselves but which should in any case not be confined to them nor left only to member state officials. We need a clear view on the judiciary of a European Union of twenty or more member states.

This organisation should enable the Courts to deal within reasonable time limits with the cases which are brought before them. The restriction of access to the Court or of the admissibility of preliminary rulings (by a filter procedure of the *certiorari* type, for example) should not be the only solutions considered for coping with a potential overload. The Court of Justice should not be kept in a position where, in order to avoid an inrush of cases, it is actually considered preferable to limit the rights of national courts to refer questions for preliminary rulings under Article 164 (**220**) or K.3 (**K.6**) conventions. To restrict the direct or indirect access of private parties to the European Courts is to limit the legal (and democratic) features of the Community system.

The existence of differentiation clauses in the EC Treaty and in the third pillar of the Treaty on European Union, together with the possibility for differentiated action under the second pillar (Common Foreign and Security Policy) symbolises the refusal of most of the member states to be prevented from progressing towards further integration. I believe that these solutions will rapidly prove to be inadequate or, at the most, of limited utility and difficult to use (see Hanf, 1995, for interesting comments on the tension between integration in a limited circle and the cohesion of the collectivity of the member states). The move to the third stage of Economic and Monetary Union will require greater political differentiation between, on the one hand, those for whom the European Union constitutes a single market and an instrument of common sectoral policies and international cooperation and, on the other hand, those who still believe in the need to build a democratic and efficient political Union.

Taking into account the current attitudes of our national bureaucracies, it is clear that the creation of such a political Union will require a qualitative change of the same order of magnitude as that which was involved in the negotiation and creation of the Economic and Monetary Union. Only then will the scale of the challenge be absolutely clear to all.

NOTES

1. See, by contrast, the German Constitutional Court's 12 October 1993 decision relating to the Maastricht Treaty, which reclaims the right to control supposedly *ultra vires* Community acts (*Entscheidungen des Bundesverfassungsgerichts*, B Ver/GE, vol. 89, p. 155, 383/182). See also, Jerdegen, 1994; Oppenheimer, 1994, pp. 526–575.
2. Or Courts, if the Court of First Instance, an economic court of great importance created by the Maastricht Treaty, is included.
3. With the exception of the granting of competence by Article K.3(2)(c) (**31**) in the context of conventions; 'Such conventions may stipulate that the Court of Justice shall have jurisdiction to interpret their provisions and to rule on any disputes regarding their application, in accordance with such arrangements as they may lay down.' The Court is also competent to interpret Article L (**46**) itself.
4. It is the case for all of the conventions mentioned in EC Treaty Article 220 (**293**). The weakening referred to in the text includes limiting the jurisdictions allowed to ask the Court questions, the transformation of the obligation for the Court as a last resort into a facultative option, and so on. The solutions adopted in the Maastricht Treaty for the role of the Court in the new Title on Free Movement of Persons, Asylum and Immigration and in the new Title VI of the Treaty on European Union on Police and Judicial Cooperation in Criminal Matters differ also from the genuine EC Treaty Article 177 (**234**), although there was some improvement towards the end of the Intergovernmental Conference on the drafts which had been circulated at an earlier stage. See new articles K7 and 73p as they resulted from the Amsterdam Treaty.
5. See *Official Journal* no. L 336, 23 December 1994, p. 1. 'GATS' = 'General Agreement on Trade on Services'. 'TRIPS' = 'Trade Related Aspects of Intellectual Property'.
6. The classic formula, as provided for by Article 14 of the Council's Rules of Procedure, is 'This Regulation shall be binding in its entirety and directly applicable in all Member States ...' The relevant clause in the current draft regulation on the introduction of the euro provides the following additional wording: 'in accordance with the Treaty, subject to Protocols no. 11 and 12 and Article 109k(1)'.
7. Once again, see Duff, 1997, p. 138. The expression, which is the translation of

'*Communauté de droit*' (just as there is a concept of the '*Etat de droit*'), is quoted by Duff from Opinion 1–91 (on the European Economic Area – Case 1–91 [1991], ECR I-6079), where the Court restated the basic features of the Community and its legal order.

REFERENCES

Club de Florence, 1996, *Europe, l'impossible statu quo*, Stock, Paris

Constantinesco, Leontin, 1965, 'La spécificité du droit communautaire', *Revue Trimestriel de Droit Européen*

Duff, Andrew, 1997, *Reforming the European Union*, Federal Trust, Sweet and Maxwell, London

European Court of Justice, 1995, *Report on Certain Aspects of the Application of the Treaty on European Union*, Luxembourg, May

Gibbon, Edward, 1985, *The Decline and Fall of the Roman Empire*, Penguin Classics Edition, London

Hanf, Dominik, 1995, 'La différenciation dans l'Union européenne: l'Europe à géométrie variable', IEE/GEPE, Brussels

Jacqué, Jean-Paul and Weiler, Joseph H.H., 1990, 'On the road to the EU. A new agenda for the IGC', *Common Market Law Review*, pp. 185–207

Jerdegen, Matthias, 1994, 'Maastricht and the German Constitutional Court: Constitutional Restraints for an Ever-Closer Union', *Common Market Law Review*, vol. 31/2, April

Labaye, Henri, 1997, 'La coopération dans les domaines de la justice et des affaires intérieures', in Manin, Philippe (ed.), *La révision du traité sur l'Union européenne. Perspectives et réalités*, Pedone, Paris

Major, John, 1994, Second William and Mary Lecture, University of Leiden, The Netherlands, 7 September

Oppenheimer, Andrew (ed.), 1994, *The Relationship between European Community Law and National Law: The Cases*, Cambridge University Press, Cambridge

Sauron, Jean-Luc, 1997, *Droit et pratique du contentieux communautaire*, Collection Réflexe Europe, La Documentation Française, Paris

United Kingdom, 1996, *Memorandum by the United Kingdom on the European Court of Justice*, HMSO, London, 25 July

Usher, John, 1997, 'Variable Geometry or Concentric Circles. Patterns for the European Union', *ICLQ*, pp. 243–73

8 For a democratic Europe

Robert Toulemon

The lack of democracy, the 'democratic deficit', is a recurrent theme in European political debate. It has been frequently remarked that the European Union would not itself meet the criteria it imposes upon candidate countries. Decisions are still taken by ministers meeting in secret, and hence beyond public opinion. The increasing involvement of the European Parliament in the EU's legislative work and the publication of the Council's voting records (though not its deliberations) incontestably represent progress. But Europe remains largely the privileged reserve of politicians, diplomats, high-ranking officials, top management and experts of all sorts who, all taken together, fall badly short of meeting the expectations of the ordinary man and woman on the 'Clapham omnibus' or, for that matter, the Brussels tram.

The gap existing between various broadly pro-European elites and the general mass of Europe's electorates was starkly illuminated in those countries which held referendums to ratify the Maastricht Treaty. On 2 June 1992 the Danish people rejected – admittedly by a narrow margin – a Treaty which the Danish Folketing had approved by a large majority. A few months later, on 20 September 1992, the French people approved the Treaty by only one percentage point, although the vast majority of France's political and economic leaders had been in favour.

Economic difficulties, mass unemployment, Europe's impotence in the face of the tragic Yugoslav crisis; all of these considerations go some way towards explaining the hesitant behaviour of European public opinion where once there was broad, if tacit, approval. And that is why, at a moment when the European construct is about to be extended to new, and far more politically sensitive fields, the old Monnet method, which gave such brilliant results, of pre-prepared decisions taken in restricted and enlightened circles, is no longer sufficient.

Increasingly, governments are finding themselves unable to hide their activities from the public gaze. Increasingly, they are finding it difficult to use enigmatic 'Brussels' as the scapegoat responsible for any and every problem. They must simultaneously render the common institutions – principally, the Council and the Commission – more transparent *and* more effective. They must, with the help of political parties, increasingly involve what has become known as 'civil society' in the great and historically unprecedented exercise which is freely and consensually uniting old nation states, several of them, it is frequently forgotten, former great powers.

The terms of the debate about the democratisation of Europe are not only institutional. The very nature of Europe is at stake, for the way in which Europe might be democratised depends on whether we choose to see it as a simple alliance of nation states, with each determined to preserve its essential sovereignty, or a Union with a federal vocation designed partially to share sovereignty.

This chapter will argue in favour of a plurinational democracy, and more for practical than for doctrinal reasons. The argument is articulated around three observations:

- the European Union can never be of real substance if it does not embody at least a partial – and effective – delegation of national sovereignty;
- democratisation of the European Union's institutions will necessarily encourage the creation of a supranational European political debate;
- the European Union will be unable to advance and consolidate its role for as long as it is unable to respond to the expectations of its citizens.

THE DELEGATION OF SOVEREIGNTY

Forty years of experience have shown that 'Europe' has only ever managed to exist, to develop common policies, to defend its common interests, where national sovereignty has been delegated to the common institutions (where, it should nevertheless be recalled, the member states play a dominant role).

From the beginning onwards – the creation of the Customs Union, its uneasy acceptance by other countries, the creation of a Common Agricultural Policy, the implementation of competition rules governing both state aids and cartels and the abuse of dominant market positions – none of these achievements would have been possible without the extraordinary efficiency of the so-called 'Community method'. This consisted essentially of an autonomous institution enjoying monopoly powers of initiative, a decision-making body made up of government representatives, and a Court of Justice designed to assure the primacy of European law. The basic system was improved, little by little, particularly through the introduction of qualified majority voting (which in effect had, through an abusive interpretation of the 'Luxembourg compromise', remained suspended from 1965 to 1985) and the belated involvement of the Parliament in the Union's legislative processes.

The impotence of intergovernmentalism

On the other hand, all attempts made to organise traditional, cooperative, intergovernmental forums outside or alongside the Community method – that is, without a common organisation enjoying the right of initiative and without majority voting – have failed, or have resulted in disappointment. Thus, from the very beginning, the statist 1962 Fouchet plan failed; the 'political cooperation' begun in 1972 enjoyed only limited success; and by most commentators' standards the two intergovernmental pillars, on common foreign and security policy and on internal security, introduced by the 1993 Maastricht Treaty, failed miserably.

Jean-Louis Bourlanges, President of the French branch of the European Movement, recently wrote that 'the intergovernmental is not an alternative to the Community method, and it will be even less so in an enlarged Europe. The two are as different as an amoeba and a human being. The Community is a complex organism, based on a sophisticated balance between the functions of initiative, decision-making, political control and jurisdictional control. The intergovernmental method is nothing more than fifteen government representatives warily watching each other and, in the absence of any external initiative, without the means of producing anything coherent' (*Societal*, March 1997).

To describe the system preferred at Maastricht, the metaphor used was of a temple composed of three columns and capped by a pediment, the European Council. This was in contradistinction to the metaphor used to describe what would have been Jacques Delors' preferred system; a tree, with different branches but a single trunk. The temple's columns were intended to represent what became known as the three pillars; the Community, the Common Foreign and Security Policy, and Justice and Home Affairs. Thereafter, the Community pillar seemed ever-stronger, whilst the other two pillars rapidly took on the appearance of paste-board.

The way forward for the Union

After Maastricht, the way towards further progress in the construction of Europe was clear. The weaker pillars had to be consolidated by gradually breathing into them the life-force of the Community pillar; in particular, by introducing majority decision-making on the basis of Commission proposals. With the perspective of imminent enlargement to the East, such reforms seem in any case to be inevitable.

However, the apparent timidity of the Maastricht Treaty and the halfway house solution adopted at Amsterdam were the result neither of chance nor of a lack of clear-mindedness among the negotiators. Ever since the French Assemblée nationale rejected the proposed European Defence Community in 1954, 'political Europe' has been a tainted subject. The failure of the 1962 Fouchet Plan did nothing to improve matters. Foreign policy and, even more, defence, are highly sensitive areas with very different national agendas. France is above all concerned about rediscovering a world role through a Europe emancipated from American supervision. The United

Kingdom places Atlantic solidarity far above European solidarity. Germany is hardly tempted by a return to power politics, even if this were to be achieved through Europe. Germany shares the French desire for independence, but cannot ignore the fact that the Americans consider the country to be their privileged partner in Europe. The other countries are divided between those with a tradition of neutrality and those who consider attachment to the Atlantic Alliance as their best guarantee against any pretension to hegemony on the part of Germany, or of France, or of the Franco-German alliance.

In other words, the progressive 'Communitarisation' of foreign policy is not self-evident. It will come from the development of a feeling of a common European destiny among the Continent's peoples, a feeling which for the moment remains embryonic at most. Europe lacks a common political *corps*; a lack that has been strongly underlined in the recent writings of Dominique Wolton.[1] Such a common political class will emerge the day that European elections give rise not to fifteen national debates but to a true debate at the Union level about the politics of the Union. Institutional reforms are essential, but they are not sufficient. The Union must adapt itself to become more responsive to the needs and desires of its citizens.

DEMOCRATISING THE INSTITUTIONS

If Europe and its citizens are to be brought closer together, the first step which needs to be taken is to give a comprehensible form to the Union's legal and institutional architecture. Yet despite all of the talk about simplification and clarification, the Maastricht Treaty and the Amsterdam Treaty have both achieved new heights of complexity and opacity. If they remain largely incomprehensible, the Union's institutions have also revealed themselves to be disappointingly ineffective, particularly in those policy areas which, due to statist prudence, have so far been kept out of the Community pillar (or only allowed halfway in). Perceived ineffectiveness has only reinforced scepticism among people who had been led to believe that 'Europe' could perform various tasks better.

An occult subject: the personality of the Union

Of all the topics on the agenda of the 1996–7 Intergovernmental Conference, this has been the one about which least has been heard. Few know that the Maastricht Treaty did not substitute the Union for the Communities. Not only do the old Communities still exist, but they enjoy their own legal personalities, as distinct from the member states, and are therefore able to conclude treaties.

The European Union created at Maastricht and consolidated at Amsterdam is more an objective than a new organisation. An obvious reform would consist of merging the three Communities (the European Coal and Steel

Community, the European Economic Community and the European Atomic Energy Community), which together constitute the so-called 'first pillar', and of integrating the fused Community into a Union with its own international legal personality. It didn't happen at Amsterdam, and if little was heard about this matter it was not without reason. The 'intergovernmentalists' feared that such a merger might, as would be logical, involve the absorption of the two intergovernmental pillars into the Community domain. The federalists, on the other hand, were afraid that such a merger might undermine the supranational aspects particular to the Community pillar.

A reasonable future compromise would consist of admitting, within a single structure, modalities particular to what are currently the second and third pillars. Thus, on foreign policy, member states would enjoy a right of initiative; on defence, each member state would be able to refuse the participation of its armed forces in actions decided on a majority basis; and on justice and home affairs, 'Communitarisation' could be accompanied by organised consultation of national parliaments and a reinforcement of their contacts with the European Parliament.

From the point of view both of democracy and of effectiveness, such a compromise could only work if accompanied by majority voting in the Council, co-decision for the European Parliament (or assent, in the case of treaty ratification), the primacy of Community law, and full competence for the Court of Justice.

The Amsterdam Treaty fell short of these requirements. However, there was some progress: for example, the possibility for the Union to conclude treaties, the association of a Vice-President of the Commission in charge of external relations with the Presidency on common foreign and security policy matters, and the promise of communitarisation of a part of the third pillar after five years.

The future of the Commission

It was France, paradoxically, which in the 1996–7 Intergovernmental Conference insisted on a reduction in the number of members of the Commission – a measure which could only have reinforced the Commission's supranationality. From the point of view of the theme of this chapter, reducing the number of members of the Commission could only have been defended if their positions had been 'denationalised' and their vocation as an emerging future government of the Union recognised.

When Paris seems to regret the alleged prudence of Germany and other member states about institutional reform, it is forgotten that Germany, in a CDU/CSU document said to be close to the Government's thinking, proposed that the Commission should become the government which Europe so cruelly lacks, particularly given the imminent existence of a central bank. The way in which this proposal was dismissed out of hand, on the specious grounds that the Commission lacks democratic legitimacy, is to be regretted.

Nominated by the governments of the member states for a limited period, most frequently drawn from the political milieu, collectively responsible before the European Parliament which, since Maastricht, approves their nomination; members of the European Commission enjoy the same democratic legitimacy as government ministers nominated by a head of state and responsible before a parliament. Nobody in France ever contested the democratic legitimacy of the Pompidou (1962–8) and Barre (1976–81) governments, and yet neither one nor the other was elected and both, when they arrived at the Matignon, were completely unknown to the French people. The truth is that the Commission is constantly done down by those who do not wish to see Europe equipped with a true government, effective and legitimate. This might be logical in the case of the United Kingdom, which has traditionally opposed any evolution which might lead to a political union. But French hostility to the political role of the Commission is inconsistent. There was, after all, nothing to stop France from calling for an increase in the Commission's accountability to the Council of Ministers or the European Council if it had so wished.

These vital questions – the future, composition, and method of appointing the Commission – were not resolved by the 1996–7 Intergovernmental Conference and have effectively been postponed until the next enlargement negotiations. The desire of the smaller member states to be represented, combined with the difficulty of entrusting major political responsibilities to an over-large and under-representative college, might well lead to the pragmatic creation of a limited 'cabinet' around the President of the Commission (perhaps composed of a number of Vice-Presidents . . .). Such a limited cabinet could, for example, be charged with the task of running Europe's foreign and defence policies, following the guidelines and under the control of the European Council.

The capital issue of the transformation of the Commission into a political executive was not discussed by the Intergovernmental Conference. The only progress made was to reinforce the position of the Commission President, whose nomination must now be confirmed by the European Parliament, who will take part in the selection of the other members of the college, and who will determine their fields of responsibility.

Council of Ministers or Council of States? The question of weighted voting. The European Council

The Council is the one institution whose membership must necessarily grow with each successive enlargement of the Union. If only for this reason, its pretensions to being the political executive of the Union are destined progressively to lose all credibility. Appointing a High Representative (the Council's Secretary General) to represent the Union can only be a provisional solution. Intended to give a face to the Union, such a measure will doubtless only serve further to cloud its image. At the least, tight cooperation will be required between the High Representative, the President of the Council (General Affairs) and the President of the European Council, whose mandate might be prolonged and detached from any national functions, in line with the proposal for a new troïka composed of this President, the President of the Council and the President of the Commission advanced by Professor Quermonne.[2] This could be considered as an intermediate stage preceding the ultimate step, perhaps at the time of an important enlargement, which would see the Union equipped with a real political executive enjoying a full range of powers – distinct from governments but accountable to them and to the European Parliament.

The future role of the Council must logically be to become an upper house of the Union's Parliament. Like the United States' Senate, the upper house would exercise a particular role in relation to the monitoring of the Union's foreign policy. But when it comes to the problem of weighted voting the German Bundesrat provides a better model than the United States' Senate. It seems perfectly right that the states should themselves decide how they should be represented in the Council, that their delegations should vote in unison, and that the number of votes attributed to each state, without being proportional to population, should avoid the risk of decisions adopted by majorities which do not represent a majority of the population. The American formula – equality of States in the Senate, strict proportionality in the House – is not suited to Europe. The overrepresentation of less populous states in the European Parliament may gradually be reduced with future enlargements, but it will never be entirely eliminated. The counterpart is a Council of States where each state disposes of a number of votes which, whilst not proportionate, takes account of population size.

To those who are against any 'reduction' of today's Council into a Council of States and upper chamber of the Parliament it should be pointed out that the states would retain, through the European Council – whose pre-eminent role nobody questions, the upper hand concerning the basic policy guidelines of the Union. The Council of States would meanwhile retain its basic role of preparing the work of the European Council and monitoring the implementation of the European Council's decisions by the Executive.

Why are such institutional reforms, which are only really of interest to specialists, so necessary if Europe and its citizens are to be brought closer together, if a genuine political debate is to be held, and if Europe is to be democratised? There are two reasons. On the one hand, people need to be able to know Europe, to know who is running it. On the other hand, Europeans want the Union to be able to act effectively in meeting their expectations. An organisation with many leaders, all in competition with one another, and one which seems unable to follow clear policies, can never be near to the citizen.

The Parliament. Powers and electoral system

Consideration of the Parliament's powers and the system used to elect it has been deliberately placed towards the end of this chapter. However necessary they may be, improvements in Parliament's role are far from being sufficient to render Europe more democratic.

By introducing parliamentary assent with regard to the composition of the Commission the Maastricht Treaty made real progress, confirmed in Amsterdam by the extension of parliamentary assent to the President's nomination. By the same logic, if there were to be a permanent Presidency of the European Council, the nomination of the Presidency would also need to be submitted to Parliament's assent. This said, the essential progress to be made in this field consists of extending co-decision to *all* those areas decided by majority vote in the Council, including those in the field of justice and home affairs.

Last, but by no means least, Parliament cannot for much longer be excluded from the constituent process. Already, the Treaties seem increasingly constitutional in nature. They should be based on the double support of the states and of the peoples, the issue of agreement between governments, national parliaments, and the European Parliament. Moreover, the European Parliament should have the right of constitutional initiative. (If the principle adopted by the European Parliament in 1984 were to be followed, amendments to the Treaties would enter into force as soon as they had been approved by a majority of states representing two-thirds of the population of the Union. Those states in the minority would have a choice between acceptance of the majority decision or association status.)

Reform of the electoral system is a basic necessity if Europe is to be democratised. Apart from the fact that the current system is in contradiction with the provisions of the Treaty of Rome, it has the effect of distancing the electors from the elected and of distorting the political balance within the Parliament. The national list system practised in several countries has the effect of giving the power of selection to parties who are frequently tempted to use the power to place the casualties of universal suffrage, and even on occasion to distance from national political life individuals judged, for one reason or another, 'awkward'. Perhaps understandable in smaller states, the net effect in larger countries is to deprive citizens of any direct relationship with the elected. Nobody knows their MEP. Even in the absence of a uniform electoral system, rendered unobtainable until recently by the British attachment to the first-by-the-post system, larger states should have been orientating themselves towards systems of proportional lists on a regional basis, and this would seem to be the intention behind the Amsterdam Treaty's amendment to Article 138.

Although raising problems of principle, an accompanying reform could contribute very effectively to the rapid evolution of a European political corps. This would consist of giving electors a second ballot paper which would permit them to vote for a fraction of the total number of MEPs – a tenth, for example – on a Union-wide basis and from obligatorily plurinational lists. This reform would have several advantages.[3] The first would be a pedagogic function in leading electors perhaps to vote for candidates from countries other than their own. The second would be a considerable political advantage, assuming the Commission's membership were to be drawn in some way from the Parliament's membership. Such plurinational lists would effectively 'pre-select' those who might be called upon to become members of the Commission. Members drawn from such lists could not easily be dismissed as having no electorally-based legitimacy. Such a system would also present a considerable democratic advantage, since it would oblige all of the major political movements to organise themselves at the Union level and to present general programmes based on broad, Union-wide political themes and not narrow programmes based on purely national themes. At a purely normative level, the old and never more than tenuous objection, that MEPs represent nations rather than peoples, no longer holds true, since nationals established in another country of the Union may now vote in European elections in their country of domicile.

These proposals and other similar ideas have been discussed in academic circles and by the media. There have been no such proposals on an intergovernmental conference's table so far, but the general trend is clear; six of the Commission's current twenty members are, in any case, former Members of the European Parliament.

Clarifying competences and the subsidiarity principle

Often announced, never achieved, a clarification of competences would render Europe less opaque, and correct the impression of an organism simultaneously distant and yet invading. Of course, a strict separation of national and Community competences is only possible in theory. Nor should the potential pedagogic role of the institutions be neglected. Through the financial assistance they provide, they can encourage reform and innovation in backward regions and those experiencing economic difficulties. In the same way, it is good that the Union should have the means to encourage exchanges of qualified and experienced people between the member states even in those areas where it has no strict competence (the teaching profession is a good example). Too strict a reading of the subsidiarity principle would have blocked entirely laudable exchange programmes of students and teachers to which the participants enthusiastically subscribe and which coincidentally facilitate the growth of links between Europe's peoples.

Clarification is nevertheless necessary. In the first place, there should be a short and easily comprehensible text setting out the constitutional norms contained in the Treaties, a text which does not excessively limit the areas of exclusive competence of the Union, particularly in the area of external relations. (Logically, for example, this area could perhaps also include everything to do with the monitoring of the external frontiers of the Union.) Given the vast field of potentially competing competences, it would doubtless be advantageous to make the distinction between areas where the Union or the states enjoy primary competence. It would be for the states and the Union to prove that action at a particular level would be appropriate and sufficient.

What legal experts like to call the 'hierarchy of norms' would help to lighten the agendas of the Council and the Parliament. The executive role of the Commission must be more broadly accepted, particularly in the areas of the so-called second pillar and the former third pillar, though clearly this would be accompanied by reinforced a posteriori control over the Commission.

The measures proposed in this chapter will doubtless seem hopelessly technical to the non-specialist. But those who work in or with 'Europe' know that the spirit, if not the letter, of these reforms is an unavoidable condition if Europe is simultaneously to be rendered more efficient whilst avoiding an indefinite deception of its peoples. Nevertheless, reforming the institutions – making them more coherent, more efficient, more democratic – will not be enough if Europe is to be brought closer to its citizens.

FOR A CITIZENS' EUROPE

As Jacques Vandamme points out later in this volume, the fundamental basis of the process of European integration is a reconciliatory peace settlement between Western Europe's 'hereditary enemies'. The process has also been much aided by the economic boom in Western Europe which enabled it to catch up with the levels of development in the United States of America. These underpinnings of peace and prosperity have formed, in their turn, the foundations on which a broad majority of European public opinion has for so long supported the process of European integration. These same factors explain the attraction which the European Union still exerts on the populations of the Central and Eastern European countries so recently liberated from the yoke of the Soviet Union.

The spectre of mass unemployment, impotence in the face of the unfolding tragic events in the former Yugoslavia, and the often unfounded but insidiously plausible campaigns against the intrusions of 'Brussels' go a long way towards explaining the increasing unpopularity of Europe. However necessary they might seem, the reforms outlined above would be unable to reverse the flow of scepticism if they were not accompanied by a range of measures aimed at encouraging and consolidating the sense and identity of Europe among its citizens.

Guaranteeing fundamental rights

The first concern of most Europeans is the guarantee of their fundamental rights, including their economic rights and, in particular, the right to a minimum standard of living. Thus, the 'problem' of accession to the European Convention of Human Rights is far from theoretical. Such a measure should be accompanied by provisions which would enable individuals to seek redress against any encroachment on their fundamental rights, as defined in the European Charter of Human Rights. In practical terms, this would consist of reducing the amount of time and limiting the cost of resorting to the Court.

The right to a minimum standard of living is now generally recognised as part of the basic standard of advanced countries. Europe would do well to recognise the importance of such a right, whilst leaving it up to each member state to ensure respect for the right, perhaps counter-balancing it with some concept of service to society. There is no need to underline the importance, and also the difficulty, of what would constitute decisive social progress if exclusion and poverty, the embarrassments of our rich and developed societies, were to be eliminated. In this context, the European Union could encourage exchanges between different national administrations, and the structural funds could be used, to the benefit of less developed member states, to encourage similar exchanges of information and experience.

Guaranteeing citizens' security

Europe's citizens expect reliability and honesty from those who govern them, which is why the Communitarisation of the third pillar is of such importance. In effect, this measure reconciles two necessities; more effective cooperation in the fight against corruption and crime, and a better guarantee of basic liberties against possible abuse by the police and home affairs authorities. Straddling Maastricht and Schengen, previous intergovernmental cooperation in this field has combined all the disadvantages of reduced effectiveness and risks for basic liberties.

The 1 October 1996 Geneva appeal of seven magistrates from different countries for a European legal area, relayed in February 1997 by more than four hundred French judges, demonstrates just how much the legal classes are aware of this problem. The creation of a European legal area in penal matters, including the creation of a European ministry of home affairs, would enable an effective fight against international organised crime, but only in the context of European laws debated by the European Parliament and under the control of the Court of Justice.

An end to anti-European pedagogy

Over the last four years, and particularly since the Maastricht European Council, Europe has witnessed what effectively amounts to an anti-European propaganda campaign. Scapegoat for any and every problem, from the retreat from the ECSC at the end of the 1950s onwards, Europe is criticised even for its achievements. Is it not paradoxical that Europe's farmers, the most obvious beneficiaries of the common market, treat the Union with such scorn?

As to the many rules and regulations held to be an abuse, it is forgotten just how often they result from the explicit requests of the member states and their administrations, frequently with justification. It is entirely logical that the defenders of migratory birds should call for protection measures to safeguard a common natural heritage. It was entirely understandable that the French producers of cheese made with unpasteurised milk called for harmonised hygiene regulations – to protect their products against the bans several member states were threatening to impose. It is entirely reasonable that water quality should be the subject of common standards.

Although regulations and directives are mostly justified, the Commission has admitted to over-zealous regulation in the past and taken measures to avoid it in the future. After all, was it not the Commission which recently proposed the annulment of some 200 directives? But the real problem is not to be found in the quantity of legislation. Rather, the problem is the failure to explain the reason for such measures when they are proposed by the Commission or adopted by the Council, but at any rate before they enter into force. Until now, there has been too little explanation, too late. Under these circumstances it is very difficult to fight against the myths and falsehoods to which 'Europe' too often falls victim, particularly in the British tabloid press. Significant budgetary resources must be devoted to the simple cause of explaining what 'Europe' is doing, and why. There is a crying need for simple information. It seems that, since the Danish 'no' in 1992, the Commission and the Parliament have become increasingly aware of the problem and have begun to take action.

Educating future European citizens

The Maastricht Treaty created European citizenship as a common right. Today's young Europeans should be made aware of their 'plural citizenship', of the fact that they belong to several communities, that closer attachment to one community is complementary and not contradictory. Such awareness is vital if they are to survive peaceably in tomorrow's increasingly complex world. From village to humankind, society's overlapping complementarity must be brought home to them. They must be helped to understand that a good citizen is open to other communities and does not seek separation or isolation from them.

Honorable mentions of 'plural citizenship' and of European citizenship in the EU's programmes and policies are starkly insufficient. Truly educational instruments must be established and used to throw light on Europe's common values. As obvious multipliers, the faculties of schools and universities should be primary targets.

Europe's universities should be progressively 'Europeanised'. I mean nothing sinister by this. Already, there exist a number of excellent and broadly appreciated Community programmes (the European Community Studies Associations, the progressive creation of Jean Monnet Chairs and course modules), and these should be consolidated and extended. Europe should be able to establish centres of excellence comparable in stature and resources with those to be found on the other side of the Atlantic. The Union should enjoy shared competences with the member states in this field, for the Union is better-placed than any individual state to help encourage the establishment of truly European centres of excellence and to endow them with the prestige and the resources necessary for the creation of international teams devoted to teaching and research.

Another initiative, currently in an experimental phase, could help to educate future European citizens and to change Europe's image. A programme of European voluntary service, open to the young of either sex and without any conditions about academic qualifications, could give youngsters of very different socio-economic backgrounds the chance to be part of a multi-national team, to learn languages, and to help a cause of their own choosing; action to help the less privileged, in or outside the Union, action to protect the environment or our cultural heritage, development cooperation in less-developed countries, humanitarian actions.

At the end of the day, it is for civil society in its entirety to make clear what it needs from and wants of the European Union. Already, a Civil Society Forum has brought together numerous organisations with very different roles and activities under the aegis of the International European Movement. The European Parliament has recently adopted a report proposing various measures designed to encourage the broadest possible debates about European issues.

Just as Europe cannot remain the domain of privileged circles, so it cannot only seek the support of the political classes. The whole of society must be involved in formulating the general will of the Union, expressed through debates and discussion in the widest possible circles. Modern communications technology – interactive television and the internet in particular – must be harnessed to these ends (on the internet, encouragingly, the European Commission has taken the lead in exploiting this new medium's immediacy).

CONCLUSION: FRAMEWORK, NOT PANACEA

'Europe' cannot be a panacea, a remedy for all ailments afflicting our economies and societies. Rather, it provides a framework within which solutions can be explored, with far greater possibilities of success than would be the case in any narrower context. Beyond expediency, the history of our peoples demonstrates that if our states are unable to unite they will be unable to preserve the originality of our cultures in all their richness and diversity. In the absence of unity, Europe cannot be the hearth of any future universal civilisation. This is no dream of neo-nationalism on a continental scale. It *is* a dream, but of participating effectively in the slow and painful construction of a peaceful and just world order based not on the hegemony of the few but on cooperation among freely-constituted regional or continental organisations. The European Union offers, if not a model, then an example of such a regional organisation, as the recent creation of such organisations as NAFTA, MERCOSUR and the D8 show.

NOTES

1 *La dernière utopie. Naissance de l'Europe démocratique*, Flammarion, Paris, 1993.
2 Jean-Louis Quermonne, 1997, *Entre mondialisation et nations. Quelle Europe?*, Bayard, Editions Centurion, Paris, p. 142.
3 It was simultaneously proposed by Elisabeth Guigou and myself. Elisabeth Guigou, 1994, *Pour Les Européens*, Flammarion, Paris, p. 224. Robert Toulemon, 1994, *La Construction Européenne*, Livre de Poche, Références, Paris, p. 204.

REFERENCES

Cohen-Tanugi, Laurent, 1992, *L'Europe en Danger*, Fayard, Paris
Duff, Andrew, 1996, *Reforming the European Union*, Federal Trust, Sweet and Maxwell, London
Gerbet, Pierre, 1994, *La Construction de l'Europe*, Imprimerie National, Paris
Guigou, Elizabeth, 1994, *Pour les européens*, Flammarion, Paris
Manin, Philippe (ed.), 1996, *La révision du traité sur l'Union européenne – Perspectives et réalités*, Pedone, Paris
Monnet, Jean, 1976, *Mémoires*, Fayard, Paris
Morin, Edgar, 1987, *Penser l'Europe*, Gallimard, Paris
Picht, Robert (ed.), 1994, *L'identité européenne*, TEPSA, Presses Interuniversitaires européennes, Brussels
Quermonne, Jean-Louis, 1997, *Entre mondialisation et nations. Quelle Europe?*, Bayard, Editions Centurion, Paris
Sidjanski, Dusan, 1993, *L'avenir fédéraliste de l'Europe*, P.U.F., Paris
Stephanou, Constantin, 1996, *Réforme et institutions de l'Union Européenne*, Bruylant, Brussels
Toulemon, Robert, 1992, *L'Europe – 50 Mots*, Desclée de Brouwer, Paris
—— 1994, *La construction européenne*, Editions de Fallois, Livre de Poche, Références, Paris
Wolton, Dominique, 1993, *La dernière utopie. Naissance de l'Europe démocratique*, Flammarion, Paris

9 Dreams come true, gradually
The Tindemans Report a quarter of a century on

Leo Tindemans

For me, European Union is a new phase in the history of the unification of Europe which can only be achieved by a continuous process. Consequently, it is difficult to lay down ... the date of completion of the European Union. It will only be achieved by means of institutions which have been adapted to its new requirements.

Leo Tindemans, 1975

The classical nation state belongs to yesterday. European Union will not be the outcome of a supranational revolution, nor of an uprooting of frontier posts, but of an acceleration of the fragmentary, functional efforts to achieve Economic and Monetary Union, Social Union and Political Union.

Willy Brandt, 1973

THE ORIGINS OF THE TINDEMANS REPORT

The December 1969 European Summit at the Hague was generally seen as the starting point of a great European revival. To a considerable extent, it was. Rebuffed by his people, an increasingly recalcitrant General de Gaulle had stalked away from power and was soon to die. His successor, Georges Pompidou, was far more amenable to elements of further integration and to the prospect of accession by the United Kingdom. The Heads of State and Government at that momentous summit decided to go way beyond a simple customs union by agreeing, in principle, to create a true Economic and Monetary Union. This was an extraordinary quantum leap in conceptual terms – easy to forget in the post-Maastricht age. In its wake, like the thaw of the polar ice fields in the summer, flowed a series of conceptual corollaries – industrial, regional and social policies, and talk of a social union. The logic was clear – Economic and Monetary Union would be unthinkable without the sort of flanking policies which would, simultaneously, make it workable and acceptable.

Flesh was put on these bare bones with the 1971 Werner Plan for Economic and Monetary Union, the Council adopting a three-stage programme, intended to culminate in the creation of a single currency in 1980. However, following the first oil crisis dollar-gold convertibility ended in August 1971, thus wrecking the whole Bretton Woods monetary system, and the Werner Plan was blown irreversibly off course by the ensuing monetary crisis. The Community again relapsed into a period of gloomy inertia.

In early 1974, I became Prime Minister of Belgium. I had always been an ardent supporter of the European integration process, and this renewed period of inertia worried me. If Europe did not progress, it would regress. A series of ministerial contacts over the summer of 1974 revealed a generalised desire for revival of the Community, particularly with regard to its political aspects. I became convinced that we stood at a turning point. In France, Valéry Giscard d'Estaing had just been elected President, whilst in the German Federal Republic Helmut Schmidt had replaced Willy Brandt as Chancellor. The two – Giscard d'Estaing and Brandt – had struck up a friendship while they had been finance ministers of their respective countries and, with the Franco-German alliance so closely aligned, there was clearly renewed potential for substantial progress. The potential was enhanced by the fact that the French were to hold the rotating Presidency of the Council in the second half of the year. It was what the French would call a *bonne conjoncture*.

In an October 1974 speech at the University of Leuven, I proposed that the Paris summit scheduled for December should appoint a group of three 'wise men', presided over by a Prime Minister in office, with the task of preparing, within one year, concrete proposals defining the contents of the European Union. The speech was designed to provoke debate at the least, and I encouraged this by following it up with a series of bilateral contacts. These included a presentation to the then British Prime Minister, Harold Wilson. He had successfully fought two elections in 1974, but victory had been bought at a price. In particular, Wilson had promised to renegotiate the terms of Britain's accession to the European Economic Community. I was under no illusions; Wilson found the delay implicit in my proposal politically convenient. On the other hand, he was genuinely interested in the mechanics of what I had proposed. He had served an important apprenticeship as assistant to William Beveridge during the drawing up of the famous plan which led to the creation of the British welfare state. Based on this experience, he suggested that the task be entrusted to one man only. Pursuing the political advantage, Wilson succeeded in convincing his continental counterparts about the desirability of my proposal and, in particular, Giscard d'Estaing, who absorbed it as a third element in his Paris summit strategy, the general aim of which was to create a European *relance*.

The December 1974 Paris summit duly agreed to the two primary elements in Giscard's plan. The first of these was to proceed to direct elections to the European Parliament, a measure envisaged by the founding fathers but which had been repeatedly blocked since the early 1960s. The second was to institutionalise the European summits in the form of a new organ, the European Council. Thus, on the one hand, the democratic nature of the Community was to be reinforced and, on the other, an overarching executive was to be created to resolve sectoral turf wars in the Council of Ministers and to determine the broad guidelines of Community action. The latter, a direct (and intergovernmental) threat to the role of the supranational Commission, was counterbalanced by the former, a reinforcement of the role of the supranational Parliament. It remained to put these reforms into their wider context, and to impart to the Community the coherence and dynamism it so badly needed. Thus, in the communiqué issued at the end of the summit, the Heads of Government stated that:

> the time has come for the Nine to agree as soon as possible on an overall concept of European Union. Consequently, in accordance with requests made by the Paris meeting of Heads of Government in October 1972, they ... request the European Assembly, the Commission and the Court of Justice to bring the submission of their reports forward to before the end of June 1975. They agreed to invite Mr Tindemans, Prime Minister of the Kingdom of Belgium, to submit a comprehensive report to the Heads of Government before the end of 1975, on the basis of the reports received from the institutions and of consultations which he is to have with the governments and with a wide range of public opinion in the Community.
>
> EC Bulletin, 12/1974

DRAFTING THE REPORT

The task entrusted to me was a considerable one. Where I had initially envisaged a team effort the summit, under Wilson's influence, had mandated me with a personal mission. I was to draw my inspiration from a series of privileged interlocutors – the other European institutions, and I was also to consult with the governments. But by far the most original – and democratic – aspect of my mission was the requirement that I should consult with 'a wide range of public opinion'. This implied a vast amount of work – all in addition to my duties as Prime Minister, and I badly needed an assistant. My choice fell on Jacques Vandamme.

Jacques possessed many appropriate qualities in a unique combination. He was a lawyer by training and profession, but had become a specialist in social policy and had an economist's brain. He was, at one and the same time, an ardent idealist and a supreme pragmatist, a patriot and a federalist. He was a Francophone by birth and a Flemish militant by conviction. He spoke fluent English and German. He had a mix of diplomatic skills and a politician's instincts. He was extraordinarily dynamic, and there was a sense of urgency about him. He was, in all respects, the man for the job, and he was to remain by my side throughout the consultation and drafting processes. We have been European comrades in arms ever since.

Once all of my consultations were complete and all of the written contributions had been assembled and digested, I realised that I faced a fundamental choice about what strategy I should adopt. I agonised for a long time before coming to a conclusion. The 1970s were not the 1950s. The idea of drafting a Spaak-type report seemed unrealistic, and therefore unproductive, to me, and I did not really consider the option. At the same time, I faced a genuine choice between a more idealistic and a more pragmatic approach. To use Jacques' own words, the more idealistic approach (to which Jacques himself tended) would have been;

> to make a report relying on the majority tendency which had emerged from the 'popular consultation', and which was in favour of substantially strengthening the European construction, with regards both to the powers and the working of the institutions. Such a report would have identified the new challenges facing the Community, and the solutions with which to deal with them, in the short and medium term. It would have been a kind of 'message' to the European people, looking further afield than the immediate prospects.
>
> Vandamme, 1989, p. 158

As I wrote to my European Council colleagues, I was strongly aware that 'almost all the people to whom I spoke stated that they could not imagine a better future for their country than that offered by the building of Europe'. Alas, I was also forced to recognise that '(p)ublic opinion is extremely sceptical on the will to establish a genuine European Union and solve the real problems of the day at European level' (Tindemans, 1976a, p. 7). In the 1974–5 period the EEC was beset by economic depression and high levels of unemployment. Though my belief in the need for European Union was undimmed, my political instincts told me that this was not the moment to proselytise. 'This', I explained

> was the reason why I deliberately refused to draw up a report claiming to be, at least in part, the Constitution for the future European Union. Nor did I wish to describe what Europe ideally should be, while remaining personally convinced that Europe will only fulfil its destiny if it espouses federalism. . . . My proposals do not directly concern the final phase of European development. They state the objectives and the methods whereby Europe can be invested with a new vitality and current obstacles can be overcome. My choice is based on the belief that at the present time any other approach would either be unworthy of our faith in Europe, or else, because of its utopian nature in the present circumstances, would lose all credibility with the parties in power. Consequently, it represents a realistic yet feasible approach.
>
> Tindemans, 1976a, p. 8

THE INITIAL FOLLOW-UP

The 1974 Hague Summit had called for an 'overall concept of European Union'. My 1975 report gave the Heads of State 'an overall picture of the European Union and of the means of achieving it' (1976b, p. 34). I shall consider the substance of those proposals below, but an immediate question arose; how could I get the member states to act on my recommendations? In the general conclusion to the report I set out a four-step procedure. In the first place, I called for the governments and European institutions to arrive at a 'political consensus on the aims and main features of the Union in terms which give expression to the deep aspirations of our peoples'. In the second place, I called for them to determine 'the consequences of this choice in the various areas of the Union's internal and external activities'. I then asked them to set in motion, 'by positive action in each of those fields, the dynamic process of attaining the Union'. Last and not least, I asked them to strengthen the 'institutional machinery to enable it to cope with the tasks awaiting it' (1976b, p. 35).

It is easy to be wise with hindsight. The European Council was then a very young institution whose role and functions were not yet entirely clear. I had fulfilled my mandate and, in submitting my report, I had proposed to the European Council a step-by-step strategy which would, I hoped, build on the recommendations contained in the report. In proposing the first step, I was consciously bowing to the pre-eminent role of the governments, since I genuinely believed that they had to be involved in any exercise to give expression to the 'deep aspirations of our peoples'. However, I had reckoned without the Council of Ministers and its preparatory bodies which, although I had addressed myself to the European Council, was where my report and its recommendations were discussed throughout 1976. Predictably, these discussions soon got bogged down on such sensitive matters as majority voting in political cooperation, economic and monetary cooperation, proposed increases in the powers of the European Parliament, and the nomination procedure for the President of the European Commission. The big picture was lost.

The year 1976 saw persistent economic and financial difficulties, so that ministers themselves were distracted. It was hardly the moment for *grands projets*. At the same time, understandably, the Luxembourg and Dutch Presidencies of 1976 did not share my proprietorial interest in the report's recommendations. The year 1976 also saw the realisation of another of the twin *volets* of Giscard d'Estaing's original 1974 European policy when, on 20 September, the Act concerning the election of representatives of the European Parliament by direct universal suffrage was signed in Brussels. Here was a concrete, and entirely laudable, measure in line, indeed, with the institutional improvements I had recommended. But in the short term the Community seemed ready to settle for this alone, whereas my report had recommended much more.

In fact, I was forced to recognise that real negotiations of the sort I had envisaged seemed increasingly improbable. Ultimately, the November 1976 Hague European Council declared the report to be of 'great interest' and recognised the necessity of arriving in due course at a 'comprehensive and coherent common political approach'. But the only immediate practical outcome was an invitation to the Council and the Commission to produce an annual report on progress achieved.

If, in the 1977–9 period, anyone had asked me to describe the results consequent on my report on European Union, then I would have been forced to acknowledge that, despite my decision to favour the pragmatic over the idealistic approach, the concrete results of all of my efforts had been minimal. In large part I believe, in retrospect, that this was because the initiative I had gained through the *bonne conjoncture* of 1974 was lost in the *mauvaise conjoncture* of 1976. At the time, this seemed an immensely frustrating end to a great deal of effort. What I did not realise then, and what time alone would demonstrate, was that many of the recommendations in my report would later come true . . .

THE RECOMMENDATIONS

The pragmatic approach I had decided to adopt in my report disappointed militant Europeans in more ways than one, and although a large majority of the February 1976 Congress of the European Movement in Brussels took note of the report's recommendations with approval, that approval was not unconditional. The recommendation which caused most controversy came in a chapter of the report devoted to European economic and social policies. I pointed out that '(i)t is impossible at the present time to submit a credible programme of action if it is deemed absolutely necessary that in every case all stages should be reached by all States at the same time. . . . were we to insist on this progress would be impossible and Europe would continue to crumble away.' I therefore argued that 'those States which are able to progress have a duty to forge ahead' (Tindemans, 1976b, p. 20). I will not enter into a detailed analysis of the ramifications of this recommendation, particularly since in Chapter 6 Wolfgang Wessels provides an extensive comparative analysis of what is now known as the concept of 'flexibility' or 'enhanced cooperation'. But I should point out that the concept has been with us since the Treaty of Rome; in particular, Article 233 allowed for both the Benelux organisation and the Belgium–Luxembourg Economic Union. Some saw in my recommendation the thin end of the wedge of a '*Europe à la carte*', despite the specific denial in the report (1976b, p. 21). If thin end there was, it began in 1957, and not in 1975!

Whatever the argument about the past, the future – in the form of the 1993 Maastricht Treaty's provisions on Economic and Monetary Union – was to provide just the sort of differentiated integration I had envisaged. Yet, frankly, how could it have been otherwise? As I wrote in 1975, '(t)he divergence of (member states') economic and financial states is such that, were we to insist . . . progress would be impossible and Europe would

136 *Leo Tindemans*

continue to crumble away' (1976b, p. 20). It seemed to me then, as it seems to me now, to be a self-evident logical truth. The Maastricht Treaty's Economic and Monetary Union provisions may have sought to encourage and even to enforce convergence. But it would never have been anything other than miraculous for all fifteen member states to satisfy the convergence criteria within the 1997–9 period and that is why – leaving the exceptions of the United Kingdom and Danish opt-ins to one side – the draftsmen made explicit provision for staggered entrance to the third stage. Was this not, in effect, what the Report on European Union had recommended almost twenty years previously?

Economic and monetary union was one of five components listed in the report's overall 'package' of recommendations. The other four were: presenting a united front to the outside world; regional and social policies; enhancing the rights of the European citizen; and reforming the institutions. For me, revisiting the recommendations of the report has been a deeply illuminating experience. Box 9.1 sets out a selection of the main recommendations with regard to a common front. The Union may still be far from a truly unified external policy but, as the box shows (the information in brackets), much of what the Report recommended has either since been realised, or has at least been broached in some way. Boxes 9.2–4 provide similar information about the other main components of the Report.

Box 9.1 Recommendations from the Tindemans Report on External Policy

---

'a united front in world discussions' . . . 'an external policy' . . . 'a comprehensive and coherent outlook'

A common foreign policy with general policy guidelines laid down by the European Council (Maastricht Treaty – Title V) and majority decision-making in the Council (Amsterdam Treaty).

A united front at multilateral trade negotiations (e.g. Uruguay Round of GATT talks leading to the creation of the World Trade Organisation).

A common reflection of the character and scope of relations between the European Union and the United States (December 1995 New Transatlantic Agenda and action plan – approved by the EU and the US).

Regular exchanges of views on defence policy (Maastricht Treaty – declaration no. 30 on the WEU, Amsterdam Treaty).

Cooperation on armaments manufacture (27 July 1995 Council decision to establish an ad hoc working group to examine options for a European arms policy, 24 January 1996 Commission Communication on defence-related industries).

Dreams come true, gradually 137

Box 9.2 Recommendations from the Tindemans Report on Economic and Social Policy

---

Revival of plans for economic and monetary union (Single European Act, Maastricht Treaty).
Pursuing such Community objectives as opening up markets (White Paper, Single European Act).
Enhanced common research policy (Single European Act, Maastricht Treaty).
Enhanced social policy (Single European Act, 1989 Social Charter, Social Protocol to the Maastricht Treaty, Amsterdam Treaty).
Enhanced role for standing committee on employment (Amsterdam Treaty Article 6 – creation of Employment Committee).
Enhanced regional policy (Single European Act, 1988 Structural Fund reform, Maastricht Treaty and creation of the Cohesion Fund).

Box 9.3 Recommendations from the Tindemans Report on a Citizens' Europe

---

'Europe must be closer to its citizens' (Adonnino Report, 1984, Maastricht Treaty).
Respect for and guarantee of fundamental rights (Amsterdam Treaty amendment to Article F).
Consumer rights (Maastricht Treaty – Articles 3s and 129a, Amsterdam Treaty).
Environment policy (Single European Act, Maastricht Treaty, Amsterdam Treaty).
The gradual disappearance of frontier controls (Single European Act, Schengen, Amsterdam Treaty).
Improved transport and communications (Maastricht Treaty, Amsterdam Treaty).
Greater integration in educational matters (Single European Act – mutual recognition, Maastricht Treaty).
Information policy (1995 and 1997 Commission reforms – though chiefly internal to DG X, European Parliament-inspired priority information actions).

138 *Leo Tindemans*

Box 9.4 Recommendations from the Tindemans Report on Institutional Reform

> Gradual increase in the European Parliament's powers 'in the course of the progressive development of the European Union' (1979 direct elections, 1980 Isoglucose Court decision, Single European Act, Maastricht Treaty, Amsterdam Treaty).
> Annual parliamentary debate on the state of the Union (Maastricht Treaty, Article D – derived debate in Parliament, Declaration no. 15 – report to the Conference of Presidents – currently defunct).
> Right for the European Parliament to consider all matters (no longer contested).
> European Council to lay down general policy guidelines (1983 Stuttgart Solemn Declaration, Single European Act, Maastricht Treaty, Amsterdam Treaty).
> General Affairs Council to coordinate Council work (1983 Stuttgart Solemn Declaration).
> Abolish the distinction between European Political Cooperation and the Council (Maastricht Treaty).
> When nominated, the Commission President should appear before the Parliament (1983 Stuttgart Solemn Declaration, Maastricht Treaty, Amsterdam Treaty).
> More coherent delegation of executive power (Single European Act, 1986 'comitology' decision, Amsterdam Treaty declaration).

It is striking just how much has since come to pass. In many areas (the Parliament's powers in relation to the appointment of the Commission and its President, for example), the integrative process has gone far beyond the steps envisaged in my report. This is perhaps the most encouraging aspect of such an assessment exercise, for it will be recalled that I deliberately opted to set out attainable courses of action which would, in turn enable further integration to take place.

LESSONS DRAWN

Over the past two years, I have felt a distinct sense of *déjà vu*. In 1995–6, I headed a group of politicians, civil servants and experts (the so-called 'Tindemans Group') which was given the task of identifying the various options open to the European Union in the run-up to the 1996–7 Intergovernmental Conference and of explaining them in accessible form to the public at large (Tindemans, 1996). A little more recently, in the first half of 1997, I was the author of a parliamentary report on the formulation of perspectives for the common security policy of the European Union

(Tindemans, 1997). In relation to both reports I like to think that I was able to bring to bear my experience in drafting the Report on European Union just over two decades before. In particular, I feel that I learnt four important lessons.

The first concerns the organic and evolutionary nature of the integration process, as described by Westlake in Chapter 2, and the natural restraints this places on the strategic choices facing integrationists. Some of the more fierce criticism of the 1975 report came from those who believed that I had made a fundamental error in opting for a pragmatic, incremental approach. For example, a Dutch critic declared that:

> It did not, as many had hoped, lay down a ready-formulated concept, to be carried out in stages, which the governments would have subscribed to, as had happened in the past with the Spaak–Beyen Report, which culminated in the EEC Treaty.
>
> Metzemaackers, 1976

Having spoken at length with them all, I do not believe that, at that time, a majority of governments wanted or expected a Spaak–Beyen-style report. Leaving this to one side, however, all of my experience since then has served to convince me that the strategy of identifying relatively small but attainable steps was, and mostly continues to be, the right one for the European Union.[1] Much as I would like to see a definitive federal union materialise overnight, I do not believe that it can happen or, at least, not in one sudden, gigantic step. If we were closer to some sort of popular high tide in support for the federalist model in the 1940s and 1950s, we were undoubtedly further away in 1974–5, and we are indisputably yet further away now. The same observation could be made about the majority of member state governments. The scope and the complexity of the negotiations at the Amsterdam European Council demonstrated how unlikely it was that a majority of governments might support a major constitutional conference leading to a fixed settlement. At the same time, an incremental strategy has much to commend it, particularly in the context of an unprecedented constitutional experiment in sharing (previously jealously guarded) national sovereignties. As Westlake writes in Chapter 2, we are 'making haste slowly'.

I should stress that this is not to argue against the Spaak method *per se*. Indeed, in my 1997 report on a common security policy for the European Union I called for a 'Messina-style' conference to discuss the possible content of a common defence policy and the implications of incorporating the Western European Union into the European Union. But there is a difference between urging the member states forward in one specific area, where the lapsing of the 1948 Brussels Treaty which created the Western European Union obliges the member states to take some sort of action in any case, and a broader constitutional conference which would question everything. I sympathise with Pinder's argument, set out in Chapter 4, that the European Parliament might be able to force the issue by using its assent powers in relation to enlargement to force a constitutional conference, but this seems an unlikely possibility. As Boxes 9.1–4 demonstrate, dreams *do* come true, but gradually.

The second lesson which I learned from my wide-ranging consultations is as applicable today as it was in 1975. We must get the people back on board! My consultations uncovered widespread, general support for the building of Europe. I have no doubt that roughly similar levels of support exist today (the latest *Eurobarometer* opinion poll shows support hovering around the fifty per cent mark), but we cannot take anything for granted. Above all, we should not mistake benign acquiescence for positive support. If we believe that integration is in the interests of the European citizen, we cannot just blithely assume that the citizen will acquiesce in the cavalier adoption of integrationist strategies by our governments and parliaments. We must spell out what we are doing and why. This largely forgotten pedagogic duty is rightly emphasised by Toulemon in Chapter 8. I do not believe that people are naturally anti-integrationist, but they *are* naturally sceptical of government. Research has shown that levels of support for integration grow in parallel with levels of knowledge. People cannot support what they do not know. It is imperative that the European Union should better inform its people about its decisions and activities and about the reasons behind them. There are two counterparts to this. The first is that the Union must not only act effectively but must be *seen* to be acting effectively. The second is that the Union must address the real needs and concerns of its citizens.

The third lesson I learned was that those of us who believe in a federal destiny must keep the debate going. I do not only mean that we must keep the flame of faith burning, but that we must seek always to set the terms of debate and, through the force of our arguments, convince the decision-makers of the day to keep to the integrationist path. In 1997, as in 1975, most of Europe is beset by economic recession, structural unemployment, and declining competitiveness in many sectors. As I wrote in 1975;

> The construction of Europe is the only all-inclusive answer to this challenge; it derives spontaneously from the wills of our peoples as embodied in the work of the Founding Fathers of Europe. It is the only answer which seeks everywhere to regain some of the control and power which is slipping from us, and to enable us to build the society in which we want to live.
>
> Tindemans, 1976b, p. 35

This leads on to the fourth lesson. I cannot claim that there is any direct causal link between the proposals in the Report on European Union and the later developments set out in Boxes 9.1–4, but I can say that those recommendations seemed to me to form a logical whole. What the experience of the past twenty-odd years has taught me is that my report was just part of a greater context, that the integrative process contains its own inexorable logic, and that my report reflected that logic. The strength of that inherent logic is demonstrated in the way that the Union has evolved along broadly the lines which were set out in my report. The Italians have a saying; *da cose nasce cose* – one thing leads to another. Even a casual glance at the many developments which have taken place since the Hague summits of 1969 and 1974 will show how very much this saying holds true for the European Union.

NOTE

1 For example, Helmut Kohl, then President of the German CDU, was very supportive of the decision I had taken. He argued that there was no alternative to the step-by-step method, and judged the proposals in the report to be realistic, constructive, and immediately applicable (Vandamme, 1989, p. 164).

REFERENCES

Metzemaackers, L., 1976, 'Het Tindemans rapport: Samenvatting en karakteristiek', *Nieuw Europa*, 1

Pryce, Roy (ed.), 1989, *The Dynamics of European Union*, Routledge, London

Tindemans, Leo, 1976a, 'Letter to European Council colleagues', sent on 29 December 1975, annexed to Tindemans, 1976b

—— 1976b, 'European Union. Report by Mr Leo Tindemans, Prime Minister of Belgium, to the European Council', *Bulletin of the European Communities*, Supplement 1/76

—— 1996, *Quelle Europe Choisir?*, Groupe Tindemans, Brussels

—— 1997, Report on the Formulation of Perspectives for the Common Foreign and Security Policy of the European Union, Session Document A4–0162/97, 23 April

Vandamme, Jacques, 1981, 'L'Union européenne et le Rapport Tindemans', *Studia Diplomatica*, vol. XXXIV, no. 1–4

—— 1989, 'The Tindemans Report', in Pryce, Roy (ed.), op. cit.

10 European federalism
Opportunity or Utopia?[1]

Jacques Vandamme

The questions of forty years ago are as relevant now as they were then. What does the European integration process mean? Where are we heading? And with what implications? In this chapter I shall attempt some sort of a personal answer to these questions. I will briefly review some of those developments in integration theory which have sought to interpret the emerging European system and hence to give answers to the above questions, before moving on to give my own view about the probable future of the European Union.

THEORIES OF EUROPEAN INTEGRATION

The 1940s and 1950s saw wide-ranging debate on the future of Europe. According to the 'statists', traditional forms of cooperation between independent states, on the model of the Council of Europe or the OEEC (later to become the OECD), were sufficient. Others, thinking on federal lines, believed contrarily that it was essential to devise new relationships between states. In particular, they believed that in certain well-defined areas they should hand over part of their sovereignty to common institutions, entrusted with management tasks in the interest of all participants.

Between 1951 and 1954, adherents of the federalist view witnessed a series of developments which encouraged them in the hope that Western Europe might finally develop into a federal state. The 1951 establishment of the European Coal and Steel Community (ECSC) was a notable first step, with six countries deciding to place their coal and steel production under a central authority with its own real powers, albeit restricted to one sector of the economy. (It should however be recalled that the primary motivation for the ECSC was *not* economic in nature. The main purpose of the 1951 Treaty of Paris was to place Franco-German reconciliation on a firm and irreversible foundation.)

In 1952, only shortly after the ECSC Treaty came into force, a new idea arose; the creation of a joint European defence through the integration of national armed forces. The agreement to establish the European Defence Community – based on the institutional model of the ECSC – was signed at the end of May 1953 by the six governments of the ECSC member states. Work immediately started on preparing a treaty to establish a political community which would have had almost all the features of a nascent federal constitution and which was intended to be a crowning achievement. But the ambitious project came to nothing when, on 30 August 1954, the French Parliament refused to ratify the draft treaty.

The Assemblée Nationale's refusal dashed the expectations of those who had hoped to be able to usher in at an early date such a new era in the history of the European peoples. It also temporarily closed down the conceptual debate about what might be the most desirable and appropriate form of institutional cooperation in Western Europe to enable the Continent to meet the major challenges of the second half of the twentieth century.

Some might infer, from the failure of these early moves to create a European Defence Community, that all of the developments which followed – the 1957 creation of the European Economic Community and the European Atomic Energy Community in particular – were forms of cooperation whose ascendants could be traced back directly to earlier types of inter-state relations. I do not believe this to have been the case.

In fact, the European Economic Community was a political compromise, not so much between advocates of inter-state cooperation and advocates of federalism but, rather, between two groups of pragmatists. On the one hand, there were those advocating the creation of a large market which, in economic terms, would replace national markets, beginning with the creation of a customs union. On the other hand, there were those advocating the partial integration of certain sectors, such as agriculture, nuclear energy and transport, and the transfer to the Community of a limited number of policy areas, such as a common trade policy and competition policy. Under this compromise, the states would retain their autonomy with regard to foreign policy and economic and social policy, and policy coordination in these areas would not go beyond what was considered necessary to achieve the Community's objectives.

The result was a system of partial and limited transfer of sovereignty, memorably described by the Court of Justice:

> Whereas the Member States have agreed to establish a Community for an indefinite period, provided with permanent institutions which are vested with actual powers as a result of the fact that the States have limited their powers or transferred them to the Community.
>
> Case 6/64 [1964] ECR 1159

Interpretations of the significance of this partial integration vary. For the so-called 'functionalists', beginning with a few specific and strictly limited areas where a common approach was acceptable to the participating states would lead ultimately and almost inexorably, because of the 'spill-over' effect, to federation. This would be, as Walter Hallstein put it, federation through 'force of circumstances'; from customs union to common market; from common market to economic union and, later, monetary union. The basic elements of national sovereignty would be progressively undermined, gradually assuring the transition to a federal state.

For others, the newly-established system already embodied maximum concessions to the concept of integration and there could be no question of any further transfers of sovereignty, unless these were the result of explicit agreements between the contracting states. This minimalist interpretation was particularly popular in France in the late 1950s. General de Gaulle, it will be recalled, had returned to power in April 1958, just four months after the EEC Treaty had come into force. He immediately summoned the most important ministers in his government and, referring to the newly-born EEC, told them that he would not 'call your trade treaty into question'.

The view reflected in his memoirs was more subtle. Looking back, he wrote that his policy had been aimed at establishing harmony among European states. By developing links of any and all kinds, solidarity among them would increase. 'On this basis there is nothing', he wrote, 'to prevent the possibility, particularly if they are all faced with the same threat, that evolution might lead on to confederation.' Whatever de Gaulle's hindsight might have led him to write, the basic idea remained the same. At most, he favoured the idea of states working increasingly closely together, perhaps leading to a confederation in the longer term.

INTERPRETING THE COMMUNITY SYSTEM

What does the experience of the partial, somewhat equivocal, integration of 1958 onwards teach us about these two different systems? How best may we judge the way the Community/Union has evolved over the past thirty years? Are there better ways of understanding what has occurred so far and what may still occur in the development of this as yet incomplete Union? To repeat a commonplace observation, integration is a process and not a condition. It is as important to consider the nature of legal development as it is to consider the status of the law.

Functionalism and its weaknesses

The apparent success of the step-by-step evolution from customs union to common market gave the impression that the functional approach might indeed be the key to progress. This impression continued until the early 1970s, when the failure of the 1970 Werner Plan for the step-by-step realisation of economic and monetary union inevitably brought into question the whole functionalist logic. (It should perhaps be recalled that the Werner proposals, approved by the Council of Ministers and the representatives of the member states on 21 March 1971, were accompanied by a formal decision to establish Economic and Monetary Union in stages over a ten-year period. At the end of that period it was envisaged that there would be a federal system of central banks and an – ill-defined – centre for economic decision-making. Few questions were posed, at that time, about the legal implications of these envisaged developments.)

Whatever the reasons which led to the Werner Plan being blown so badly off course, it is clear that functionalists generally failed to take adequate account of what Stanley Hoffman described as 'the ability of national bureaucracies to resist the transfer of power' (1982), and of the inertial desire of states to retain control of 'high politics'. Functionalist and neo-functionalist theorists also paid too little attention to the political efforts which would be necessary for the achievement of a technical, economic, step-by-step approach:

> The neo-functionalists appeared strangely uninterested in evaluating how far any particular functions needed to be performed by supra-national institutions ... Nor did the neo-functionalists seem much concerned about the form of democratic control by European institutions that can be seen as a corollary of the most far-reaching transfers of competence.
>
> Pinder, 1986, p. 51

Inter-state cooperation

The relative failure of functionalist theory does not mean that the European treaties should be interpreted as simply a new form of cooperation between states – far from it. In the first place, repeated rulings of the Court of Justice have emphasised both the primacy and the autonomy of the Community order in a system of partial transfer, with direct applicability, of competence. One of my Leuven University colleagues, Koen Lenaerts, convincingly argued that, because of the unanimity requirement in Article 100 (**94**), the Community consisted effectively of a confederal system of legislation, accompanied by the quasi-federal actions of the Court of Justice. (Lenaerts' conclusion was that such a hybrid system was untenable in the longer term and that the departures from it, as represented by the Single European Act and the Maastricht Treaty, were necessary and inevitable – Lenaerts, 1988.) As Joseph Weiler has remarked, 'What is remarkable in Europe is the high level of compliance, the automatic acceptance of Community supremacy and Community obligations in almost all cases, even against the interests of the governments concerned' (Weiler, 1988).

The Single European Act seemed to revive the school of inter-state cooperation. Baroness Thatcher – 'Our Lady of Bruges', as she was dubbed in these parts – became the school's principal spokeswoman, championing the argument that 'willing and active cooperation between sovereign states is the best way to build a successful European Community':

> I am the first to say that on many great issues Europe should try to speak with a single voice. I want to see the countries of Europe work more closely on the things we can do better together than alone. Europe is

stronger when we do so, whether it be in trade, defence or in our relations with the rest of the world.

Thatcher, 1988

Lady Thatcher went on to argue that 'working more closely together does not require all power to be centralised and decisions to be taken by bureaucrats'. She was thus referring not only to the politics but to the management of the Community. In the case of the latter, the federal doctrine does not require everything to be centralised. On the contrary, the essence of federalism lies in the decentralisation of authority and the distribution of the broadest possible powers to the lowest possible levels, in accordance with the now ubiquitous principle of subsidiarity.

In fact, none of the earlier schools of thought – from functionalism through to inter-state cooperation – could offer an entirely convincing analytical interpretation of the Community/Union system, where allowance must simultaneously be made for the specific legal legitimacy conferred by the Court of Justice and the political legitimacy which, since the 1979 direct elections to the European Parliament, has involved not only the states but also the peoples.

International regime theory

International regime theory was principally developed by American authors, notably Stanley Hoffman (for a general discussion, see Breckinridge, 1997), in the literature of the 1970s and early 1980s. It portrayed the then European Economic Community as consisting of something more than a typical exercise in international cooperation, but involving less than full-blooded integration:

> It is a set of norms of behaviour and of rules and policies covering a broad range of issues, dealing both with procedures and with substance, and facilitating agreements among the members. From the viewpoint of the participants, such a regime provides both restraints and opportunities. It limits the State's freedom of unilateral action. But it provides the participant with external support.
>
> Hoffman, 1982, p. 33

Such an interpretation was understandable in the situation of relative political and institutional stagnation which characterised the Community in the 1970s and the earlier 1980s. It had the considerable advantage of considering the significance of the inter-state dimension from a new, modern perspective, beginning with an analysis of the role and the function of the nation state in modern society. However, such an interpretation did not allow for the internal dynamics of the system; for example, the quest for regime-legitimacy including, in that specific context, the burgeoning role of the directly elected Parliament. The theory also neglected the achievements made in monitoring the application of Community law by the Court of Justice.

Cooperative federalism

This theoretical model gradually gained ground in the United States during the second half of the nineteenth century. According to the model, the constitution gives Congress the power to regulate national affairs of 'interstate commerce'. In such areas, the states may not intervene, although Congress can authorise the states to regulate in certain areas. In the EEC/EU context, only limited powers are assigned to the Community, while the states are prohibited from doing certain things, unless obliged to harmonise legislation. As another Leuven University colleague, Henri Brugmans, once notably remarked, 'European federalism is federalism in reverse'.

The characterisation of the European integration process as cooperative federalism attracted many adherents in Europe, particularly in Germany. For example, Wolfgang Wessels described how:

> By the term 'cooperative federalism' we mean the 'pooling' and 'mixing' of national sovereignty with Community competences. In a system of cooperative federalism, the two levels (in our case the Community and the national) are not clearly separated in terms of their areas of action. By contrast, the traditional notion of federalism implies that each level operates on its own without taking into account the other level. In a cooperative federalist system, both levels share in the responsibility for problem solving.
>
> Speech delivered at the European University Institute, Florence, 1985

This interpretation surely stemmed in part from a descriptive analysis of the way in which the relationship between the member states and the Community had evolved over the preceding twenty years, characterised by conflicting state policy aims. On the one hand, states have felt a need to broaden the scope of Community activities in order to help them fulfil their public service function (for example, effective environmental policy entirely restricted to a single member state is a nonsense – collective action is obviously necessary to deal with such phenomena as acid rain or the greenhouse effect). On the other hand, the same states have been extremely reluctant to relinquish their powers of policy control and supervision.

Wessels believes that the modern welfare state system (together with its public service function) is now firmly re-established and that there is therefore little willingness to replace it with an independent European system. Almost twenty years before, Stanley Hoffman had already described how the Community system had, in effect, revived the threatened nation state; 'the EEC regime has served not only to preserve the nation states but paradoxically to regenerate them' (Hoffman, 1982, p. 35).

The limited integrative function posited by the theory of cooperative federalism, if taken together with the apparent consolidation of the nation state, are twin factors which any theory must now take into account. But cooperative integration can be criticised on normative grounds. Would not such a system, with all of its checks and limitations, lead to a kind of permanent negotiation between the states and the Community, between national and European bureaucrats? In such a system democratic legitimacy would be entirely absent and democratic institutions – the European Parliament above all – would lose out.

WHAT FUTURE?

To what extent are these theories and interpretations relevant to the future of the European Union and to its further expansion? Three elements should be considered here. The first is the concept of the European Union itself. The second concerns proposals for the granting of a constitutional mandate to the European Parliament. The third concerns the experiments embodied in the Single European Act and the Maastricht Treaty and, most recently, the Amsterdam Treaty.

The European Union

Paradoxically, the more the term 'European Union' is used, the more amorphous it becomes. Some argue that this is an advantage; 'European Union' means whatever you want it to mean, and can thus be used without giving offence to anybody. Contrarily, others would argue that because it has lost whatever precision it might have had its usage should be dropped. This reasoning coincides with the argument of those who might be termed the 'pragmatic progressionists' – those who favour progress but hope that it can be done without provoking offence among politicians in those member states sensitive to the use of such a potently significant term as 'European Union'.

The European Parliament's 1984 Draft Treaty Establishing the European Union (the so-called 'Spinelli Treaty' – European Parliament, 1984) undoubtedly went furthest in its conceptual use of the term. Many commentators felt that the Spinelli Treaty was a true model of a European constitution. Among the draft Treaty's innovations were provisions relating to the division between competing and exclusive powers of states and the Community which emulated, if they did not quite match, those of fully-fledged federal systems. On the other hand, the draft Treaty displayed pragmatism in distinguishing between matters for cooperation between the states and those which would fall within the Community's competences. The draft Treaty envisaged that the European Council, as the supreme intergovernmental body, would be entrusted with deciding whether to switch, in certain areas, from inter-state cooperation to the Community system.

The 1975 Tindemans Report on European Union was more modest in its ambitions. Although a number of the concepts Tindemans considered necessary to European Union were listed and analysed, the term itself was not defined. The overall approach of the Report implied strongly that European Union should be considered as a new step in the integration process, starting with political decisions (rather than treaties) that qualitative progress should be made in certain areas – external relations, internal development and the institutions – which at a later date would be converted into binding rules. Most commentators hesitated to define such an approach as being federalist, seeing it at most as an intermediate stage. This echoed Tindeman's logic:

> I deliberately refused to draw up a report claiming to be, at least in part, the Constitution for the future European Union. Nor did I wish to describe what Europe ideally should be, while remaining personally convinced that Europe will only fulfil its destiny if it espouses federalism. . . . My proposals do not directly concern the final phase of European development. They state the objectives and the methods whereby Europe can be invested with a new vitality and current obstacles can be overcome. . . . Consequently, it represents a realistic yet feasible approach.
>
> Tindemans, 1976, pp. 5–6

Any cumulative definition of European Union would also have to include the 19 July 1983 Stuttgart solemn declaration of the Heads of State or Government on European Union which, in vague wording, urges deepening and broadening but, above all, places the emphasis on the institutionalisation and expansion of the tasks of the European Council, a quintessentially inter-governmental body.

The draftsmen of the 1986 Single European Act contented themselves with a general cross-reference to the 1983 Stuttgart Solemn Declaration. The 1993 Maastricht Treaty created the European Union as a Treaty-based term, but fell far short of defining what it was supposed to be. Article A (**1**) gave its foundation and objectives in very broad terms, whilst Articles B and C (**2** and **3**) set out the Union's aims in general terms. The 1997 Amsterdam Treaty went little further.

From all of the foregoing, it seems clear that the concept of European Union remains a loose political objective, a multi-faceted concept comprising both substantial and institutional progress in terms of integration, but which still falls short of the federal model. It is, at most, a political and legal unity which is aimed at evolving into a federal state. Federalists have found this sort of definition increasingly useful; as the prospect of a 'one-stop-shop' constitutional settlement has faded, so the attractiveness of step-by-step development has grown. But as Pinder has pointed out, the federalists generally failed to allow for intermediate stages 'between normal inter-state relations and normal intra-state relations'. They have traditionally placed too much emphasis on the constitutional process laid down in acts, and not enough on the evolutionary process described by Westlake in Chapter 1.

The European Parliament

In the 1950s, one of the European Parliament's direct ascendants was co-opted into becoming a Treaty draftsman and the Parliament has rarely lost the habit since then. The 1984 draft Treaty establishing the European Union was but one of a series of examples of blueprints drawn up by the Parliament over the past twelve years (the others include the 1989 Herman Report, the 1991 Martin Reports, and the 1996 Bourlanges/Mendez de Vigo Report).

One of the particularities of the 1989 Herman Report was its invitation to the member state Governments to hand over to the Parliament the task, after the June 1989 European elections, of formulating a new draft Treaty. Needless to say, the member state Governments did not follow the Parliament's invitation. Subsequently, in the run-up to the 1996–1997 Intergovernmental Conference, the Parliament uncharacteristically decided against adopting a draft constitution, preferring instead to adopt a relatively brief 'shopping list' of constitutional and institutional demands. Although the lack of draft Treaty provisions may have been only a temporary step back, based on astute readings of the political situation at the time, the prospect of the European Parliament ever fulfilling the role of constituent assembly seems distant.

On the other hand, Parliament's role as an inveterate drafter of constitutional blueprints should not be underestimated. The ability, metaphorically speaking, to take a step back and to look at the overall picture is a rare privilege and one which, unfortunately, the participants at intergovernmental conferences and European Councils rarely, if ever, enjoy. Nor should the benefits of such exercises be underestimated. It was the Parliament, after all, which first introduced the now ubiquitous concept of subsidiarity into the EU's lexicon (in its 1984 draft Treaty).

However, there is irony in the Parliament's previous insistence that it would be best placed to draft the ultimate Treaty – effectively to act as the Union's constituent assembly. Whereas, under the theoretical approach of cooperative federalism, the Parliament would have been all but excluded, with the parliamentary constitutional approach it would be the member states which would find themselves excluded from the constituent process. Both extremes seem highly unlikely developments. In normative terms they would also be highly undesirable. Legitimacy must be assured by both peoples and states. Hence, even if the Parliament is destined never to play the role of constituent assembly, its assent should be sought in relation to constitutional change. The Amsterdam Treaty's failure to introduce such a provision ranks among the most glaring of the Treaty's many disappointments. It is easy to see the logic that agreement among sixteen is more difficult than among fifteen, but recent experiences would seem to indicate that the European Parliament is as able to muster majorities as the member states and their parliaments.

Its possible roles as constituent and assenter aside, it seems clear that the Parliament will exercise an increasing role in the Union's policy and legislative processes. Its persistent ambition – to become an 'institutional co-player' – is entirely consistent with Parliament's continued belief that the European Union's institutional arrangement will ultimately evolve into a bi-cameral system. As the Amsterdam Treaty illustrated, further progress in that direction is still possible.

The Single European Act and beyond

The success of the Single European Act was bound up in the happy combination of an economic necessity and an institutional requirement. The economic necessity was the need for the creation of a genuine internal market and, as a corollary of this, the establishment of re-distributory mechanisms designed at maintaining social and economic cohesion. The institutional requirement, vital if the internal market were to be created, was the need for effective decision-making in the Council – hence the explicit introduction of qualified majority voting. As Jacques Delors himself once remarked, the Single European Act marked a return to the Monnet style of functionalism, with substantial progress linked to institutional reform. The Maastricht and Amsterdam Treaties have continued in the same vein.

The European Parliament was more involved in the preparations leading to the 1996–7 Intergovernmental Conference than had been the case with previous intergovernmental conferences. Even so, its role fell far short of the direct participation it has always demanded. As was noted above, the Heads of State or Government at Maastricht and Amsterdam failed to grant the Parliament assent powers over constitutional reform. I believe it is only a matter of time before the Parliament's wishes are belatedly granted. (The lateness is regrettable, since the Parliament's views on constitutional reform have demonstrated a consistence and coherence rarely evident in the past three intergovernmental conferences.) Were the European Parliament to be more effectively involved in negotiating constitutional reform and in giving its assent to the outcome, then the treaties would collectively become a legal instrument based at once on the legitimacy of the states and their governments and on that of the European peoples.

Whether or not one believes that Economic and Monetary Union will necessarily lead to political union, it is clear that monetary union will have important political and constitutional ramifications. If all of these elements are taken together – substantial progress, incremental institutional reform (particularly the steady extension of qualified majority voting), a growing constitutional role for the European Parliament, Economic and Monetary Union and its constitutional ramifications, then in my opinion we are no longer very far from a federal model adapted to European reality. This model might be dubbed 'federal union'. At the institutional level, the Council (and hence also the Commission and the Parliament) would no longer be hampered by the unanimity requirement, whilst one of the most important policy areas – Economic and Monetary Union – would effectively be under federal control.

The difference between the concept of a federal union and that of a federal state is that the creation of a federal state would involve the transfer of *all* of the most important components of national sovereignty, with compulsory means of implementation at the level of the central authority. This would include such vital policy areas as foreign and defence policy. Any witness to the painfully slow progress made at Milan, Maastricht and Amsterdam would know just how idealistic such a prospect remains. But it is not unthinkable. It is even, I would venture, predictable – in the longer term. We can – must – dream about future freedoms, but we must also live with the restraints of the present. We should be informed by the constitutional experiences of others but we do not need slavishly to follow them. Federal union is Europe's own constitutional experiment. As Leo Tindemans points out in his chapter, we might have hoped that we could move further, faster, but it is extraordinary just how quickly we have come so far.

I would like to conclude with the motto of William of Orange, which has inspired me throughout my life: 'No need for hope in order to act, nor for success in order to persevere.'

NOTE

1 An earlier version of this chapter was first delivered as Jacques Vandamme's valedictory lecture to the Faculty of Law at the University of Leuven. The chapter has been updated by the editor.

REFERENCES

Breckinridge, Robert E., 1997, 'Reassessing Regimes: The International Regime Aspects of the European Union', *Journal of Common Market Studies*, XXXV, 2

De Gaulle, Charles, 1970, *Mémoires d'espoir. Le Renouveau*, Plon, Paris

European Parliament, 1984, Resolution on the Draft Treaty Establishing the European Union, *Official Journal* no. C 77, 19 March

Hoffman, Stanley, 1982, 'Reflections on the Nation-State in Europe Today', *Journal of Common Market Studies*, XXI, 1 and 2

Lenaerts, Koen, 1988, 'Outlook for a Comparison', in Lenaerts, Koen (ed.), infra

Lenaerts, Koen (ed.), 1988, *Two Hundred Years of the U.S. Constitution and Thirty Years of the EEC Treaty*, Kluwer, Deventer

Pinder, John, 1986, 'European Community and Nation-State: a case for neo-federalism', *International Affairs*, 1

Thatcher, Margaret, 1988, 'The European Family of Nations', reproduced in Holmes, Martin (ed.), 1996, *The Eurosceptical Reader*, Macmillan, London

Tindemans, Leo, 1976, 'European Union. Report by Mr Leo Tindemans, Prime Minister of Belgium, to the European Council', *Bulletin of the European Communities*, Supplement 1/76

Weiler, Joseph H.H., 1988, 'The Future of the European Community in the Light of the American Experience', in Lenaerts, Koen (ed.) op. cit.

Index

absolute majority requirement 26–7
accession 57
Accession, Act of (1972) 55, 110
AETR doctrine 102
Albania 70
amendments 22–4, 25, 27, 29
Amsterdam European Council 27, 30
Amsterdam Intergovernmental Conference *see* IGC (1997)
Amsterdam Treaty (1997) 29, 38, 105, 118; and Britain 39, 44–5, 46; closer cooperation provisions 77, 78, 79, 80, 83–4, 85–6, 92, 94–5; and co-decision procedure 20, 21, 52; and complexity 94–5, 119; and Court of Justice 109, 110–11; criteria for distinguishing between 'ins' and 'outs' 83; disappointments 120, 150; and European Parliament 92, 150; and flexibility 2, 44–5, 74, 78–9, 108; and human rights 53; importance of 45; negotiations leading to 71; and non-participating states 88, 89–90, 91
Atlantic Alliance 119

Balladur, Edouard 42
Belgium 8
Beveridge, William 35, 131
Bevin, Ernest 35
Blair, Tony 46
blueprints (constitutional): role and importance 2, 27, 28–30
border controls: abolition of 40
Bosnian crisis 70
Bourlanges, Jean-Louis 118
Brandt, Willy 49, 130, 131
Britain 34–46, 119; accession to Community 36, 55; and Amsterdam Treaty 39, 44–5, 46; battle against European partners (1996) 41; Blair's government and Europe 45–6, 59; Churchill's view of Europe 34, 35; and Economic and Monetary Union 41, 46; and EEC 35–6; electoral system 2, 38–9; and flexibility 40–1, 43, 44–5; history of policy approach towards Europe 35–7; inconsistency of European policy 37–8; and Maastricht Treaty 38, 39, 40; and national sovereignty 35–7, 40; as Union reform 38; opposition to Germany's 'hard core' proposal 42, 43; opposition to proposals for strengthening of Union at IGC (1996–7) 41–4, 58–9; Presidency of Council 45; referendum (1975) on Europe 37; relationship with European Community 2, 37, 38
Brown, Gordon 46
Brugmans, Henri 147
Brussels Treaty (1948) 139
budgets 50, 51, 72

CFSP (Common Foreign and Security Policy) 61, 68, 70–4, 82, 103, 118; and citizens' rights 69; and Commission 66–7, 71; limitation of effectiveness 70–1, 72–3; link with EC 72, 73–4; and qualified majority voting issue 45, 66, 71
Chirac, President 42, 46
Churchill, Sir Winston 34, 35
citizens 4–5, 54–5, 125–8; and Community law 112; education of regarding Europe 127–8, 140; guaranteeing of security 126; and IGCs 57; importance of to Union

democracy 56–7; needs of 54–5; and rights 53, 54, 69, 126, 136; support for reform proposals 58; and Tindemans Report 136, 137
Civil Society Forum 128
'co-decision procedure' 19, 20, 21, 28, 52, 58, 59
Commission, European 20, 48, 92, 103, 125, 132; and closer cooperation 86, 92; enhancement of role 50, 93; and EPC 64; and European Parliament 52; and foreign policy 66–7, 71; future of 120–1; and IGC (1996–7) 43, 44, 121; and legislation 50–1; role 50–1
Common Agricultural Policy 50, 117
Common Foreign and Security Policy *see* CFSP
Community law 112; characteristics 101; and citizens' rights 53, 54; primacy over national law 4, 101–2, *see also* Court of Justice
Conservative party 34, 38
'consistency concept' 64–5
Constantinesco, Professor Leontin 101
constitutional change 2, 16–30; and avoidance of extinction 25–6; as cumulative process 19, 20–2; evolutionary nature of 17, 19–22; mechanism for 22–5; and progress 27; role and importance of blueprints 2, 27, 28–30
cooperation, closer 76–95; and Amsterdam Treaty 77, 78, 79, 80, 83–4, 85–6, 92, 94–5; conclusions 93–5; and consensus principle 85; criteria for distinguishing 'ins' from 'outs' 82–4; and EC Treaty 85–6, 92; limitation in progress 94; and Maastricht Treaty 40–1, 78, 79, 80, 81, 84, 87–8, 89, 90, 92, 93; and non-participating states 87–91; and qualified majority in Council 86–7; role of Union institutions 91–3; and Schengen agreement 81; and Tindemans Report 76–7, 78, 79, 80–1, 84, 85, 87, 94, 95
cooperative federalism 147–8, 150
COREU 66
Council, European 19, 36, 102, 118, 121–2, 125, 132, 152; appointment of High Representative 121–2; and EPC 64; and foreign policy 72; future role 122; and IGC (1996–7) 44; and legislation 52; and Maastricht Treaty 91; preclusion from being a federal executive 53; procedures for closer cooperation 86–7, 91–2; and qualified majority voting 27, 43, 45, 50, 51, 53, 58, 86–7, 91, 151; strengthening of role 50, 103; and Tindemans Report 134, 138
Council of Europe 17, 76, 142
Council of Ministers 20, 72, 132, 134
Court of First Instance 103, 106
Court of Justice 4, 19, 48, 99–114, 145; achievements 102; and Amsterdam Treaty 109, 110–11; and appointment of judges 105; and citizens' rights 53; and closer cooperation 87, 92, 93, 109; and Community law 52–3; and definition of the Community's legal order 101–2; and differentiation 109–11; and ECSC 100, 101; and IGC (1996–7) 44, 104–6, 109; intergovernmentalism and limits on 103–6; and 'loyalty clause' 4, 102, 113; and Maastricht Treaty 103, 104, 110–11; problem with average length of proceedings 106; reasons for creation 100; reform proposals 106–7; role of under Paris and Rome Treaties 99–101; trends for the future 112–14
Customs Union 117

Darwin, Charles 16–17
Davignon Reports 62, 63
Dawkins, Richard 16–17, 18, 19, 28
De Charette, Hervé 43
De Gasperi, Alcide 48
de Gaulle, General 49, 51, 130, 144
defence 55, 58, 69–70, 118, 120
Delors, Jacques 1–2, 21, 151
Denmark: referendum on Maastricht Treaty (1992) 4, 23, 25, 55–6, 116; referendum on Single European Act 23, 55
differentiation 40, 76, 94, 113; and Amsterdam Treaty 84; and commitment to Economic Monetary Union 108–9, 135–6; and Court of Justice 109–11; and Maastricht Treaty 17, 103, 107–8, 109; and Tindemans Report 94; *see also* cooperation, closer

Duff, Andrew 106

Eastern Europe: collapse of Communist regimes 26
EC 63, 65–6; and CFSP 72, 73–4; relations with EPC 63, 64–5
EC Treaty 80, 84, 85–6, 92, 102, 109; *see also* EEC Treaty and Rome Treaty
Economic and Monetary Union (EMU) 108, 109, 111, 114; Britain's attitude towards 38, 41, 46; and differentiation 108–9, 135–6; and Maastricht Treaty 76, 82, 136; and political union 151; and Werner Plan 130–1, 144–5
economic sanctions 65, 66, 72
ECSC (European Coal and Steel Community) 11–12, 48, 50, 61; and Britain 35; and Court of Justice 100, 101; creation 10, 142; and intergovernmentalism 103
ECSC Treaty (1952) 62, 142
EDC (European Defence Community) 25, 48, 55, 63, 118, 142–3
EDC Treaty 48, 55
Eden, Anthony 35
EEC (European Economic Community) 11–12, 61, 63, 146; and Britain 35–6; creation 10–11, 49, 143; structure 62
EEC Treaty (1958) 11, 49, 50, 51, 100; *see also* EC Treaty and Rome Treaty
'empty chair crisis' (1966) 63
EPC (European Political Cooperation) 62, 63–5, 66, 67, 68–9, 71, 103
Euratom (European Atomic Energy Community) 49, 143
euro 3, 73, 74, 111
Euromissiles 68
European Central Bank 46, 103, 109–10
European Coal and Steel Community *see* ECSC
European Commission *see* Commission, European
European Convention of Human Rights 126
European Council *see* Council, European
European Defence Community *see* EDC
European Economic Community *see* EEC
European integration *see* integration, European

European Monetary Institute 103
European Monetary System 40, 49
European Movement 128, 135
European Parliament 48, 53, 59, 93, 122, 123–4, 125, 128, 132, 150–1; and accession of applicant states 3, 57; appointment of Commission 52; assent powers 3, 26–7, 28, 57, 68, 123, 140; and British MEPs 39; and closer cooperation 92; and constituent process 29, 123, 150–1; and Court of Justice 105; direct elections to 19, 21, 51, 131, 134; enhancement of powers 26, 27; and EPC 68; evolution of role 20, 21; and foreign policy 68, 69, 72; future 151; growth of budgetary powers 51–2; and human rights issues 26; and IGC (1996–7) preparations 151; increasing democracy of 57–8; and legislation 19, 20, 21, 52, 117; need for reform of electoral system 123–4; and nomination of Commission President 123; and Tindemans Report 138
European Political Cooperation *see* EPC
European Union: attraction 125; concept 148–50; consequences of undemocratic nature of 54–5; enlargement 25, 48; factors for survival 56; need for more democracy 56–8, 116; personality 119–20; way forward 118–19
Europol 104
Exchange Rate Mechanism 40, 88–9, 113

Falklands crisis 65, 68, 72
federal state: and federal union 5, 55, 152
federalism 142–52, 147; and cooperative federalism 147–8, 150; and functionalism 144–5, 151; and inter-state cooperation 145–6; and international regime theory 146–7; steps towards 142–4
federalists 29, 55, 149
fish quotas 41
flexibility 2, 3, 40–1, 42–3, 76–7; and Amsterdam IGC 108; and Amsterdam Treaty 2, 44–5, 74, 78–9, 108; and IGC (1996–7) 42–3, 44, 56; and Maastricht Treaty 4, 78–9; and Tindemans Report 76–7, 78, 79, 84,

135; *see also* cooperation, closer; differentiation
foreign policy 3, 61–74, 118, 119, 120; and the Commission 66–7, 71; criticism of 71; and economic sanctions 65, 66, 72; and EPC 62, 63–5, 66, 67, 68–9, 71; and European Parliament 68, 69, 72; future 73–4; initiatives for more effective 65–7; jeopardising of by 'opting out' clause 66; and joint actions 66; and Maastricht Treaty 61, 66, 68–9, 69, 70–1, 118; and national sovereignty 3, 61; origins 61–3; and the Presidency 67, 68; problems 61–2, 72–3; *see also* CFSP
Fouchet Plan (1962) 118
France 144; and Commission 120, 121; concentric circles proposal 42; and monetary union 49; referendum on Maastricht Treaty 116; rejection of European Defence Community 55, 63, 118, 143; relations with Germany 54, 59, 131, 142
Francovich case (ECoJ) 102
free trade 54
functionalism 144–5, 151

GATT 105
Genscher–Colombo plan (1983) 64
GEPE (*Groupe d'Etudes Politiques Européennes*) 13, 14
Germany 119; Basic Law 25; and Commission 120; 'hard core' proposal 42; and monetary union 49; relations with France 54, 59, 131, 142
Gibbon, Edward 99
Giscard d'Estaing, Valéry 131
green movements 47–8
Group of Reflection *see* Reflection Group

Hague summit (1969) 40, 130; (1974) 134
Hallstein, Walter 143
Hänsch, Klaus 43
'hard core' concept 42, 43, 56, 81, 84
Heath, Edward 36, 37
Helsinki Conference (1975) 64
Herman Report (1989) 150
High Authority 50, 100, 103
Hoffman, Stanley 145, 146, 147
Holland 51

Howe, Geoffrey 38
human rights *see* rights

IGC (intergovernmental conference) (1985) 20, 22; (1990) 49 IGC (1996–7) 25, 30, 56, 58, 120; Britain's opposition at 41–4, 58–9; and Commission 43, 44, 121; and Court of Justice 104–6, 109; differentiation and flexibility 42–3, 44, 56; prominent issues 76
IGC (1997) (Amsterdam) 3, 27, 61, 70, 73, 105, 108, 109
IGCs 22, 28, 47–9; achievements 48; and citizens' representatives 57; difficulties encountered 55, 57; success 23, 25; tabling and adopting amendments 23, 24, 27, 29; and unintended consequences 26
institutions, European 50–3, 57; and democratisation 5, 119–25; role in closer cooperation 91–3; Tindemans Report and reform 91, 92, 138; *see also* individual names
integration, European 29, 30; differing view on pace of 3–4; and evolutionary theory 19–22; public support for 3; theories of 142–4; *see also* cooperation, closer
'inter-institutional agreements' 26
inter-state cooperation 145–6
Intergovernmental Conference *see* IGC
intergovernmentalism 11–12, 17; and Community method 103–7, 118; impotence of 117–18
International European Movement *see* European Movement
international regime theory 146–7
Isoglucose ruling (ECoJ) 20, 21
Italy 71

Jenkins, Roy 36, 38
Juppé, Alain 42

Keynes, John Maynard 35
Kinkel, Klaus 43
Kissenger, Henry 67
Kohl, Helmut 42, 46

Labaye, Henri 103–4, 105
Labour Party 38, 59
Lamers, Karl 42
law *see* Community law
Lenaerts, Koen 145

Liberal Democrats 38
Liberals 39
London Report (1981) 63–4, 68, 69
'loyalty clause' 4, 102, 113
Luxembourg Compromise 36, 44, 87, 103, 117
Luxembourg Treaty 21

Maastricht Treaty (1993) (Treaty of European Union) 24, 27, 82, 127; and *AETR* doctrine 102; and Britain 38, 39, 40; and closer cooperation 40–1, 78, 79, 80, 81, 84, 87–8, 89, 90, 92, 93; co-decision procedure 19, 20, 21, 52; and complexity 119; and constitutional change 23, 24; and Council 91; and Court of Justice 103, 104, 110–11; Danish referendum (1992) 4, 23, 25, 55–6, 116; and differentiation 17, 103, 107–8, 109, 113; and Economic and Monetary Union 76, 82, 136; and economic sanctions 72; and EPC 65, 103; and European Union term 149; and flexibility 4, 78–9; and foreign policy 61, 66, 68–9, 70–1, 118; and human rights 53; and intergovernmentalism 103; modesty of institutional reforms 56; referendums on 116; subsidiarity principle 109
Macmillan, Harold 35
Major, John 38, 42, 108
Marx, Karl 10
MEPs 123, 124
Messina Conference (1955) 12, 18, 90
Metzemaackers, L. 139
Mitterrand, François 30
monetary union 49–50, 151; *see also* Economic and Monetary Union
Monnet, Jean 48, 55, 76
Mounier, Emmanuel 10

national sovereignty 3, 61, 71, 117–19, 139, 142, 144, 152; and Britain 35–7, 40
NATO (North Atlantic Treaty Organisation) 40, 69, 70
neo-Darwinian theory 2, 17, 18, 25, 27
non-participating states 87–91, 93, 108–9; appeals for annulment 111; and closer circle 88–9; obstacles for opting in 89–90; problems for 87–8; support for 90–1

OEEC 142
OSCE 70

Paley, William 16, 17
Paris summit (1972) 37, 40; (1974) 131–2
Parliament *see* European Parliament
political cooperation *see* EPC
Pompidou, Georges 49, 130
Powell, Enoch 37
Presidency 67–8, 72, 123

qualified majority voting (QMV) 59, 117; and CFSP 45, 66, 71; and Council 27, 43, 45, 50, 51, 53, 58, 86–7, 91, 151

Reflection Group 42, 58, 70, 71
rights 26, 53, 54, 69, 126, 136, 137
Rome Treaty (1957) 18, 19, 36, 40, 61; and Court of Justice 101; and European Parliament 19, 21, 62; and flexibility 135; strengthening of role of Council 103

Schäuble, Wolfgang 42
Schengen Agreement 40, 81, 103
Schmidt, Helmut 131
Schuman declaration 47, 99
Schuman Plan 35
security 54, 55, 69–70
single currency 49, 50, 54, 56
Single European Act (1986) 2, 28, 38, 49, 104, 145, 151; and concept of 'consistency' 64–5; Danish referendum 23, 55; and differentiation 40, 107; and EPC 64, 103; and extension of qualified majority voting 21, 51, 52, 151; success 151; on unanimity 28; and unintended consequences 26
Social Democratic Party (SDP) 38
Social Protocol 107, 108, 110
Solemn Declaration of Stuttgart *see* Stuttgart Solemn Declaration
sovereignty *see* national sovereignty
Spaak, Paul-Henri 48
Spaak Report 12
Spinelli, Altiero 48
'Spinelli Treaty' (1984) 148
Stability Pact 113
Stuttgart Solemn Declaration (1983) 21, 69, 149
subsidiarity principle 124–5

TEPSA (Trans-European Policy Studies Association) 1, 14, 29
Thatcher, Margaret 38, 145–6
Thorn, Gaston 21
Tindemans, Leo 11, 12, 13
Tindemans Group 138
Tindemans Report (1974) 76–95, 130–41; approach adopted 13, 133, 139; approach possibilities 12–13, 133; and citizens 136, 137; and closer cooperation 76–7, 78, 79, 80–1, 84, 85, 87, 94, 95; and concept of European Union 149; consultations involved 12; criticism of 139; distinguishing 'ins' and 'outs' 82–3, 85; drafting 132–3; economic and social policy 137; external policy 136; initial follow-up 134–5; and institutional reform 91, 92, 138; lessons learned 138–41; and monetary cooperation 40; 'new approach' 4, 76, 77, 94; and non-participating states 87, 89, 90–1; origins 130–2; recommendations 29, 134, 135–8; and safeguard clauses 85; and Vandamme 11–13, 132–3
Trans-European Policy Studies Association *see* TEPSA
Treaty of Amsterdam *see* Amsterdam Treaty
Treaty of European Union *see* Maastricht Treaty
Treaty of Rome *see* Rome Treaty
troika system 64, 66, 67

unanimity principle 27–8, 51, 70, 71, 91, 102, 145, 152; replacement by qualified majority voting 50, 51
United States 122; and cooperative federalism 147; mechanisms for constitutional change 22, 23–4
Uruguay Round (1994) 102, 105
Usher, John 102, 110, 111

Van Gend & Loos case (1963) 101
Vandamme, Charles 6, 7
Vandamme, Elsa 6
Vandamme, Jacques 1, 5–15, 47, 60, 99; career 10, 13; childhood 6–7; early career 9; and GEPE 13, 14; influence of personalism 9–10; military antecedents 6; personal life 9, 11, 14; philosophy 8, 10; qualities 5, 132; 'retirement' 14–15; and Second World War 7–9; and TEPSA 1, 14; and Tindemans Report 11–13, 132–3
Vandamme, Marguerite 9, 11
Vanhaeverbeke, Guy 14

Weiler, Joe 145
welfare state 147
Werner Plan 130–1, 144–5
Wessels, Wolfgang 14, 147
Westendorp Reflection Group *see* Reflection Group
Western European Union (WEU) 35, 40, 58, 70, 139
William of Orange 59–60, 152
Wilson, Harold 38, 131
Wolton, Dominique 119